Bermuda

a Lonely Planet travel survival kit

Glenda Bendure
Ned Friary

Bermuda

1st edition

Published by
   Lonely Planet Publications
   Head Office: PO Box 617, Hawthorn, Vic 3122, Australia
   Branches: 155 Filbert St, Suite 251, Oakland, CA 94607, USA
                  10 Barley Mow Passage, Chiswick, London W4 4PH, UK
                  71 bis rue du Cardinal Lemoine, 75005 Paris, France

Printed by
   Colorcraft Ltd, Hong Kong

Photographs by
   Cathi Below   Bermuda Department of Tourism
   Glenda Bendure   Ned Friary   Bob Krist

   Front cover: Bob Krist, architectural detail
   Title page: Mark Butler, Bermuda Cathedral

Published
   March 1997

Although the author and publisher have tried to make the information as accurate as possible, they accept no responsibility for any loss, injury or inconvenience sustained by any person using this book.

National Library of Australia Cataloguing in Publication Data

Bendure, Glenda.
   Bermuda.

   1st ed.
   Includes index.
   ISBN 0 86442 417 5.

   1. Bermuda Islands – Guidebooks. I. Friary, Ned.
   II. Title. (Series: Lonely Planet travel survival kit).

917.299

Glenda Bendure & Ned Friary

Glenda grew up in California's Mojave Desert and first traveled overseas as a high school AFS exchange student to India.

Ned grew up near Boston and studied Social Thought & Political Economy at the University of Massachusetts in Amherst.

After meeting in Santa Cruz, California, where Glenda was finishing up her university studies, they took to the road and spent years traveling throughout Asia and the Pacific, including long-term stints in Japan, where Ned taught English and Glenda edited a monthly magazine. They eventually came back to the States, settled down on Cape Cod in Massachusetts and began to write for Lonely Planet.

In addition to this Bermuda book, Ned and Glenda are the authors of Lonely Planet's guides to *Denmark, Micronesia, Hawaii, Honolulu* and the *Eastern Caribbean*, and they write the Norway and Denmark chapters of Lonely Planet's *Scandinavian & Baltic Europe on a shoestring*.

From the Authors

We'd like to thank the following people who answered questions, dug through their files or otherwise helped us with our research: William H Cook and LeYoni Junos, at the Department of Agriculture, Fisheries & Parks; island historian Brendan Hollis; David Wingate, of the Bermuda Audubon Society; Connie Dey, of the Bermuda National Trust; Colin Benbow, curator of the Bermuda Historical Society Museum; Joy Sticca and Charles Webbe, of the Bermuda Department of Tourism; Camilla Jones, of the Bermuda National Trust Museum; and Alexandra Martinengo, Rosemary LaPorte, Gayl LeMay, Mark Anthony Basden, David Abraham, Leonard Pedro, Gerald Bean and Eddie DeMello.

A special thanks to island musician Gene Ray, and his wife, Candy, who graciously spent a night on the town with us, and to former Bermuda News Bureau chief Bill Breisky, and his wife, Barbara, who shared their stories of Bermuda and piled us high with reference materials.

From the Publisher

This first edition of *Bermuda - travel survival kit* is a product of Lonely Planet's US office in Oakland, California. Don Gates was the project editor, with Carolyn Hubbard proofing text behind him. Alex Guilbert created all of the maps. Hayden Foell took charge of layout and, with fellow artists Mark Butler and John Fadeff, illustrated the book. Hugh D'Andrade produced the cover and, along with Scott Summers, contributed many hours of design advice and effort. Thanks to each and all.

Special thanks to Cathi Below for on-island investigation above and beyond the call of duty.

Warning & Request

Things change - prices go up, schedules change, good places go bad and bad places go bankrupt - nothing stays the same. So, if you find things better or worse, recently opened or long since closed, please tell us and help make the next edition even more accurate and useful.

We value all of the feedback we receive from travelers. Julie Young coordinates a small team that reads and acknowledges every letter, postcard and email, and ensures that every morsel of information finds its way to the appropriate authors, editors and publishers. Everyone who writes to us will find their name in the next edition of the appropriate guide and will also receive a free subscription to our quarterly newsletter, *Planet Talk*. The very best contributions will be rewarded with a free Lonely Planet guide.

Excerpts from your correspondence may appear in updates (which we add to the end pages of reprints); new editions of this guide; in our newsletter, *Planet Talk*; or in the Postcards section of our website - so please let us know if you don't want your letter published or your name acknowledged.

Contents

Map Legend

BOUNDARIES

—··—··—··— Parish Boundary

HYDROGRAPHIC FEATURES

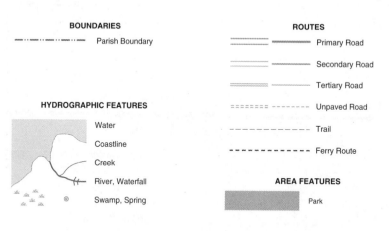

Water

Coastline

Creek

River, Waterfall

Swamp, Spring

ROUTES

Primary Road

Secondary Road

Tertiary Road

Unpaved Road

Trail

Ferry Route

AREA FEATURES

Park

SYMBOLS

✪ **HAMILTON**	✈ Airfield	🚩 Gas Station	⊓ Picnic Area
VILLAGE, TOWN	✈ Airport	⌐ Golf Course	★ Police Station
	∴ Archaeological Site, Ruins	✚ Hospital, Clinic	🛏 Pool
	⑤ Bank, ATM	❶ Information	✉ Post Office
	⚾ Baseball Diamond	⚚ Lighthouse	❶ Public Toilets
■ Hotel, B&B	⚑ Beach	✔ Live Music	∴ Ruins
▲ Campground	✦✦ Border Crossing	☀ Lookout	⤳ Shipwreck
♙ Chalet	● Bus Depot, Bus Stop	⚑ Monument	❖ Shopping Mall
♙ Hostel	⊞ Cathedral	▲ Mountain	🏛 Stately Home
⌗ RV Park	⌂ Cave	🏛 Museum	⚓ Surfing
♙ Shelter	✝ Church	← One-Way Street	✡ Synagogue
▼ Restaurant	◗ Embassy	⌂ Observatory	☎ Telephone
🍷 Bar (Place to Drink)	● Ferry Terminal	▣ Parking	■ Tomb, Mausoleum
☕ Cafe	⋈ Foot Bridge	✿ Park	🏃 Trailhead
	✿ Garden	)(Pass	🐘 Zoo

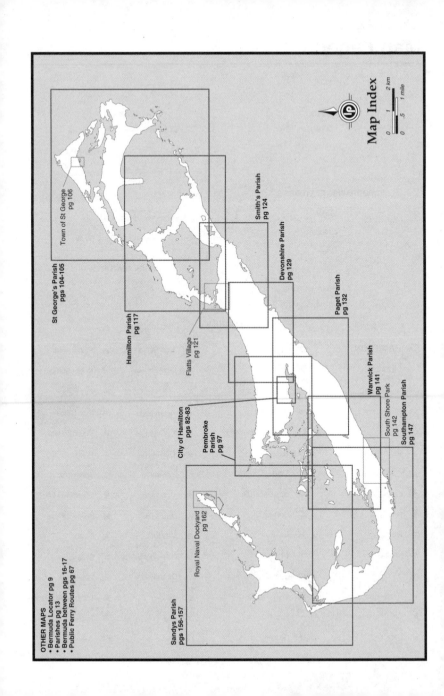

Map Index

0   1   2 km
0   .5   1 mile

Introduction

Tidy pastel cottages, pink-sand beaches, businessmen in Bermuda shorts, cricket matches and afternoon tea – Bermuda's stereotypes are its reality as well.

With just 60,000 inhabitants and 21 sq miles of land, tiny Bermuda is one of the more isolated island groups on earth. Far from urban pollution, Bermuda enjoys clear skies and clean turquoise waters.

Bermuda is often confused with the Caribbean, which lies nearly 1000 miles to its south, but it shouldn't be. Bermuda is not a tropical island, but a subtropical one. The weather is warm-to-hot from April to October, which is the main tourist season and the time for swimming and water activities. It's much cooler in the 'winter' or 'low season', with a mild climate similar to spring or fall in temperate countries – a time when the beaches are best suited for strolling.

Bermuda is a getaway island, a hospitable place with a well-established tourism industry. The majority of visitors arrive from North America for short visits of three to seven days. Many are looking for nothing more than peace and quiet, which is easily found on tranquil Bermuda.

But for active vacationers there is plenty to do. Bermuda lays claim to the world's northernmost coral reefs, which not only harbor colorful fish, but have been the cause of scores of shipwrecks over the centuries – all of which makes for good diving and snorkeling. There are sailing opportunities, sightseeing cruises, hiking trails,

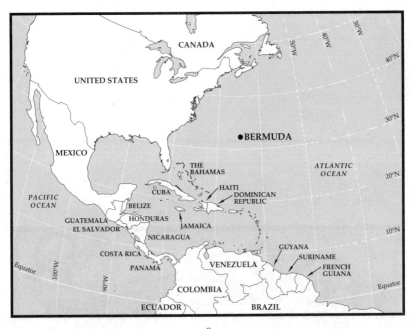

9

world-class golf courses, deep-sea fishing, tennis and horseback riding.

With a British colonial history that dates back nearly four centuries, Bermuda offers numerous historic attractions. The coast is rimmed with old forts, while the town of St George, Bermuda's original 17th-century capital, exudes period charm.

Although Bermuda is made up of several islands, all of the main ones are linked by bridges, forming one continuous entity, and no place on Bermuda is more than an hour from the modern capital of Hamilton. There is an efficient public bus and ferry system, or visitors can hop on mopeds to get around.

Despite its ties to Britain, Bermuda is geographically closer to the USA and is thus influenced by both. It's often said that Bermuda seems very British to American visitors, but American-like to British visitors. Of course, it's both – but it's uniquely Bermudian most of all.

Facts about Bermuda

HISTORY

Bermuda takes its name from the Spanish sea captain, Juan de Bermúdez, who sighted the uninhabited islands around 1503. The Spanish, in search of gold in the Americas, took no interest in settling the sparse island chain. In fact, there is no indication that the Spanish ever deliberately landed on Bermuda in the 16th century, although misadventures at sea cast them ashore at least a few times.

During the 16th century, Spanish galleons sailing between Havana and Spain commonly set a course that took them north along the Florida coast and then east out to sea. Although the extensive reefs surrounding Bermuda posed a potential hazard to their ships, there were no other islands in the mid-Atlantic that sea captains could use to take bearings, so Bermuda became an important navigational landmark. Once Bermuda was spotted, the ship's course could be reset east-northeast to follow a straight line to the Azores and Spain.

As long as the weather was fair, sailing past Bermuda was generally uneventful. However the winds of hurricanes and other powerful storms occasionally swept ships from their intended course and onto Bermuda's shallow reefs. Scores of Spanish ships, their hulls loaded with gold bullion, never completed the journey from the New World to Spain. Just how many went down near Bermuda remains unknown. Among the earliest traces of Spanish presence on Bermuda is a rock that was found on the south shore carved with the date 1543; the rough etching is speculated to have been the work of a shipwrecked sailor.

The treacherous reefs around the islands gained such an ill reputation among mariners that by the mid-16th century Bermuda was appearing on some Spanish charts with the nickname *'Islas Demonios'*, or 'Isles of Devils'.

One well-documented shipwreck occurred in 1603, when a Spanish galleon, carried north by storm gales, struck a rock off Bermuda. The captain, Diego Ramirez, managed to navigate the damaged ship through the reef and into the Great Sound, the large body of water at the west end of Bermuda. Ramirez and his crew spent three weeks on Bermuda making repairs before returning to sea. The area where the Spanish sailors are believed to have camped, two miles northwest of present-day Hamilton, still bears the name Spanish Point.

Sir George Somers

On June 2, 1609, Admiral Sir George Somers, under the employ of the Virginia Company, set sail from England for North America with a fleet of nine ships carrying supplies and colonists to the recently established British settlement at Jamestown, Virginia.

En route, Somers, who was in command of the flagship *Sea Venture*, got caught in a fierce storm and lost contact with the rest of his fleet. The *Sea Venture*, badly damaged by the storm, eventually shipwrecked on a reef three-quarters of a mile off the eastern shore of Bermuda. Using skiffs, Somers was able to safely land all 150 people on board, coming ashore on the beach near the present-day Fort St Catherine.

The castaways salvaged much of the wreckage from the *Sea Venture* and almost immediately began construction on two new ships. Aware of the gloomy Spanish accounts of the island, the shipwrecked English colonists expected the worst, but instead found Bermuda to be surprisingly agreeable. The native cedar trees provided a suitable timber for the new ships, palmetto trees supplied thatch for shelters and the abundant nearshore fish proved an easy catch.

Much to their surprise, the colonists

The Pocahontas Connection

Pocahontas, the Powhatan Indian woman who befriended the English settlers in Jamestown, Virginia, has an interesting – if indirect – connection to Bermuda.

One of the men aboard the shipwrecked *Sea Venture*, which brought those first English settlers to Bermuda, was John Rolfe. His wife gave birth on the island to a baby girl, whom they named Bermuda. Little Bermuda Rolfe died soon after birth, however, and the baby's mother died not long after the Rolfes reached Jamestown, their original destination.

John Rolfe became a successful tobacco farmer in Virginia, and it was there that he first met Pocahontas. The two fell in love and married in April 1614, with the approval of both the Virginia governor and tribal chieftains, who hoped the marriage would help soothe tensions between Native Americans and English colonists. ■

found the island rife with wild hogs. Some historians speculate that the hogs were accidentally released during an earlier shipwreck, but it's quite possible that early Spanish explorers had deliberately released the animals to provide a supply of fresh meat for Spanish ships that might pass by

at a later date. However they got there, the hogs provided an easy source of food, and that in turn allowed Somers to concentrate on his main goal – building replacement ships to carry the colonists to their original destination.

In 1610, the two new ships, the *Deliverance* and the *Patience*, set sail to continue the journey to Jamestown, their holds loaded with fresh supplies of dried fish and meat. A couple of men were left behind on Bermuda, in part to establish an English claim to the islands. Later that year, Somers returned to Bermuda with the intention of picking up more food to resupply the Jamestown colony, but he fell ill and died not long after landing. Although the title failed to stick, the British officially named the islands the Somers Islands, in honor of the admiral.

First Settlements

Back in England, the officers of the Virginia Company took a keen interest in the promising reports they were given on the island's suitability for colonization. The fact that Bermuda was uninhabited weighed heavily in its favor, especially in light of the Indian sieges and consequential famine that nearly decimated the Jamestown settlement. The Virginia Company decided to amend its charter to include Bermuda as part of its New World holdings, and it organized a party of 60 settlers to establish a permanent colony there.

The new settlers landed in Bermuda in 1612, under the leadership of Governor Richard Moore, an able carpenter who went about building the village of St George. In 1620, the parliamentary Sessions House, which still stands in St George today, began to hold meetings of the colonial legislature. The only previous British possession with such a legislature was Jamestown, giving Bermuda claim to being one of the earliest self-governing colonies under the British flag.

The Bermuda colony was divided into parishes, each named for a major stockholder of the Virginia Company. The

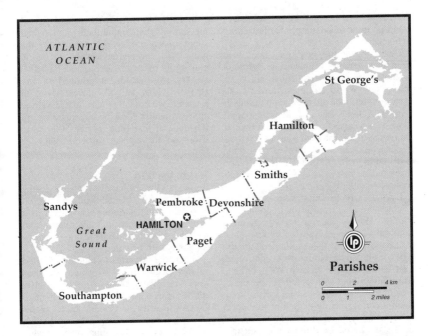

parishes were further divided into plots that were in turn leased to settlers. Crops were planted and the first slaves were brought to Bermuda, but agriculture was severely limited by the shallowness of the topsoil and the reliance upon rainwater. Bermuda's lack of rivers left it without a reliable water source to carry farmers through unexpected dry periods and also prevented sugar cane, a water-thirsty crop, from being successfully introduced. In the end, Bermuda became reliant upon food imports, mostly from the American colonies, to augment its meager harvests.

In many ways the Virginia Company ruled Bermuda like a fiefdom – people were told what crops they could grow, trade was controlled by the company and those who violated the rules could be forced into indentured servitude. Over time, the settlers became weary of all the restrictions that the Virginia Company and its successor, the Bermuda Company, placed upon them and

took their case to London, where they successfully sued to have the charter rescinded in 1684. After that date, Bermuda was ruled as a British crown colony in much the same vein as the American colonies.

Slavery

The first slaves were introduced to Bermuda in 1616. While the vast majority came from Africa, there were also American Indians, mainly Mahicans, taken from the American colonies. All came against their will, being captured and torn from their homelands and forcibly brought to the islands. The Atlantic crossings were so brutally inhumane that many of the slaves, chained in the suffocating hulls of the ships, died en route.

For those who made it to Bermuda, the dehumanizing conditions continued after arrival, permeating every aspect of life. Slaves were buried in a separate part of the cemetery, away from whites, and as late as the early 19th century island ministers could be imprisoned simply for preaching to blacks.

Degrading as the conditions may have been, they were not as hideous on Bermuda as they were elsewhere. Unlike slaves in other New World colonies, most of the slaves on Bermuda did not end up toiling in sweltering fields but instead were put to work as servants, construction workers and sailors. Some of the slaves became skilled tradespeople and were able to pass their skills on to their children – a circumstance that would assure them opportunities in the trades long after the end of slavery.

By the early 1800s, slavery was being assailed by abolitionists in London, and the anti-slavery movement was gaining widespread support. Spurred by changing sentiments, the British Parliament finally took on the sugar barons who controlled vast estates in the British West Indies. Throughout the 18th century, the great wealth of these sugar barons had assured them a corresponding degree of influence in affecting legislation in London, but by the beginning of the 19th century, sugar's heyday was clearly on the wane and the political clout of plantation owners significantly diminished.

In 1807, the British Parliament passed legislation that immediately abolished some aspects of slavery, most notably the trade itself, and phased out slavery on the plantations over a broader period. By 1834, slavery was no longer allowed in any British colony and all slaves living in Bermuda were finally emancipated. Of the approximately 9000 people residing on Bermuda at that time, nearly 5000 were listed on the census roles as black or 'coloured'.

Ties to the USA

Bermuda's history has always been closely tied to that of the United States, a situation that at times put Bermuda in a squeeze as it struggled to balance its trade relationship with the American mainland and its political bonds with Britain.

When the American colonies rebelled against Britain in 1775, some islanders were sympathetic to the American cause, but Bermuda nonetheless remained loyal to the crown. After the Continental Congress enacted a ban on trade with all British colonies that failed to support its struggle for independence, a Bermuda delegation sailed to Philadelphia to request an exemption so that it could import American food

Turks Islands & the Salt Trade

After agriculture proved a meager option on Bermuda, many settlers turned to the sea for their hopes of wealth and riches. Sailing their own ships made of Bermuda cedar, they tried to notch out a place for trading with the American colonies. The Bermudians needed to secure a commodity that was highly valued by the Americans – but resource-scarce Bermuda had little to offer. Eventually, the traders found what they were looking for in salt.

Around 1670, a party of Bermudians sailed to the Turks Islands, some 900 miles to the south, and began a lucrative business harvesting sea salt. The salt, which was shipped back north, brought a handsome price from the American colonists, as it was essential to preserve winter stores of fish and meat.

The salt works proved so profitable that nearly 1000 colonists and slaves were active on the Turks Islands raking, drying and shipping the salt. For a time, the salt traders even entertained the idea of turning the Turks Islands into a colony of Bermuda. However, that plan, which would have placed a colony (Turks Islands) under the domain of another colony (Bermuda), proved too unorthodox for British officials. Instead, by the beginning of the 19th century the British had incorporated the Turks Islands as part of the Bahamas colony and Bermuda's role in the salt industry slipped into history. ■

staples. The Congress made that exemption conditional upon receiving the stores of gunpowder held in the Bermuda magazine. In one of the more daring escapades of the day, in August 1775 a group of Bermudians stole up to the St George arsenal, carried away the gunpowder kegs and rowed them out to a waiting Boston-bound ship.

During the War of 1812, Bermuda once again found itself, as a loyal British colony, at odds with the United States. In August 1814, the British Navy used Bermuda as a base to launch the Chesapeake Bay Campaign that was responsible for torching the US White House and burning down much of Washington DC. The Americans, offended by the brazen attack, took revenge where they could. Under the rules of war as they were practiced during the period, American ships were free to confiscate the cargo of any ship flying the British flag. As a result, Bermuda provided lucrative booty for American privateers, who made an easy catch of much of Bermuda's merchant fleet. The losses were devastating for the Bermudian economy, which was heavily dependent upon trade.

While the War of 1812 spelled hard times, the US Civil War (1861-65) provided an economic boon for Bermuda, which was thrust into the lucrative role of serving as a center for blockade runners. The Confederacy of the southern states was heavily dependent upon the sale of cotton to finance its rebellion against the northern states. After President Lincoln imposed a blockade on southern ports in 1861, the south was forced to employ small, fast vessels to outrun the gunboats of the northern navy. These vessels were not capable of handling trans-Atlantic shipping, however, and it became necessary to use intermediate islands such as Bermuda and the Bahamas to transship the cotton to England, where it provided the raw material for hundreds of clothing mills. There was tremendous money to be made, as the cotton, which was worth five cents a pound in the south, fetched 10 times that price on the English market. Likewise, the guns and

ammunition brought back from England commanded a premium in southern ports.

At the height of the US Civil War, the town of St George enjoyed unprecedented prosperity. The waterside warehouses overflowed with goods, while stores and taverns cropped up to cater to seamen carrying fat wads of cash. The sea captains and traders made fortunes. Then, in 1865, victories by the northern forces ground the blockade runners to a halt. As it had sided with the now-defeated south, Bermuda's shipping industry, reliant as it was upon trade with the USA, all but collapsed after the war.

Advent of Tourism

Princess Louise, daughter of Queen Victoria and the wife of the Governor General of Canada, is credited with putting Bermuda on the map for North American tourists. Anxious to escape the long, cold Canadian winters, the princess paid an extended visit to Bermuda in 1883. The press took note of her stay, and journalists – including perennial traveler Mark Twain – followed in her wake. In 1884, Bermuda's first seaside resort, named – not surprisingly – The Princess Hotel, opened in Hamilton.

By the turn of the century, Bermuda was well on the way to becoming a trendy winter destination for 'snow birds', who flocked aboard steamers crossing regularly from New York to Hamilton. The crossing in winter, when stormy Atlantic seas are common, was rough enough that Twain compared his journey to 'going through hell' in order to reach paradise. Still, until the introduction of airplane service, it was winter – not summer – that was the main tourist season in Bermuda.

World War II

Bermuda, with its strategic mid-Atlantic location, became a center for Allied military and intelligence operations during WWII.

Even though the war had ground tourism to a halt, island hotels were brimming with activity. The Princess Hotel, Bermuda's

US Presence in Bermuda

At the outbreak of WWII, Britain was concerned with securing its shipping channels to the USA and saw Bermuda as a strategic Atlantic station. As the island was located much closer to the USA than it was to Britain, it seemed inevitable to military planners that the USA take over primary responsibility for developing military bases on the island.

In March 1941, US and British authorities, meeting in London, signed a 99-year lease that handed the US military a substantial chunk of Bermudian real estate, including the lion's share of St David's Island. The Bermudians, who were not given a voice in the negotiations, were so taken aback by the lengthy terms of the lease and the magnitude of territory involved that rumors ran wild that Bermuda was on the verge of being taken over as a US possession.

While the USA had no intention of laying claims to Bermuda, its presence there did bring rapid and permanent change to the sleepy colony. By the end of 1941, scores of Bermudians had found work on military construction projects, including the building of Bermuda's first airport. The US military introduced the widespread use of motor vehicles, which had heretofore been forbidden from Bermuda's streets. In the postwar period, the airport opened to civilian traffic, giving islanders easy access to the US East Coast and opening Bermuda as a weekend getaway for American tourists.

With the end of the Cold War, the US bases in Bermuda – which included 1040 acres on St David's Island and 250 acres in Southampton Parish – no longer provided any legitimate military need. In the 1980s, US news programs took a fancy to exposing golf junkets to Bermuda by military brass. The bad press helped add Bermuda to the shortlist of base closures necessitated by post-Cold War cutbacks in US military budgets. On September 1, 1995, the USA ended its military presence on Bermuda by turning over 1330 acres, some 10% of Bermuda's total land mass, to the island government. ∎

largest, was taken over by British intelligence agents, who turned the basement into an operations center. There, tucked out of view, scores of codebreakers interpreted mail and other correspondence passing between the USA and Europe, in an effort to uncover Axis espionage operations and decode secret messages. Because of the need to painstakingly pry open suspected mail without damaging the seal, examine the letter and then quickly get it back into circulation, more than 1000 people were employed in this operation alone.

In addition to intelligence gathering operations, Bermuda also served as a port for Britain's Royal Navy, which patrolled the North Atlantic for German submarines and battleships that threatened vital US-UK shipping lanes.

At the onset of the war, the USA also established a presence on Bermuda, most notably with the construction of an air base on St David's Island. The base, comprising some 1040 acres in all, was so large that it added another 1.25 sq miles to the island in the form of reclaimed land, boosting Bermuda's total land mass by more than 5%.

Postwar Changes

In the wake of WWII, many of the old colonial assumptions that prevailed in the British Empire were called into question. On Bermuda, the long-held political and economic preferences given to white males, at the expense of women and blacks, came under fire.

While blacks had been granted the right to vote in the 19th century, franchise qualifications and other prejudices kept them from achieving any significant political power. Indeed, in the 100 years between emancipation and WWII, only a dozen blacks had been elected to Parliament. Women, on the other hand, had been completely blocked from the political arena until 1944, when the right to vote was finally extended to them. Even after that,

GLENDA BENDURE

Gombey dancer's cape

BOB KRIST

Unloading zone

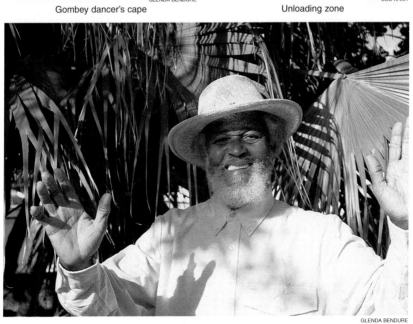
GLENDA BENDURE

Johnny Barnes bids you welcome to Bermuda.

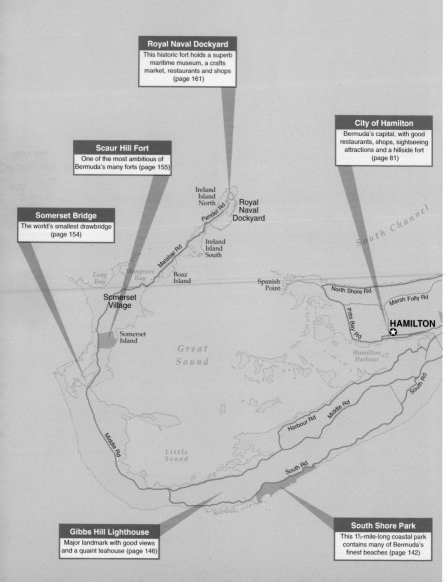

ATLANTIC
OCEAN

Royal Naval Dockyard
This historic fort holds a superb
maritime museum, a crafts
market, restaurants and shops
(page 161)

City of Hamilton
Bermuda's capital, with good
restaurants, shops, sightseeing
attractions and a hillside fort
(page 81)

Scaur Hill Fort
One of the most ambitious of
Bermuda's many forts (page 155)

Somerset Bridge
The world's smallest drawbridge
(page 154)

Ireland
Island
North

Royal
Naval
Dockyard

Pender Rd

South Channel

Ireland
Island
South

Malabar Rd

Long
Bay

Mangrove
Bay

Boaz
Island

Spanish
Point

North Shore Rd

Marsh Folly Rd

Somerset
Village

Pitts Bay Rd

HAMILTON
★

Somerset
Island

Great
Sound

Hamilton
Harbour

South Rd

Harbour Rd

Middle Rd

Middle Rd

Little
Sound

South Rd

Gibbs Hill Lighthouse
Major landmark with good views
and a quaint teahouse (page 146)

South Shore Park
This 1½-mile-long coastal park
contains many of Bermuda's
finest beaches (page 142)

Regiment Band member in full regalia

Park ranger

Business as usual, Bermuda style

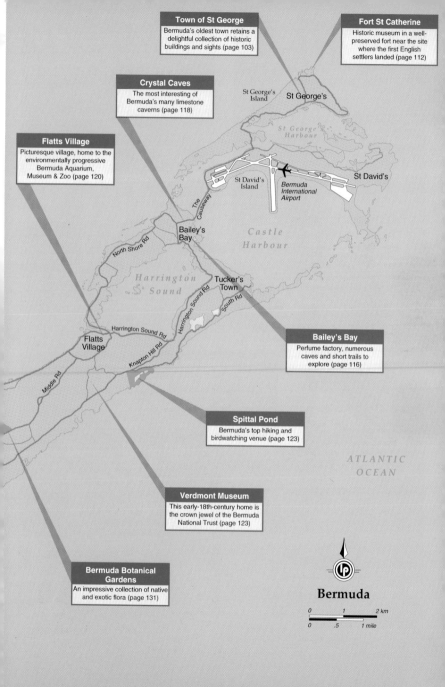

Town of St George
Bermuda's oldest town retains a delightful collection of historic buildings and sights (page 103)

Fort St Catherine
Historic museum in a well-preserved fort near the site where the first English settlers landed (page 112)

Crystal Caves
The most interesting of Bermuda's many limestone caverns (page 118)

Flatts Village
Picturesque village, home to the environmentally progressive Bermuda Aquarium, Museum & Zoo (page 120)

Bailey's Bay
Perfume factory, numerous caves and short trails to explore (page 116)

Spittal Pond
Bermuda's top hiking and birdwatching venue (page 123)

Verdmont Museum
This early-18th-century home is the crown jewel of the Bermuda National Trust (page 123)

Bermuda Botanical Gardens
An impressive collection of native and exotic flora (page 131)

St George's Island

St George's

St George Harbour

St David's Island

Bermuda International Airport

St David's

The Causeway

Castle Harbour

Bailey's Bay

North Shore Rd

Harrington Sound

Tucker's Town

Harrington Sound Rd

South Rd

Harrington Sound Rd

Flatts Village

Knapton Hill Rd

Middle Rd

ATLANTIC OCEAN

Bermuda

0   1   2 km
0   .5   1 mile

voter registration for both sexes was restricted to property owners, leaving fewer than 3000 Bermudians eligible to vote.

Blacks in Bermuda faced policies of segregation that were not dissimilar to those found in the USA – with the exception that Bermudian blacks were well entrenched in the trades. In the 1950s, buoyed by their clout in the trade movement, black Bermudians began to emerge as a political and social power to be reckoned with.

In 1959, intent on putting an end to segregation, blacks successfully boycotted movie theaters and restaurants to force them to integrate. Under pressure, hotels and other businesses that had practiced discriminatory hiring practices began to open job opportunities to blacks.

In 1960, a grassroots movement called the Committee for Universal Suffrage sparked widespread support with a drive to extend the voting right to the 75% of the adult population that didn't own 'qualifying property'. Conservatives, unable to block the movement, were nonetheless able to amend the legislation so that property owners were granted the right to cast two votes. Still, in the 1963 general election, every adult Bermudian age 25 and over could finally vote, swelling the voting rolls fourfold to more than 20,000.

Before universal suffrage was introduced, Bermuda's political arena so narrowly represented the interest of white landowners that it was free of political parties and rival platforms. In 1963, the first political party in Bermuda, the Progressive Labour Party (PLP), was formed, in part to represent the interest of nonwhite Bermudians.

The PLP, which advocated total independence from Britain, won support from newly enfranchised voters and captured six House seats in the 1963 general election. Many of the remaining independent members, wary of the potential bloc vote that the PLP could cast, united to form a counter party, the United Bermuda Party (UBP), which appealed to the interest of businesspeople and professionals.

In the years that followed, under encour-agement from Britain, the UBP, PLP and independent parliamentary members joined together to produce a constitution, which took effect in 1968. The new constitution provided for full internal self-government on all matters from health and finance to immigration, while leaving control of security, defense and diplomatic affairs to the crown.

Independence Issue
Although Bermuda prides itself on the relative harmony that exists between blacks and whites, in the 1970s racial antagonisms sometimes flared into violent confrontations. In 1977, responding to heightened unrest and race riots, the government moved to end de facto discrimination and to open talks on independence from Britain.

In the decade that followed, the independence movement became the dominant issue in Bermuda politics. Not only did the minority PLP support independence, but the more conservative UBP split on the issue after the premier, Sir John Swan, threw his support behind the independence campaign.

On August 16, 1995, in a referendum called by the premier, the issue of Bermudian independence from the crown finally came to a vote. With 16,369 votes cast against it and only 5714 votes in favor, the Independence Referendum was resoundingly defeated. Despite the years of fractious debate that the independence issue had evoked, just 25% of the electorate had voted in favor of breaking ties with Britain. In the wake of the election, Sir John Swan, who had made his political future contingent upon the passage of the referendum, announced his resignation after having led the government for 13 years.

The reasons behind the referendum defeat were varied, but in the end many Bermudians, regardless of their political affiliations, were apprehensive about the potential political and economic cost of independence. Certainly many had concerns about the financial strain that statehood would bring to an island of a mere

60,000 residents – everything from the need to maintain their own overseas diplomatic missions to the possible loss of commercial advantages with the UK.

Bermuda's long history of political and social conservatism undoubtedly played a significant role in the final vote. Employment concerns also weighed into the decision to stick with the status quo, since many of the best-paying jobs rely on upscale tourism, which commonly plays up a genteel colonial image, and upon offshore businesses. Indeed, many of the foreign companies operating in Bermuda, including British insurance firms and US financial services, let it be known that they found security in the current system of British law.

GEOGRAPHY & GEOLOGY

Bermuda lies in the North Atlantic, 570 miles off the coast of North Carolina, the nearest land mass.

Bermuda is comprised of a cluster of some 150 small islands, which collectively total just 21 sq miles in area. The eight largest islands – St George's Island, St David's Island, Bermuda Island (or the 'main island'), Somerset Island, Watford Island, Boaz Island, Ireland Island North

and Ireland Island South – are connected by causeways and bridges to form a continuous fishhook-shaped land area that stretches 22 miles in length. In contrast, its width averages less than a mile across and at its widest it barely reaches two miles. Together these connected principal islands contain more than 95% of Bermuda's land mass.

Bermudians tend to treat the connected islands as a single geographic entity and commonly refer to Bermuda simply as 'the island'. Only about a dozen of the other islands are inhabited. Most of the uninhabited islands are little more than rocks, and some are so small that there's not a general agreement, even among government departments, as to the exact number of islands in the colony!

All of the islands are of volcanic origin, the emerged tips of a volcanic mountain mass that rose from the sea floor several million years ago. They have a limestone cap, which is comprised of coral deposits and the bodies of billions of shell-bearing creatures that gradually built up around the edges of the submerged volcanic peaks. From a combination of accumulating deposits and lowering sea levels the mountain tops eventually emerged as islands and gave rise to the fringing coral reefs that surround them. Over time the action of the surf has pounded the limestone shells and coral into grains of sand that have amassed in the numerous bays and coves along the shoreline, giving Bermuda a generous string of pinkish-white sand beaches.

Although some sections are flat, Bermuda has a largely hilly terrain. The highest point is a 259-foot hill called The Peak, which is in Smith's Parish.

CLIMATE

Because of the warming effects of the Gulf Stream, Bermuda enjoys a mild, agreeable climate.

The average annual high temperature is 75°F, while the average annual low temperature is 68°F. In the warmest months, July to September, the average high tempera-

Distance from the Neighbors

Set in the isolated North Atlantic, Bermuda enjoys a wide berth from its neighbors. The nearest lies nearly 600 miles away at Cape Hatteras, North Carolina. And even though many people unfamiliar with Bermuda often mistakenly connect it with the Caribbean, nearly a thousand miles of ocean separate Bermuda from its tropical Caribbean neighbors to the south. In fact, Nova Scotia to the north is a bit closer!

As far as the motherland goes, London is a distant 3450 miles to the east. Not surprisingly, the places most frequently visited by Bermudians are not in the UK, but are New York and Boston, which are a cozy 750 and 775 miles, respectively, from sleepy Hamilton. ■

ture is 85°F and the average low is 75°F. The coldest months, January to March, have an average high temperature of 69°F and an average low of 60°F.

Bermuda is frost free; the lowest temperature on record (February 1993) is 40°F. The highest temperature on record is 92°F, which has been reached in August on several occasions.

Relative humidity is high all year round, ranging from an average of 75% in March to 84% in August. The mean annual rainfall is 57 inches, which is distributed fairly evenly over the year with no identifiable rainy season.

While Bermuda is not in the main hurricane belt that whips across the Caribbean, it does occasionally get nipped by such storms if they blow back out to sea in a northerly direction.

For a recorded two-day weather forecast, updated every four hours, dial ☎ 977. Call ☎ 977-1 for current weather, ☎ 977-2 for a marine forecast and ☎ 977-3 from June to November for tropical storm warnings. From overseas, you can get the weather information by calling ☎ 441-297-7977.

ECOLOGY & ENVIRONMENT
Bermuda is a small island with limited resources and a relatively high population density. Those conditions, along with the need to accommodate half a million visitors each year, inevitably cause stress on the environment.

In the waters surrounding the Bermuda islands, overfishing practices decimated the populations of numerous reef-fish species, scallops and other edible marine life. The Nassau grouper, for example, which was once the mainstay of the island fishing industry, has been fished to commercial extinction. Turtle hunting, still prevalent until the 1960s, was responsible for wiping out Bermuda's entire nesting green sea turtle population.

In recent decades, Bermuda has made a concentrated effort to raise the level of environmental awareness, ranging from introducing natural history into the school curriculum to enacting strict regulations protecting marine life.

The 1966 Coral Reef Preserves Act set up marine preserves that protect plants and fish in substantial tracts of Bermuda's reef waters. Subsequent marine protection orders have extended coverage to other environmentally sensitive areas by restricting fishing, spear fishing and the taking of lobsters.

Other programs to restore native fauna are also making headway. The yellow-crowned night heron has been successfully brought back; turtle conservation projects are underway; and West Indian topshells, a type of mollusk, have been reintroduced. The cahow, an endemic seabird once thought to be extinct, is on the comeback, and a concerted effort to increase the number of nesting boxes has resulted in a growing number of eastern bluebirds.

In terms of environmental aesthetics, Bermuda has long been in the forefront – it is free of polluting heavy industry and does not allow billboards or neon signs. The use of public buses and ferries is encouraged and the ownership of cars is strictly limited. Only one automobile is permitted per household – regardless of the number of drivers in the family! Bermudians have been known to concoct creative schemes to circumvent the spirit, if not the letter, of the law – such as dividing a home into two separate apartments – but that only stands as testimony to how effective the law actually is.

Recycling is encouraged, and there are drop-off centers for most household recyclables, including glass, aluminum, tin cans, newspaper, cardboard, motor oil and car batteries.

Even though tourism is an integral part of the economy, it is subject to environmental controls as well. No more than four cruise ships are allowed in Bermuda at one time; they are required to hook up to the local sewage system and are not allowed to emit soot while docked. There's also a moratorium on new hotel construction, though this may have as much to do with economic issues as the environment, as Bermuda's hotel occupancy rates are relatively low.

Although open space is at a premium, Bermuda nonetheless maintains a growing number of parks and nature reserves and is making efforts to restore some of the unpopulated islands, particularly Nonsuch Island, to their precolonial ecology.

FLORA & FAUNA
Flora
Bermuda, with its subtropical frost-free climate, is abloom with colorful flowers year round. Since temperatures usually stay within the range of 50°F to 90°F, tropical plants imported from the West Indies thrive here, and so do many of the flowers found in temperate climates.

In all, about a thousand different flowering plants can be found in Bermuda. Some of the more common are bougainvillea, hibiscus, oleander, morning glory (called 'bluebell' in Bermuda), poinsettia, freesia, nasturtium, chalice vine, garden geranium, night-blooming cereus, Mexican poppy, corallita (or chain-of-love, for its heart-shaped flowers), passion flower and bird of paradise. Easter lilies, introduced in 1853, are used locally to make perfume and are exported around Eastertime.

One of the few endemic flowers is the Bermudiana, a tiny blue-purple iris with a yellow center and grass-like leaves, which resembles the blue-eyed grass of North America. It blooms from mid-April through May.

Old-style roses – including the multiflora, tea and bourbon varieties – have remained popular since the 1700s. Notable rose collections can be seen at the Bermuda National Trust's Waterville office and in the Bermuda Botanical Gardens, both in Paget Parish.

Among the curiosities you'll find on the island is the prickly pear cactus, which is common in St George's near the seaside forts and in other coastal areas around Bermuda. The prickly pear produces the islands' only native fruit.

Shrubs & Trees Bermuda's most whimsically named shrub is the match-me-if-you-can, so called because no two leaves – in mottled colors of red, yellow and green – have the same pattern. Other common shrubs are croton, shrimp plant, blue sage, red sage bush (lantana) and pittosporum, the latter boasting perfumed white flowers in winter and early spring. Fragrant rosemary, with tiny blue flowers, is prolific as a landscape planting.

The umbrella-shaped royal poinciana tree has gorgeous scarlet blossoms from late May through early October, while the smaller scarlet cordia tree has orange-red flowers in the midsummer months. The pink shower, golden shower and Sydney golden wattle all produce attractive blooms in summer. Other flowering trees include the cassia, with golden flowers year round; frangipani (plumeria), with fragrant waxy flowers in summer; fiddlewood, with leaves that turn red in the spring before dropping; and yucca, with white flowering spikes in July.

The bay grape, abundant along the south shore, has fruit that hangs in grape-like bunches at year's end and round green leaves that turn red and gold before falling. Another easily identifiable tree is the pandanus, or screw pine, which has spiny leaves, fruit that resembles pineapples and a trunk that's anchored with multiple aerial roots.

Endemic trees include the Bermuda cedar, which once covered vast tracts of the islands; olivewood bark, an evergreen found on rocky hillsides; and the Bermuda palmetto, Bermuda's only native palm tree. Early settlers made liquor from the sap of the Bermuda palmetto and from the berries of the Bermuda cedar.

Fast-growing casuarina (beefwood) trees, native to Australia, were planted throughout the island as a replacement for the many Bermuda cedar trees that were stricken by cedar-scale infestation in the 1950s. Prevalent in island parks, casuarina has long, needle-like leaves with a soft feathery appearance.

The Onion Patch
Onions were first planted in Bermuda in 1616 from seed brought from England. By the 17th century, onions from Bermuda were being shipped to the West Indies, though large-scale cultivation did not start until the 1830s. By this time, Bermuda onions were grown in both red and white varieties, using seed imported from the Madeira and Canary Islands. The climate and soil conditions unique to Bermuda helped produce onions that were notably tasty.

By the late 19th century, exported Bermuda onions had become so well-known, particularly in New York markets, that Bermuda was nicknamed 'The Onion Patch' and Bermudians themselves were sometimes lightheartedly referred to as 'Onions'.

Bermuda no longer exports onions, however. The major downfall came from increased competition by 'Bermuda onions' grown commercially in Texas starting around 1900. In addition, protective US tariffs, crop damage from insects and disease, and a loss of Bermuda farmland to growing numbers of homes and hotels sealed the demise of onion exports. Indeed, there are indications that as early as 1908, Bermuda was importing 'Bermuda onions' from Texas! ■

For a close-up view of Bermuda's varied flora, the Bermuda Botanical Gardens in Paget is a great place to start – there you'll find the widest variety of both native and introduced species.

Food Crops Bermuda's soil is limestone in origin, so it tends to be strongly alkaline. Soil depths are very shallow, seldom more than two to three feet in the relatively fertile valleys and as little as an inch elsewhere. Because of this shallowness, the soil has a limited capacity to hold water, and droughts, which can last a month or more in summer, create unique challenges for farmers.

Nonetheless, just about all of the major vegetable crops found in temperate climates grow in Bermuda, including lettuce, broccoli, cauliflower, peas, potatoes, pumpkins, tomatoes, beets, cabbage, onions, carrots, beans, cucumbers, corn, celery and kale.

Cassava, a root crop resembling sweet potatoes, is also grown on the island and used to make cassava pie, a local Christmastime favorite.

Citrus trees – orange, lemon, grapefruit, lime, tangerine and tangelo – are popular in home gardens. Another island favorite is the loquat tree, the small yellow-orange fruit of which is used in pies, jams and liqueur.

Other edible fruits grown on Bermuda are avocados, grapes, figs, papayas (locally called paw-paw), Surinam cherries, sugar apples (sweetsop), guavas, strawberries and bananas.

Fauna
Bermuda has no native land mammals. The endemic Bermuda rock lizard, a brown skink, was the only nonmarine land animal on Bermuda prior to human contact.

Introduced lizards include the Jamaican anole, which puffs out a showy orange throat sac as a territorial warning; the Warwick lizard, a foot-long lizard with golden eye rings; and the Somerset lizard, identifiable by its black eye patches. All of the lizard species are harmless, and there are no snakes, poisonous or otherwise, on Bermuda.

There are two kinds of whistling tree frogs: the *Eleutherodactylus johnstonei*, which is about one-inch long, and the slightly larger but less common *Eleutherodactylus gossei*. Both are brown, nocturnal, live in trees close to the ground and were introduced to Bermuda around the turn of the century. The frogs create a musical chorus of loud, bell-like whistles that fill the night from April to November, so long as the temperature is above 67°F.

The giant toad *(Bufo marius)*, imported

from Guyana in the late 1800s to control cockroaches, is most often seen squashed flat on the road, hence its local nickname 'road toad'.

Butterfly species common to Bermuda include the monarch, cloudless sulphur, buckeye, gulf fritillary, red admiral and cabbage white. There's also a wide variety of nocturnal moths.

Birds Of the land birds that once inhabited Bermuda, only a single endemic species survives: chick of the village *(Vireo griseus)*, a subspecies of the white-eyed vireo.

Of course, there are a number of introduced species that are now common. Perhaps the most notable is the kiskadee, a noisy yellow-breasted flycatcher that is often spotted on hotel grounds. The kiskadee was introduced from Trinidad in 1957 in hopes of bringing the lizard population down so that beetles introduced to prey on the cedar-scale insects would have a better chance of getting established.

Other common introduced land bird species include starlings, house sparrows, European goldfinches, catbirds and mourning doves. Two other birds, the northern cardinal and the eastern bluebird, were common on Bermuda until the 1950s, but the loss of cedar habitat coupled with increasing competition from kiskadees and sparrows have brought drastic declines in their populations.

While Bermuda's resident species may be limited, the island hosts a wide variety of migrant birds. The checklist of some 300 birds includes three dozen warblers, numerous shorebirds, herons and ducks. Graceful white-tailed tropicbirds, more commonly called longtails on Bermuda, can be seen swooping and gliding along the shore from March to October. In addition, sandhill cranes and a number of other exotic birds, such as the Pacific fairy tern, make the occasional visit.

In spring, terns, storm petrels, jaegers and four species of shearwaters (greater, sooty, Manx and Cory's) pass by, often in flocks that number in the thousands. The peak of the spring seabird migration occurs in May and June.

Still, fall is the most varied time for birds, with the migrations reaching their peak in October. At that point, most of the shorebirds and herons and some of the land birds, ducks and coots have arrived. Among the birds spotted during this period of migration are osprey, ring-necked duck, double-crested cormorants, eastern wood peewee, yellow-bellied sapsucker, scarlet tanager, rose-breasted grosbeak, gulls, thrushes and sparrows.

Marine Life Bermuda being so far north, it may surprise to some visitors to learn that many tropical fish common to the Caribbean can also be spotted in the waters that surround Bermuda.

Some of the more colorful fish include the clown wrasse, queen angelfish, rainbow parrotfish, rock beauty, spotted puffer, blue chromis, foureye butterflyfish, blue tang, triggerfish and orange spotted filefish.

The key to all this marine life is Bermuda's coral formations, which grow in the clear shallow waters surrounding the islands. These are the northernmost corals found in the Atlantic and owe their existence to the warm ocean currents carried north by the Gulf

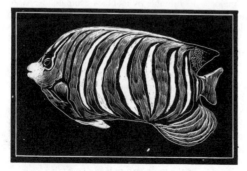

Angelfish are seen in a variety of colors and patterns.

Stream. In all, Bermuda has 24 species of hard coral, including brain coral and tree coral, and another two dozen species of soft coral such as sea fans and sea rods.

In addition to pretty fish, Bermuda's coral reefs also harbor more menacing-looking creatures, including green moray eels that grow up to 10 feet long. While moray eels may provide a bit of a shock to snorkelers who suddenly come upon them, they are generally nonaggressive and the intimidating mouth-chomping motions that they make are not meant for defense but are in fact a mechanism for breathing, pumping water across their gills. Three other species of eels are also found in Bermuda's waters: the speckled moray, brown moray and conger eel.

Much more dangerous than eels are the jellyfish-like Portuguese man-of-wars, which are sometimes found in Bermuda's waters, especially from March to July. Waters where they've been seen recently should be avoided (see Dangers & Annoyances in the Facts for the Visitor chapter).

Bermuda's waters also hold brittle stars, sea horses, sea spiders, sea cucumbers, sea hares, sea anemones, sea urchins, squids, conchs, slipper lobsters and spiny lobsters.

Land crabs, active along the shoreline at night, make telltale burrows in dunes above the beach, particularly along the south shore. The females release their larvae into the ocean at least once each summer, often on nights following the full moon.

Humpback whales, migrating north from the Caribbean, can sometimes be seen off the south shore in March and April. Less common, but not unknown, are sightings of Cuvier's beaked whales and sperm whales. Various species of dolphins and porpoises are sometimes found in deeper waters as well. Green sea turtles, hawksbill turtles, loggerhead turtles and leatherback turtles are sometimes seen near the reefs.

A great place to go for an introduction to Bermuda's marine life is the Bermuda Aquarium, Museum & Zoo in Flatts Village, where you'll find tanks identifying more than 100 species of fish.

Endangered Species

Hundreds of miles from the nearest land mass, Bermuda's flora and fauna evolved in an isolated environment with limited competition and few predators. Consequently, when the first human settlers arrived on the scene 400 years ago they had a devastating impact.

Free-roaming pigs, left by passing sailors in the 16th century, and rats, cats and dogs introduced by the first permanent settlers in the 17th century, spelled havoc for many species of endemic plants as well as ground-nesting birds. Still, it was the humans who brought some species to extinction.

One bird that offers a haunting testimony to species devastation is the Bermuda petrel, or cahow *(Pterodroma cahow)*. These quail-size seabirds were abundant when the first settlers landed, but they had no natural fear of people. Diego Ramirez, the Spanish captain who spent three weeks on Bermuda in 1603, noted that his men were able to make a ready catch of thousands of the plump little birds. When the English arrived six years later, they too developed an appetite for the cahow. The birds made such an easy catch – indeed, they would even land on the colonists' arms – that they all but disappeared within a few decades.

After three centuries without sightings, the cahow, which was officially listed as extinct, was rediscovered in 1951. Subsequent research identified 20 nesting pairs of the birds on four of the smaller uninhabited Castle Harbour islets. Although environmentalists were initially encouraged, the islands were found to be a marginal habitat for the ground-nesting birds, as rats preyed upon their eggs and the soil was so eroded that it was no longer sufficient for burrowing nests. The cahows had adapted by nesting in natural holes in the cliffs, but they had to compete for these nesting sites with more aggressive longtails, a large tropicbird. Because the longtails nested later in the season, the cahows were sometimes forced to abandon their nests before they had a chance to rear their chicks.

To create more favorable odds for survival, special baffles were installed in the opening of the cahows' cliffside nesting holes, reducing the size of the entrance so as to prevent longtails from entering. In addition, naturalists created artificial nesting burrows, hollowed into the islands' rocky surfaces and roofed with concrete, in the hopes of returning the cahows to ground-level burrows and reducing competition with the longtails. In conjunction with these efforts, rats and other predatory mammals were eradicated from the four islets where the cahows nest.

The cahow, which lays but a single egg each year, is making a slow, precarious comeback. There are currently 49 pairs of cahows and they remain one of the rarest seabirds in the world.

National Parks

In 1986, legislation was enacted establishing a national parks system to protect, maintain and enhance the natural and historic character of environmentally sensitive areas. Bermuda now has dozens of parks and nature reserves, collectively accounting for nearly 1000 acres.

Although none of the parks are extensive, a handful of properties – most notably Spittal Pond Nature Reserve, the Bermuda Botanical Gardens and South Shore Park – are large enough to provide for an hour or so of walking.

GOVERNMENT & POLITICS

Bermuda is an internally self-governing British dependency with a bicameral parliamentary government.

The official head of state is the British monarch. The crown is represented on Bermuda by an appointed governor who is responsible for external affairs, defense, internal security, and police. Otherwise, the governor's role is largely symbolic, acting on the advice of the cabinet. The current governor, Lord Waddington, is a former member of Margaret Thatcher's cabinet.

The premier, who is the leader of the majority party, heads the government and appoints the cabinet, a 12-member ministerial body responsible for government administration.

Parliament, which is responsible for enacting legislation, is divided into two bodies: the House of Assembly, which has 40 elected members, and the Senate, which has 11 members. Five of the Senate members are selected by the premier, while three each are selected by the leader of the opposition and the governor. Both branches of Parliament sit for five-year terms. To be enacted, legislation must be passed by the House, approved by the Senate and signed into law by the governor.

Bermuda has two major political parties: the United Bermuda Party (UBP), which generally promotes a conservative platform, and the Progressive Labour Party (PLP), which is supported by labor and has a large black membership. Although the PLP has held as many as 18 of the 40 House seats, the UBP has been the majority party since Bermuda's Parliament divided into parties in the mid-1960s.

The current premier is David Saul, a former finance minister who took office in 1995 following the resignation of Sir John Swan.

ECONOMY

Bermuda has a gross domestic product (GDP) of $1.8 billion and a workforce of 34,300 people. The average income on Bermuda is $32,200.

Since the turn of the century, tourism has been the cornerstone of the economy; it accounts directly for about 4000 jobs and indirectly for perhaps twice that number. Bermuda receives nearly 600,000 visitors per year, about 30% of whom arrive aboard cruise ships. The 70% who arrive by air have an average stay of six days. Slightly more than 80% of the visitors come from the USA, while the rest are tourists from Canada and visitors from the UK and Europe.

In recent years a growing number of international finance operations, attracted by the absence of corporate and income taxes, have set up offshore operations in Bermuda. These include mutual funds services, investment holding firms and insurance companies specializing in reinsurance, a type of catastrophic insurance that protects conventional insurers against natural disasters.

The USA is the leading trade partner, accounting for more than half of Bermuda's international trade. Most food and clothing are imported, and it is this situation, compounded by high customs duties (Bermuda's main tax source), which gives Bermuda an unusually high cost of living.

Until recently the US military had a small but significant presence on the island. In late 1995, when the Americans pulled out of Bermuda, the island government was forced to take over operation of the airport, which had previously been maintained by the US Navy. Hoping to cover the approximately $10 million in annual operating expenses, a new departure tax of $20 was instated. To soften the loss of about $50 million annually that the USA once pumped into the local economy, the government is contemplating a small industrial park on a portion of the former base lands that border the airport.

POPULATION & PEOPLE

Bermuda's population stands at approximately 60,000. About 25% of Bermudians are under the age of 20, 65% are between the ages of 20 and 64 and the remainder are 65 years of age or older.

Approximately 75% of all islanders were born in Bermuda. Of those who are foreign-born, about 30% were born in the UK, 20% in the USA, 13% in the Azores or Portugal, 10% in Canada and 10% in the Commonwealth Caribbean.

Most Bermudian blacks can trace their ancestry to slaves brought to the island in the 17th and 18th centuries. Blacks have been in the majority since colonial times and currently comprise about 61% of the population. Most of the remainder of the population is white, but there is also a small minority that is of American Indian descent.

EDUCATION

Bermuda has a literacy rate of 98%.

Education is free and compulsory for all children ages five through 16. The curriculum borrows from both British and US systems. The school year runs 40 weeks from September to June, with Christmas, spring and summer breaks that parallel those in the USA. Most schools are coed and all students are required to wear uniforms.

Postsecondary education is available at the Bermuda College and through an extension program offered by Webster University of Missouri.

ARTS
Dance

Gombey dancing is an art form that is unique to Bermuda. While it has roots in West African tribal music, Gombey dancing also incorporates influences from Christian missionaries, the British military and, most visibly, American Indians, from whom the Gombey dancers have adapted their colorful costumes.

A Gombey group consists of men and boys, referred to as a 'crowd'. The young boys are called 'warriors' and wear short capes and carry wooden tomahawks. The older boys are called 'Indians' and carry bows and arrows, while the head males, or 'chiefs', wear long capes, carry whips and command the show. The capes of all the dancers are brightly colored, decorated with sequins, yarn fringe and trailing ribbons. Their tall headdresses are elaborately ornamented with glitter and peacock feathers, while long sleeves, gloves, scarves and masks keep their bodies covered from head to toe.

Military influence can be found in the use of a fife, which is customized from a beer bottle, and in whistles and snare drums. The beat is also carried by a goatskin drum that has a billy goat skin on one side and a nanny goat skin on the other.

To the uninitiated, the Gombey dancers may just look like wildly costumed characters acrobatically jumping up and down to loud music, but in fact the dancing is carefully choreographed to specific rhythms. Pantomimes often portray stories from the Bible, such as fights between David and Goliath, or Daniel in the lion's den.

There are four Gombey groups in Bermuda. To be part of one, you either have to be born into a family of dancers or have some other significant connection.

Gombey dancers traditionally take to the streets throughout Bermuda on Boxing Day and New Year's Day – when islanders hear their drums they come running out of their homes to watch the dances. If you're lucky enough to be in Bermuda during these holidays, you can catch the Gombeys dancing in the street. Otherwise, winter visitors can watch a free performance of Gombey dancers every Tuesday afternoon from November to March in the main cruise ship passenger terminal on Hamilton's waterfront.

Arts & Crafts

Bermuda's pastel houses and gentle landscapes have long inspired both local and international artists.

Among the more renowned artists who have captured Bermuda scenes over the years are Americans Georgia O'Keeffe, whose best-known island works depict banana flowers and banyan trees in charcoal and pencil; Winslow Homer, who created 21 paintings on the island, concentrating on seaside scenes; and Andrew Wyeth, who focused on the people of Bermuda. Canadian Jack Bush used watercolors to create robust scenes with a tropical motif, while the French cubist artist Albert Gleizes worked in gouache and watercolors.

One of Bermuda's best-known contemporary watercolorists is the deceased Alfred Birdsey, whose prolific art still fills galleries both on the island and abroad. His daughter Joanne Birdsey Linberg, an artist herself, continues to maintain the family gallery. Other well-known local painters who have their own galleries are Jill Amos Raine, Carole Holding, Michael Swan, Sharon Wilson and Joan Forbes.

Bermuda's most highly regarded contemporary sculptor is Desmond Fountain, who casts graceful, life-size figures of playing children and female nudes in bronze. His sculptures can be seen at Hamilton's city hall and at several of the island's upmarket hotels. Bermuda's other leading sculptor, Chesley Trott, works in native cedar at his studio in the Bermuda Arts Centre at the Royal Naval Dockyard.

The Dockyard is also the home of Island Pottery, a pottery shop where both ornamental and utilitarian pieces, such as vases, pitchers and dishes, are handcrafted and painted with island designs. The Bermuda Glassblowing Studio in Bailey's Bay specializes in colorful handblown glass items, ranging from ornamental tree frogs to tableware and paperweights.

There are dozens of other craftspeople on Bermuda, making jewelry, wall hangings, dolls, hand-dipped candles, trinkets, toys and the like. The largest collection of works by these craftspeople can be found at the Bermuda Craft Market in the Royal Naval Dockyard.

Architecture

One of the first things to strike visitors upon arriving in Bermuda is the charming uniformity of island homes – quaint cottages painted in pastel hues with stepped white roofs.

While it may seem that the houses were designed solely for their pleasing aesthetics, their unique qualities are a consequence of local conditions, both in terms of available building material and the island's reliance upon rainwater.

The houses are built of locally quarried limestone. The roofs are cleverly designed to gather rainwater and direct it via angled stone gutters into a catchment tank that provides the residents with drinking water. The bright bleached-white color of the roofs is the result of their being painted with a limestone wash that acts as a water purifier. The appearance of the bright textured roofs has earned them the nickname 'cake icing'.

The simplicity of the homes, free as they are of embellishments, is necessitated by the smooth limestone surfaces. Jalousied wooden window shutters provide the main ornamental feature. One decorative indulgence is the 'eyebrow', an inverse letter V, above the windows of some homes.

Another notable architectural feature is the moongate, a round limestone gate often found at the entrance to Bermuda gardens. Thought to be of Chinese origin, passing through the moongate is said to bring good luck.

Literature

Bermuda can claim ties to a number of significant 20th-century writers who either vacationed or lived on the island.

Nobel prize winner Eugene O'Neill (1888-1953), who had a place in Warwick Parish, wrote a number of works while on Bermuda, including *Strange Interlude*. One of O'Neill's neighbors was the English playwright and composer Noel Coward (1899-1973).

American novelist, poet and biographer Hervey Allen (1889-1949) wrote the novel *Anthony Adverse* during his stay at Felicity Hall, a mansion in Somerset.

James Thurber (1894-1961), author and cartoonist for the *New Yorker* magazine, wrote the fairy tale *The 13 Clocks* and other stories during long stays on the island. He was a frequent contributor to *The Bermudian* magazine.

Munro Leaf (1905-76), an author and illustrator of books for children, had a home in Somerset. He wrote *The Story of Ferdinand*, about a Spanish bull, while living in Bermuda in the 1930s.

Peter Benchley, a frequent visitor to the island during the 1960s, wrote *Jaws* on Bermuda and found a setting for a second novel, *The Deep*, while diving in Bermuda. Benchley also used Bermuda for the setting of the suspense novel *Beast*, published in 1991.

SOCIETY & CONDUCT

Bermuda culture is a blend of British and African heritage. The British influences solidly predominate in institutional ways, including the form of government, educational system and legal framework. Politicians and judges still wear powdered wigs, bobbies direct traffic, afternoon tea is a ritual and a pint of ale at the local pub is a common way to cap off a day's work. Cricket is Bermuda's most popular sport. Fashion and manners remain conservatively British.

The African influence is more subtle, but can be found in island music and dance, most notably in the rhythm of Gombey dancers. Other African-related influences come by way of the West Indies, such as the popularity of reggae, steel drum and calypso music.

Bermuda Shorts

Bermuda shorts are the closest thing Bermuda has to a national dress for men. Unlike other places around the world where these nearly knee-length style of shorts are equated with casual wear, on Bermuda the namesake shorts are an element of formal dress.

The rest of the outfit consists of socks that reach just below the knee, a dress shirt and a tie and jacket. The knees remain exposed. As for coordinating the various pieces, the shorts and jacket should be different colors, while the socks can compliment either.

The shorts, incidentally, were inspired by British soldiers in tropical outposts such as India, who took to trimming the lower half of their trousers off to make their uniforms more bearable in the heat. By the early 20th century, British soldiers stationed on Bermuda were wearing such shorts as standard uniform and in the years that followed the more upscale Bermudian version began to make an appearance. Today, it's standard wear for bankers, insurance executives and other conservatively dressed community leaders. ■

Dos & Don'ts

For visitors, neatness in dress and politeness in attitude go a long way. You should never stop someone on the street for directions without first greeting them with 'Good morning' or 'Good afternoon' . . . a simple 'Excuse me, could you tell me the way to the beach' is considered abruptly rude. Even ordering a drink from a bar should be prefaced with a friendly 'hello'.

Dress is relatively formal, with bathing suits and skimpy beachwear inappropriate any place other than at the beach or swimming pool. In fact, it's an offense for men to appear in public without a shirt or for woman to wear a bathing suit top in place of a blouse. Nude and seminude bathing is not allowed anywhere in Bermuda.

RELIGION

The majority of islanders are Christian. Although the number of people affiliated with the Anglican church has dropped to 28% (from 45% in 1970), it remains the largest denomination. This is followed by Roman Catholic at 15%, African Methodist Episcopal at 12%, Seventh-Day Adventist at 6% and Methodist at 5%. Other houses of worship on Bermuda include Jehovah's Witness, Baptist, Presbyterian, Christian Science and Muslim.

LANGUAGE

English is spoken on Bermuda with a predominantly British accent. The interchange of 'w' for 'v' is not uncommon, so that welcome is often pronounced as 'velcome'.

Facts for the Visitor

PLANNING
When to Go
Bermuda can be visited year round, but the busiest tourist season, referred to as the 'summer season' or 'high season', is from April through October. This is the time when Bermuda enjoys its warmest air and water temperatures and when the best conditions exist for water sports such as swimming, snorkeling and diving. It's also the most vibrant time on the island, with a livelier hotel scene, greater entertainment options and more visitors milling about.

The winter is a bit too cool for most people to enjoy ocean swimming, and many tourist-related activities, such as diving tours and glass-bottom boat cruises, suspend operations for at least part of the season. Even a number of guesthouses and small hotels close for a month or two, with January being the deadest period.

That doesn't necessarily mean that winter is a bad time to visit Bermuda – it depends on what your interests are. Golfers and tennis players will find temperatures more pleasant in the winter. Also on the plus side, there are far fewer visitors to compete with, and getting a table at your favorite restaurant will be much easier. In addition, winter visitors are treated to free 'November to March' activities sponsored by the Bermuda Department of Tourism – these include Gombey dancing, guided walks in Hamilton and St George, and a skirling ceremony at Fort Hamilton by kilted bagpipers of the Bermuda Islands Pipe Band.

Not surprisingly, most hotels drop their rates in winter, and if you shop around you can find some good deals, even at the biggest resorts. Not that winter has all the bargains – in summer there are more airlines flying into Bermuda and consequently fare wars tend to keep airfares lower than in winter.

For detailed climate information, see the Climate section in the previous Facts about

Bermuda chapter. For specific events taking place throughout the year, see the Special Events section later in this chapter. Also see the Outdoor Activities chapter for seasonal information on specific sports.

Maps
The Bermuda Department of Tourism's free *Bermuda Handy Reference Map*, updated annually, is indeed handy and may be all you'll need for a short visit or limited sightseeing. It shows major roads and the location of hotels, sightseeing attractions, beaches and the like. It can be obtained from the Department of Tourism (see Tourist Offices, below) in advance of your trip or picked up at any of the Visitors Service Bureaus in Bermuda after you arrive.

The most detailed fold-out map, however, is *The Bermuda Islands Tourist Map* by Island Maps ($4.95). It shows all public roads, parks, beaches, golf courses, nearshore shipwrecks, gas stations and larger hotels, and can be purchased at bookshops and hotel sundry shops.

If you prefer a paperback atlas, the 80-page *Bermuda Islands Guide* ($4.95) by Clarion Enterprises shows virtually every road, beach and tourist attraction in Bermuda – it even shows pay phones and public restrooms. Unfortunately, it hasn't been updated since the first edition in 1982, so some of the newer places aren't marked and a few of the older ones no longer exist. It's sold at larger bookshops, such as the Bookmart in Hamilton, and at Trimingham's stores.

What to Bring
Bermudians dress conservatively. What clothing to bring depends not only on the season you visit, but on where you stay and what sort of dining you have in mind.

Casual sportswear is acceptable daytime attire most anywhere in Bermuda, including lunchtime dining in restaurants.

A number of fine-dining spots will require dressing up for dinner, so men who plan on dining in fancy restaurants are best advised to bring along a jacket and tie and women are advised to bring a nice dress. This also holds true if you book into a hotel-dining package that includes fine dining.

Otherwise, particularly in the summer, lightweight clothing made of cotton, which breathes best in hot weather, is the most suitable. In winter, it's wise to pack an autumn-weight jacket, a sweater and other light woolens as well.

If you plan on renting a moped, you'll appreciate having a windbreaker for cooler evenings and to offer limited protection in the event of a rainstorm. Another good thing for moped riders to bring is a bungee cord, so you can strap down a small bag in the basket of your moped, securing it from wind and the hands of any potential drive-by thief.

A good pair of walking shoes will be appreciated if you decide to thoroughly explore the towns of St George and Hamilton, or take one of Bermuda's longer hikes, such as the one to Spittal Pond.

Be sure not to forget your swimsuit. Divers should bring their certification card and log book. If you plan on doing a lot of snorkeling, you might want to bring your own snorkel, mask and fins; of course, these can be rented in Bermuda, but the prices tend to be high. Likewise, tennis players can save rental fees by bringing their own racquets and tennis balls, and golfers by carting along their own clubs and golf balls. Keep in mind that some tennis courts insist on players wearing 'tennis whites'.

Birdwatchers will no doubt appreciate having a pair of binoculars. A Swiss Army knife, or similar knife with a corkscrew, can be handy for picnics. Bring a camera and film, as Bermuda is very picturesque.

Zip-lock plastic sandwich bags in a couple of sizes are indispensable for keeping things dry. You can use them to protect your film and camera equipment, to seal up airline tickets and passports, and to keep wet bathing suits away from the rest of your luggage.

Airlines do lose luggage from time to time, but you've got a better chance of it being retrieved if it's tagged with your name and address *inside* as well as outside. Outside tags can always fall off or be removed. But take heart: Should you lose something or simply forget to pack it, you'll be able to find most anything you'll need after your arrival in Bermuda.

HIGHLIGHTS

The **Town of St George** is unique for its well-preserved period character. No trip to Bermuda would be complete without spending at least an afternoon strolling its crooked streets and poking into its churches, museums and historic sites.

While the **City of Hamilton** has a more modern, businesslike facade, it also has plenty to offer visitors, including an excellent selection of restaurants and quality shops, an art museum, a history museum and scenic views from the hilltop Fort Hamilton.

The **Royal Naval Dockyard** is the top sight at the western end of Bermuda. Its inner fort has been turned into the island's best historic museum, the Bermuda Maritime Museum, and other buildings have been converted into craft shops and atmospheric restaurants.

Pink-sand beaches are certainly a highlight in Bermuda. The most dazzling array is found at **South Shore Park**, with the turquoise waters and gentle, curving sands of Horseshoe Bay being arguably the most picturesque.

Other top natural sights include the **Bermuda Botanical Gardens** in Paget, which displays hundreds of specimens of flora, and the **Crystal Caves** at Bailey's Bay, where you can walk deep into an underground cave and see impressive stalactites and stalagmites. Also interesting to visit is the **Bermuda Aquarium, Museum & Zoo**, with its tanks of colorful fish, Galápagos turtles and endangered-species breeding program.

TOURIST OFFICES
Local Tourist Offices

The Bermuda Department of Tourism (☎ 292-0023, fax 292-7537) has its administrative office at Global House, 43 Church St, Hamilton. The mailing address is PO Box HM 465, Hamilton HM BX, Bermuda. When calling from outside Bermuda, prefix the 441 area code to the local number.

The chamber of commerce, in cooperation with the tourism department, staffs walk-in tourist offices called Visitors Service Bureaus all year round in the City of Hamilton, the Town of St George, the Royal Naval Dockyard and the airport. There's also a Somerset office open from April through October.

Tourist Offices Abroad

Before you visit Bermuda, you can contact the Bermuda Department of Tourism to receive a standard packet of visitor information covering accommodations, activities and seasonal events. Upon request, the department will also send specific information on family activities, honeymoon packages, golf courses and yachting. In addition, if you have a fax machine you can call the New York toll-free number listed below to receive fact sheets on a score of different topics via fax.

The Bermuda Department of Tourism operates the following overseas offices.

Canada
   1200 Bay St, Suite 1004,
   Toronto, Ontario M5R 2A5
   (☎ 416-923-9600, 800-387-1304,
   fax 416-923-4840)

UK
   1 Battersea Church Rd,
   London SW11 3LY
   (☎ 0171-771-7001, fax 0171-352-6501)

USA
   Head office:
   310 Madison Ave, Suite 201,
   New York, NY 10017
   (☎ 212-818-9800, 800-223-6106,
   fax 212-983-5289)

Regional offices:
245 Peachtree Center Ave NE, Suite 803,
Atlanta, GA 30303
(☎ 404-524-1541, fax 404-586-9933)

44 School St, Suite 1010,
Boston, MA 02108
(☎ 617-742-0405, fax 617-723-7786)

150 N Wacker Drive, Suite 1070,
Chicago, IL 60606
(☎ 312-782-5486, fax 312-704-6996)

3151 Cahuenga Blvd W, Suite 111,
Los Angeles, CA 90068
(☎ 213-436-0744, 800-252-0211 from CA,
800-421-0000 from elsewhere in the USA,
fax 213-436-0750)

VISAS & DOCUMENTS
Passport

A passport is the preferred document for entry into Bermuda and is required of visitors from all countries that require a passport for re-entry purposes.

Your passport should remain valid until well after your trip. If it's about to expire, renew it before you go.

Applying for or renewing a passport can take anything from a few days to several months, so don't leave it till the last minute. Bureaucracy tends to grind faster if you do everything in person rather than rely on the mail or agents. Find out beforehand what is required: passport photos, birth certificate, exact payment in cash, whatever.

Australian citizens can apply at a post office or the passport office in their state capital; Britons can apply at major post offices; Canadians can apply at regional passport offices; New Zealanders can apply at any district office of the Department of Internal Affairs; and US citizens must apply in person (but may usually renew by mail) either at a US Passport Agency office or at some courthouses and post offices.

From the USA Visitors from the USA must present one of the following types of identification. Note that if you're presenting identification that doesn't have a photo, such as a birth certificate, you'll need to also present a driver's license or similar photo ID. (Children 16 and under who are traveling with their parents may present an official birth certificate without a photo ID.)

- US passport – it needn't be valid, but if it has expired the photo should be recent enough that it still resembles the bearer
- An official birth certificate with a raised seal, or a certified copy issued by a municipal authority
- US Naturalization Certificate
- US Alien Registration Card
- US Re-entry Permit

From Canada Visitors from Canada must present one of the following types of identification:

- A valid Canadian passport
- An official birth certificate or a certified copy, along with a photo ID
- Canadian Certificate of Citizenship, or other official proof of Landed Immigrant status

From Other Countries Visitors from other countries, including the UK, Western Europe, Australia and New Zealand, must present a valid passport.

Visas
Visas are not required of citizens of most countries, including the USA, Canada, the UK, Australia, New Zealand and Western European countries.

Visas are required for citizens from the former Soviet Union, most countries in North Africa and the Middle East (but not Israel or Egypt), Albania, Bosnia-Herzegovina, Bulgaria, Cambodia, China, Croatia, Cuba, the Czech Republic, Haiti, Mongolia, Nigeria, North Korea, Romania, Serbia, Slovakia, Slovenia, Sri Lanka and Vietnam. Visitors from these countries should contact a British embassy or consulate in their home country for visa information.

Visa Extensions Immigration authorities at the Bermuda International Airport will determine your permitted length of stay. They commonly grant a stay of up to 21 days. Extensions can be applied for at the

Immigration Headquarters (☎ 295-5151), 30 Parliament St, Hamilton.

Onward Tickets
All visitors landing in Bermuda must be in possession of a return or onward ticket.

Other Documents
A driver's license can be useful as an ID, however you won't get much mileage out of it in Bermuda, as the only vehicles that can be rented are mopeds, and no driver's license is required to rent them.

If you're a member of the National Trust in Australia, Barbados, Britain or another Commonwealth country, you'll get free entry into Bermuda National Trust sites by showing your membership card.

Divers should bring along their certification cards.

Photocopies
It's a good idea to make photocopies of your passport, birth certificate or other ID, as well as your airline tickets and traveler's checks serial numbers. Stash a copy at home before you go and leave another in your guest room in the event you should lose any of these items on your trip.

Travel Insurance
Your travel agent can sell you a travel insurance policy to cover losses you might incur should you unexpectedly have to cancel your trip or change your itinerary. Keep in mind that many airlines, cruise lines, hotels and package tours have hefty penalties for cancellations or changes, and some are totally nonrefundable.

A good travel insurance policy also provides coverage for lost luggage and medical emergencies. Your travel agent can explain the various options. For further details, see the Health section later on in this chapter.

It's a good idea to purchase travel insurance as early as possible. If you buy it the week before you leave, you might find, for instance, that you're not covered for delays to your departure caused by strikes or other industrial action that may have been in force before you took out the insurance.

Paying for your ticket with a credit card often provides limited travel accident insurance, and you may also be able to reclaim the payment if the operator doesn't deliver. Ask your credit card company what it will cover.

EMBASSIES
Embassies Abroad
Bermuda's diplomatic representation is handled by British embassies and consulates around the world.

Foreign Consulates in Bermuda
While there are no embassies in Bermuda, Portugal and the United States maintain consulates. Portugal's consulate (☎ 292-1039) is in the Melbourne House, 11 Parliament St; USA's consulate (☎ 295-1342) is at Crown Hill, 16 Middle Rd, Devonshire.

In addition, several countries have designated 'honorary consuls' in Bermuda, including Belgium, Chile, Denmark, Finland, France, Germany, Greece, Italy, Jamaica, the Netherlands, Norway, Spain, Sweden and Switzerland. The addresses and phone numbers can be found in the blue pages of the Bermuda phone book.

CUSTOMS
Visitors to Bermuda may bring in duty free: 200 cigarettes, 50 cigars, one pound of tobacco, one quart of liquor and one quart of wine, as well as all clothing, sports equipment, cameras etc intended for personal use. Each visitor is also entitled to a $30 gift allowance.

Visitors are allowed to bring in up to 20 pounds of meat per person for their own consumption. Because of the high price of imported food, bringing in frozen meat may be an option to consider if you are staying in a place with cooking facilities.

Bermuda restricts or prohibits the importation of animals, plants, fruits, vegetables, pornography, firearms, spear guns, offensive weapons and drugs. For inquiries about customs laws, contact the Customs House at ☎ 295-4816.

MONEY
Costs
Unlike many vacation destinations where airfare represents your most substantial expense, the largest slice of your travel costs in Bermuda is likely to be for accommodations. Bermuda's high cost of living is reflected in the rates charged by island hotels – by the time service charges and taxes are added to the tariff, there are only a few places in Bermuda where you can squeak by for much less than $100 a day . . . and the average is easily twice that!

If you plan to stay seven days or less, look into package tours that include both airfare and hotel, as they will often work out cheaper than buying the airfare and paying for the hotel separately. Although it's not heavily advertised, with many tour operators you can also create your own 'package tours' for stays of longer than seven days – so even if you're staying for a couple of weeks, this may be an option worth pursuing.

Eating in Bermuda can be a hefty expense as well. Most of the food consumed in Bermuda is imported, and prices are generally about 50% higher than those in the USA. Snacking on simple fare from grocery stores, or getting a place with kitchen facilities and cooking some of your own meals, can help keep costs relatively low.

In terms of dining out, some of the best-value meals can be found on weekdays in the City of Hamilton, where lunch deals for under $10 abound. However, dinner at these same restaurants might well run you up a $25 tab for a solid meal. And if you stick with the resort restaurants, you can easily pay twice these amounts.

If you plan to eat meals in the restaurant where you're staying, note that many guesthouses and hotels offer discounted meal plans that include breakfast and dinner. Some of the better plans offer a 'dine around' feature whereby guests are allowed to take their meals at a handful of affiliated restaurants.

Carrying Money

It's most convenient to carry US currency, as both US dollars and US dollar traveler's checks are accepted by most businesses. Other foreign currencies will need to be exchanged at a bank.

Major credit cards, such as Visa and MasterCard, are accepted by most shops and restaurants, and the American Express charge card is accepted by many. Hotels and guesthouses are more fickle on credit cards; the larger resort hotels accept them, but a number of the smaller places do not. If you intend to pay off your room bill with a credit card, be sure to inquire at the time of booking your reservation as to whether it will be honored – surprisingly, even some of the high-end places don't accept them.

Currency

The legal tender is the Bermuda dollar, which is pegged at a 1:1 ratio with the US dollar. The US dollar is also in general circulation in Bermuda and is accepted at face value at hotels, restaurants and shops.

The Bermuda dollar is divided into 100 cents (¢). Coins come in denominations of 1¢ (penny), 5¢ (nickel), 10¢ (dime), 25¢ (quarter) and one dollar. The coins have island designs: there's a hog on the back of the copper penny, an angelfish on the nickel, an Easter lily on the dime, a longtail tropicbird on the quarter and a sailboat on the bronze $1 coin.

Bills come in $2, $5, $10, $20, $50 and $100 denominations.

Changing Money

The Bank of Bermuda will cash up to $500 in US dollar, Canadian dollar or British pound traveler's checks free of service charges. There's a 1% commission if you cash more than $500 in a single transaction. While the bank does not accept other foreign traveler's checks, it will exchange cash in other major currencies.

You can change money during normal banking hours, which are from 9:30 am to 3 pm Monday to Thursday, from 9:30 am to 5 pm on Friday. In addition, the Bank of Bermuda has 24-hour ATM machines in several locations – including the airport, Hamilton, St George and Somerset – which will accept Cirrus and Plus system ATM cards and MasterCard or Visa credit cards.

Tipping & Bargaining

The usual restaurant tip is 15%, which most restaurants automatically add onto the bill – if not, you should add the tip yourself. Hotels typically tag on a 10% service charge to your room bill, which covers gratuities to hotel workers. For taxi drivers, hair stylists and the like, a tip of about 10% is appropriate.

Bargaining is not a common practice in Bermuda.

Taxes

A 7.25% occupancy tax is added on to hotel bills upon check out. For information on departure taxes, see the Getting There & Away chapter.

POST & COMMUNICATIONS
Postal Rates

Airmail letters cost 60¢ for the first 10 grams and 30¢ for each additional 10 grams when sent to the USA, Canada, Mexico, Central America, Venezuela, Colombia or the Caribbean.

The cost is 75¢ for the first 10 grams, and 40¢ for additional 10 grams, for letters sent to the UK, Europe, North Africa and most of South America.

To other destinations – including Australia, Asia and most of Africa – the cost is 85¢ for the first 10 grams, 50¢ for additional 10 grams.

Postcards cost the same as a 10-gram letter. Aerograms cost 55¢ to any destination.

For mail sent within Bermuda for local delivery, the cost is 20¢ for a postcard and 25¢ for a letter of up to 20 grams.

Sending Mail

There are post offices in every major village and town, from St George to Somerset. As a general rule, airmail posted by 9:30 am at the General Post Office in Hamilton will leave the island the same day.

Receiving Mail

Most hotels will hold mail for their guests. In addition, mail can be received in your name, c/o General Delivery, General Post Office, Hamilton HM PM, Bermuda. Items not collected at the GPO in Hamilton within 30 days will be returned to the sender.

Telephone

Local telephone numbers have seven digits. All calls made on Bermuda to another place on Bermuda are local calls and cost 20¢.

There are pay phones all around the island, including in most shopping centers, hotel lobbies, ferry terminals and the Bermuda International Airport departure lounge. Public phones accept both coins and phone cards. In addition to Bermuda coins, many public phones will accept US coins. For making international calls, pay phones will accept Visa, MasterCard and American Express cards as well.

Phone cards (also called cash cards) can be quite convenient if you're going to be making a lot of calls or are making overseas calls, as you won't need a pocketful of coins. Phone cards are available in $10, $20 and $50 denominations and can be purchased from tourist offices, telephone company offices and the Cable & Wireless office at 20 Church St in Hamilton.

Yachters and other visitors can register for cellular phone service by calling ☎ 292-6032.

Bermuda's country code is 1 and its international access code is 011, the same as it is in the USA, Canada and some Caribbean countries.

Calls to Bermuda Bermuda's new area code is 441, which must be added to all seven-digit local numbers when calling from overseas. (The older area code 809 may still appear on some brochures, but it is no longer in use.)

You can call Bermuda direct from the USA, Canada and those Caribbean coun-

Aerial Sea Mail

The Bermuda postal system offers one of the more unusual 'sea mail' services. What is peculiar about it is that ships are not involved in the service, but the mail is instead airlifted from Bermuda to the country of destination.

To make sure people don't overly take advantage of the discounted 'sea mail' rates, all surface mail is held in Bermuda until a closing date, which is equivalent to the scheduled date that the imaginary ship would leave Bermuda, plus the additional time – two days for mail to the USA, four days for mail to the UK – that it would normally take for a ship to sail between Bermuda and the destination.

The Bermudians take it all quite seriously – the closing date for sea mail is displayed in all post offices. If you manage to get something off shortly before the closing date, it can actually be an efficient way to mail things and the rates are roughly half those of regular airmail. ■

tries sharing the same direct-dialing system by dialing 1 + 441 + seven-digit local number.

To call Bermuda from anywhere else in the world, dial the international access code for the country you're calling from + 1 + 441 + seven-digit local number. For instance, the UK access code is 00, so from the UK dial 00 + 1 + 441 + local number.

Calls from Bermuda From Bermuda, you can call direct to the USA, Canada and some Caribbean countries by dialing 1 + area code + local number.

To call direct to other parts of the world, dial 011 + country code + area code + local number. For example, the country code for the UK is 44, hence: 011 + 44 + area code + local number. Some other country codes are: Australia 61, France 33, Germany 49, Italy 39, Japan 81, New Zealand 64.

Rates to the continental USA and Canada range from 80¢ to $1.15 per minute, while rates to most other countries cost $2 per minute. A chart of international long-distance charges can be found listed by country at the front of Bermuda phone books.

In addition to placing direct-dial calls, you can also call home using the 'country direct system', which will charge the call to your home phone bill or calling card. To make long-distance calls via AT&T's USADirect Service, dial ☎ 1-800-872-2881, via MCI's WorldPhone service dial ☎ 1-800-623-0484.

Emergency & Information For police, fire and ambulance emergencies, dial ☎ 911; the call is free from public phones. For ocean rescues or information on overdue boats, call Bermuda Harbour Radio at ☎ 297-1010. Lifeline, a 24-hour counseling service, can be reached at ☎ 236-0224 from 9 am to 5 pm and at ☎ 236-3770 from 5 pm to 9 am.

Dial ☎ 411 for local directory assistance. For directory assistance to the USA, dial ☎ 1 + area code + 555-1212. For directory (and other) assistance for other countries, dial ☎ 0 for the overseas operator.

Fax & Telegraph
You can send or receive faxes and telegrams at the Cable & Wireless office, 20 Church St, Hamilton. To send a fax, the cost is $2 for the first page and $1 for each additional page, plus the cost of the phone call. To receive a fax, the cost is $1 per page; faxes from overseas should be sent to ☎ 441-295-7909. The office is open from 9 am to 5 pm Monday to Saturday.

Also, there are public fax terminals in the tourist offices in Hamilton and St George, at the General Post Office in Hamilton, at the cruise ship terminals in Hamilton, in the airport departure lounge and at the Clocktower Mall at the Royal Naval Dockyard. These fax terminals accept MasterCard, Visa and American Express cards only.

Guests can usually send and receive faxes at their hotels, but it's wise to check the rate in advance.

BOOKS
There are numerous books about Bermuda, both fiction and nonfiction, which can provide insights on the island. If you aren't able to find any of these books before your trip, you can easily pick them up at bookstores in Bermuda.

History & Culture
Bermuda's Story by Terry Tucker, the island's most highly regarded historian, is a short and easy-to-read history book covering the period from Bermuda's founding to the 1960s. A more in-depth treatment of history can be found in Tucker's *Bermuda Today & Yesterday (1503-1978)*.

School-age children might enjoy reading Willoughby Patton's *Sea Venture*, which tells the story of the famed shipwreck from the perspective of a boy on board the ship.

Held in Trust by the Bermuda National Trust is an attractive book that details the historic homes, nature reserves and other property under the auspices of the Trust.

Natural History
Bermuda's Marine Life by Wolfgang Sterrer, former director of the Bermuda Biological Station, is an excellent 300-page book with color photography and detailed descriptions of fish, crustaceans and other local marine life.

Wonders of the Deep – Underwater Bermuda by Michael Burke, Stephen Kerr et al, is a hardcover coffee-table book with lovely underwater photos of Bermuda's fish, coral and anemones.

A Guide to the Reef, Shore and Game Fish of Bermuda by Louis S Mowbray, who was curator of Bermuda's aquarium for 25 years and a pioneer of game fishing in Bermuda, describes local fish, complete with drawings.

Bermuda Shipwrecks by Daniel and Denise Berg is a well-researched book detailing many of the shipwrecks found in Bermudian waters. It's a must for divers who intend to do wreck diving.

While there are a number of books about Caribbean flora that include some Bermuda flowers, *Flowers of Bermuda*, a compact book by Hans W Hannau, is specific to Bermuda, with photos and text that feature some of the more common flowers found on the island.

If you're more interested in the origin of plants on Bermuda, Jill Collett's *Bermuda, Her Plants & Gardens (1609-1850)* gives a historic background on flora, farming and gardening on the island.

The best book for birdwatchers is *A Guide to the Birds of Bermuda* by Eric Amos, which describes more than 300 species of birds that have been seen on Bermuda and gives detailed information on birding sites around the island.

General
While Peter Benchley was on Bermuda writing his best-known novel *Jaws*, his diving outings inspired him to later write *The Deep*, an adventure novel set in Bermuda. It incorporates an interesting mix of island life and fiction and makes a good beachside read.

Bermuda in Full Color by Hans W Hannau gives general background on the people and places of Bermuda, complete with color photographs.

Bermuda Abstracts by photographer Graeme Outerbridge is an artistic book that captures the charm of Bermuda's unique architecture.

There are several books about the Bermuda Triangle, including *Bermuda Triangle Mystery Solved* by Lawrence David Kusche, which will provide interesting reading for those fascinated with the mysteries of vanished ships and planes.

Outerbridge's Original Cookbook by Alexis Outerbridge has 150 pages of recipes for drinks, soups and various other dishes using sherry peppers sauce. *Bermudian Cookery*, a 190-page spiral-bound book published by the Bermuda Junior Service League, has recipes on a variety of favorite island foods.

Bookstores
There are a number of bookstores on Bermuda. The best and biggest, The Bookmart, can be found in the City of Hamilton in the Phoenix Centre at 3 Reid St. Another good Hamilton bookstore is the Bermuda Book Store on Queen St. At the eastern end of the island, the best bookstore is The Book Cellar, on the corner of Water St and Barbers Alley in St George. All three have good selections of books on Bermuda, as well as travel books and novels.

ONLINE SERVICES
The Bermuda Department of Tourism can be reached at www.bermudatourism.com for general tourist information. The *Bermuda Sun* website is a gold mine of information at www.bermudasun.org/news; it allows you to access a wide array of information on Bermuda, including weather, news, arts and entertainment, sports, email directories and general tourist information.

Bermuda's tranquil waters are an artist's inspiration.

MR Onions, a restaurant on Par-la-Ville Rd in the City of Hamilton, has computers at its bar that can connect you to the Internet for a reasonable usage fee.

FILMS

There are several videos geared for tourists to Bermuda. *The Bermuda Channel* is an hour-long video with information on sightseeing, history, shopping and the like, complete with commercial advertising. It can be ordered for $25 from The Bermuda Channel, PO Box HM 2032, Hamilton HM HX.

The video tapes in the 'Island of Bermuda' series – which includes *Bermuda Highlights*, *Dive Bermuda* and *Bermuda Anti-Stress Video* – cost $30 each and can be ordered from Panatel VDS (☎ 238-3738), 15 Wellbottom Rd, Warwick WK 01.

Although it's dated, a good film to look for in your local public library is *Bermuda* by Van Arsdale's Video Travel Guides, which offers a glimpse of some of the island's main sights and hotel options.

A few Hollywood movies have been shot on Bermuda, including *The Deep* (1977), based on Peter Benchley's novel of the same name, starring Jacqueline Bisset and Nick Nolte; *Chapter Two* (1979), an autobiographical comedy by Neil Simon, starring Marsha Mason and James Caan; and *That Touch of Mink* (1962), starring Cary Grant and Doris Day.

NEWSPAPERS & MAGAZINES

The leading Bermuda newspaper, the *Royal Gazette*, has both local and international news and is published Monday to Saturday.

The island also has a couple of weeklies, published on Fridays, that focus almost solely on island issues: The *Mid-Ocean News* is a sister paper of the *Royal Gazette*; the *Bermuda Sun* is the best source of entertainment happenings; and the *Bermuda Times* presents a perspective on local matters that is geared to the black community.

A handy item to pick up as soon as you arrive is *This Week In Bermuda*, a free weekly publication loaded with visitor-related information, including an events schedule, sightseeing details and ads aplenty. If you don't find one at the airport, it can be readily found around the island at hotels and other businesses that cater to tourists.

Bermuda, a full-color magazine published quarterly and geared toward visitors, has an interesting range of feature articles about Bermuda. Annual subscription rates are $14.80 in the USA, $22.80 outside the USA, including postage, from Bermuda Magazine (☎ 292-7279), PO Box HM 2032, Hamilton HM HX.

The Bermudian, a full-color magazine in its sixth decade of publication, is geared more to Bermudians, with articles on business, local personalities and homes and gardens. An annual subscription in any country outside Bermuda costs $40, postage included, from The Bermudian Publishing Company (☎ 295-0695), PO Box HM 283, Hamilton HM AX.

You can also find a range of international newspapers, such as the *New York Times*, the *Boston Globe*, the *Wall Street Journal*, the *Globe & Mail*, the *Guardian* and London's *Sunday Times*.

RADIO & TV

Bermuda has American-influenced cable TV, which includes the major US networks ABC, CBS, CNN, Fox, HBO, NBC, PBS and numerous other channels. Local news is shown at 7 pm on channel 3 (ZBN) and channel 4 (VZB), and followed at 7:30 pm with CBS network news on channel 3 and NBC news on channel 4. Bermuda weather service broadcasts continuous weather and tide forecasts on channel 11.

Bermuda has two radio broadcasting companies. The Bermuda Broadcasting Company operates at AM 1230 and 1340, both with mixed music, and at FM 89, with rock and contemporary music. DeFontes Broadcasting operates at AM 1160, with BBC World Service and local public affairs; AM 1280, with religious programming; AM 1450, with country music; and FM 106.1, with contemporary music.

PHOTOGRAPHY & VIDEO

Print film is readily available on Bermuda, although slide film can be more difficult to find. As with most items on Bermuda, prices are on the high side – a 36-exposure roll of Kodak Gold print film will cost you around $8 – so it's best to bring an adequate film supply along with you.

If you want to develop your print film while on Bermuda, there are shops in Hamilton that have same-day processing at moderate prices. Otherwise, consider bringing along processing mailers to send film to a lab back home and have your photos waiting for you when you return from your vacation.

When taking pictures, keep in mind that sand and water are intense reflectors and in bright light they'll often leave foreground subjects shadowy. You can try compensating by adjusting your f-stop or attaching a polarizing filter, or both, but the most effective technique is to take photos in the gentler light of early morning and late afternoon. Also, be careful not to leave your camera in direct sunlight any longer than necessary.

Bermuda uses the same VHS video system as in the USA and Canada. Video tapes and batteries can be purchased at Stuart's (☎ 295-5496) on Reid St in the City of Hamilton, which is also an authorized service center for JVC and Sony camcorders. If you need to rent a video camera, Jensen's (☎ 295-3663) in the Washington Mall can arrange rentals.

TIME

Bermuda is in the Atlantic Standard Time zone, which is four hours behind Greenwich mean time and one hour ahead of Eastern Standard Time.

When it's noon in Bermuda, it is 11 am in New York and Toronto, 10 am in Chicago, 8 am in Los Angeles and Vancouver, 2 am in Sydney, midnight in Hong Kong and 4 pm in London.

Daylight-saving time is in effect in Bermuda from the first Sunday in April to the last Sunday in October.

ELECTRICITY

Electric current operates on 110 volts and 60 cycles, and a flat, two-pronged plug is used – the same as in the USA. Some hotels have adaptors for electric shavers.

WEIGHTS & MEASURES

Although a conversion to metric has been undertaken in such areas as the posting of speed limits, Bermuda still uses the imperial system of measurement for many applications. Newspapers print temperatures in degrees Fahrenheit and most weights are measured in ounces and pounds.

For those unaccustomed to either system, there's a conversion table on the inside back cover of this book.

LAUNDRY

While most hotels offer laundry services, these tend to be quite expensive. You'll save by using coin-operated laundries, which can be found in most parishes.

HEALTH

Bermuda is a healthy place to live and visit, and travelers don't need to take any unusual health precautions.

If you're visiting in the summer season and are new to the heat and humidity, you may find yourself easily fatigued and more susceptible to minor ailments. Acclimatize yourself by slowing down your pace and drinking plenty of liquids.

Bermuda's 324-bed King Edward VII Memorial Hospital is on Point Finger Rd in Paget. For medical emergencies dial ☎ 911 to get an ambulance; the call can be made free from public phones. For nonemergency medical services call the Red Cross at the hospital (☎ 236-2345).

Predeparture Preparations

Health Insurance A travel insurance policy to cover theft, loss and medical problems is a good idea. There is a wide variety of policies, and your travel agent will have recommendations. Some policies offer lower and higher medical expenses options. Check the small print.

• Some policies specifically exclude 'dangerous activities', such as scuba diving and motorcycling.
• A policy that pays doctors or hospitals directly may be preferable to one where you pay on the spot and claim later. If you have to claim later, make sure you keep all documentation. Some policies ask you to call back (reverse the charges) to a center in your home country, where an immediate assessment of your problem is made.
• Check if the policy covers ambulances or helicopter rescue, and an emergency flight home. If you have to stretch out you will need two seats, and somebody has to pay for them!

Medical Kit A small, straightforward medical kit is a good thing to carry. A kit might include the following items.

• Aspirin or Panadol – for pain or fever
• Antihistamine (such as Benadryl) – useful as a decongestant for colds, allergies, to ease the itch from insect bites or stings or to help prevent motion sickness
• Kaolin preparation (Pepto-Bismol) or Imodium – for possible stomach upsets
• Antiseptic and antibiotic powder or similar 'dry' spray – for cuts and grazes
• Calamine lotion – to ease irritation from bites or stings
• Bandages and Band-Aids – for minor injuries
• Scissors, tweezers and a thermometer (note that mercury thermometers are prohibited by airlines)
• Sunblock and insect repellent

Health Preparations If you wear glasses, take a spare pair and your prescription.

If you need a particular medication, take an adequate supply, as foreign prescriptions cannot be filled in Bermuda. If you do run out of medication or forget to bring it, a pharmacist can refer you to a local doctor, who can write you up a new prescription. Getting replacements will be easier if you have brought a copy of the prescription itself, or part of the packaging showing both the generic and the brand name.

For all controlled drugs you're bringing into Bermuda, it's a good idea to have a legible prescription to show that you legally use the medication. Always keep the medication in its original container. If you're carrying a syringe for some reason, have a note from your doctor to explain why you're doing so.

A Medic Alert tag is a good idea if your medical condition is not always easily recognizable (heart trouble, diabetes, asthma, allergic reactions to antibiotics etc).

Immunizations Immunizations are not required to enter Bermuda.

Basic Rules

Water Although several of Bermuda's largest resort hotels have their own desalination plants, the rest of Bermuda depends upon rain for its water supply. As the rain is caught on rooftops and directed into individual storage tanks the bacteria count in the water can vary. If you're staying at a guesthouse or smaller hotel, it's best to inquire with the manager about the water's suitability for drinking.

If in doubt you can always treat the water first. The simplest way of purifying water is to boil it thoroughly for 10 minutes.

Simple filtering will not remove all organisms, so if you cannot boil water it can be treated chemically. Chlorine tablets (Puritabs, Steritabs or other brand names) will kill many but not all pathogens. Iodine is very effective for purifying water and is available in tablet form (such as Potable Aqua), but follow the directions carefully and remember that too much iodine can be harmful.

In hot weather, make sure you drink enough – don't rely on feeling thirsty to indicate when you should drink. Not needing to urinate or very dark-yellow urine is a danger sign. Carry a water bottle on outings. Excessive sweating can lead to loss of salt and therefore muscle cramping. Salt tablets are not a good idea as a preventative, but in situations where salt is not used much, adding salt to food can help.

Bottled water is sold in grocery stores.

Food Stomach upsets are a possibility anywhere you travel, but in Bermuda these are likely to be relatively minor.

but, where possible, avoid bandages, which can keep wounds wet.

Coral cuts are even more susceptible to infection because tiny pieces of coral can get embedded in the skin. These cuts are notoriously slow to heal, as the coral releases a weak venom into the wound.

Unless you're allergic to them, bee stings are usually painful rather than dangerous; calamine lotion will give relief and ice packs will reduce the pain and swelling. Mosquitoes may be a nuisance, but mosquito-borne diseases such as malaria are unknown in Bermuda.

If you are stung by a jellyfish or a Portuguese man-of-war, quickly remove the tentacles and apply vinegar or a meat tenderizer containing papain (derived from papaya), which act to neutralize the toxins – in a pinch, you could use urine as well. For serious reactions, including chest pains or difficulty in breathing, seek immediate medical attention.

Women's Health
Some women experience irregular periods when traveling, due to the upset in routine. Don't forget to take time zones into account if you're on the pill; if you run into intestinal problems, the pill may not be absorbed. Ask your physician about these matters.

Poor diet, lowered resistance due to the use of antibiotics for stomach upsets and even the use of contraceptive pills can lead to vaginal infections when traveling in hot climates. Wearing skirts or loose-fitting trousers and cotton underwear will help to prevent infections.

TOILETS
Bermuda has standard western-style toilets. Public toilets are easy to find in major tourist areas, such as central St George and Hamilton, and at the more frequented beaches.

WOMEN TRAVELERS
Women travelers are no more likely to encounter problems in Bermuda than they

are elsewhere, but the usual common-sense precautions certainly apply when it comes to potentially dangerous situations like walking alone at night, accepting rides from strangers etc. Also, keep in mind that skimpy clothing is not the norm in Bermuda anywhere other than on the beach, and it could elicit unwanted attention.

GAY & LESBIAN TRAVELERS
While Bermuda is certainly not a mecca for gay travelers, a century-old criminal code that outlawed homosexual behavior was finally superseded by a gay rights amendment in 1994, and homosexuality in Bermuda is no longer against the law. Still, public displays of affection may well draw unwanted attention; discretion is advised.

Attitudes, a bar and dance spot in the City of Hamilton, is the main gay meeting place on the island.

DISABLED TRAVELERS
Physically challenged travelers might want to get in touch with national support organizations in their home country. These groups commonly have general information and tips on travel and are able to supply a list of travel agents specializing in tours for the disabled.

For wheelchair users, Bermuda's larger resort hotels generally have the greatest accessibility with elevators, wider doorways and the like, and some smaller places also have wheelchair-accessible guestrooms and common areas. Visitors with special needs should make their requirements known at the time of booking.

The Bermuda Red Cross (☎ 236-2345) at King Edward VII Memorial Hospital rents walkers, wheelchairs and crutches.

The Bermuda Physically Handicapped Association (☎ 292-5025), PO Box HM 08, Hamilton HM AX, can assist disabled visitors with sightseeing. It has a volunteer-operated bus with a hydraulic lift that can be used by manual wheelchairs; the bus is available on a first-come, first-served basis.

Wheelchair access on public transport is quite limited – the public buses do not have hydraulic lifts and the ferry service has only limited accessibility. However, the Hamilton ferry terminal is wheelchair accessible, so a ferry could be boarded there and taken simply as a cruise. The Hamilton-Paget ferry, for example, would make for a scenic 30-minute roundtrip tour. Another possibility is to take the ferry from Hamilton to the Royal Naval Dockyard, where the terminal, restaurants, museum, shopping center and restrooms are all wheelchair accessible.

SENIOR TRAVELERS
Bermuda is a popular destination any time of the year for senior travelers.

In addition to the usual off-season deals that are open to everyone, the Bermuda Department of Tourism tries to attract senior visitors in February by declaring it the 'Golden Rendezvous Month' and offering special events geared for travelers over 50. There's something happening for seniors every day of the week in February, including bridge games, ballroom dancing, island bus tours and lectures on architecture, local history or flora and fauna.

TRAVEL WITH CHILDREN
Although Bermudians are quite family oriented, Bermuda can pose some challenges to travelers with children. For instance, families who are accustomed to renting a car and piling all the kids inside will be dismayed to learn Bermuda has no car rentals. Large resort hotels don't place restrictions on children, but many other hotels and guesthouses tend to be formal and gear their activities solely for adults; a few don't accept children at all.

Travelers with babies will readily find baby food, formula and disposable diapers at local supermarkets, although prices will be higher than at home. Some hotels can provide cribs and high chairs; if not, they can be rented from the Bermuda Red Cross (☎ 236-2345) at the King Edward VII Memorial Hospital in Paget. If you expect to need a stroller, bring one from home.

For more information on traveling with children, pick up a copy of Lonely Planet's *Travel with Children* (1996) by Maureen Wheeler.

USEFUL ORGANIZATIONS
The Bermuda Audubon Society (☎ 293-6153 or 297-2623), PO Box HM 1328, Hamilton HM FX, puts out a quarterly newsletter that lists upcoming events such as birdwatching field trips and lectures on local environmental projects. The membership fee is $10, but a $15 donation is suggested for overseas members to cover the cost of airmail postage.

The Bermuda National Trust (☎ 236-6483), PO Box HM 61, Hamilton HM AX, is the island's leading preservation organization. For a $15 annual membership fee ($30 per family), you can receive the Trust newsletter and be entitled to free admission to Trust properties in Bermuda and in other Commonwealth countries, from Australia to Zimbabwe.

The Bermuda Zoological Society (☎ 293-2727), PO Box FL 145, Flatts FL BX, is a support organization for the Bermuda Aquarium, Museum & Zoo. The $25 annual dues ($35 for a family) not only help with the organization's various conservation efforts, but entitle members to a quarterly newsletter and free entrance to the Bermuda Aquarium, Museum & Zoo.

For information on social and business clubs, such as the Kiwanis Club, Rotary Club and Lions Club, see the yellow pages of the Bermuda phone book.

DANGERS & ANNOYANCES
Although Bermuda is a relatively safe place, it has issues with crime and drug abuse just like anyplace else. Violent crime has been on the rise in recent years and tourists are occasionally targeted for muggings. Travelers should use the standard precautions they would use anywhere when walking alone at night, especially in poorly lit areas. Women carrying purses should keep them close to their bodies to prevent purse snatchings.

Still, the most common problem encountered by visitors is moped thefts, which are at epidemic proportions on Bermuda. An average of 200 bikes are stolen each month – so great of a problem that it's virtually impossible to get theft insurance on mopeds anymore. Many of the bikes end up in 'chop shops' where they are stripped for parts, although some just end up being taken for a joy ride before being dumped over a cliff. If you rent a moped, you can cut down on the odds of having it stolen by locking it every time you stop and by parking in well-lit public places.

Visitors should be aware that Bermuda has very strict laws prohibiting of possession of illegal drugs, including marijuana, and penalties can be strict. Customs officers sometimes conduct body searches and students on spring break are given particular scrutiny. Those on cruise ships are not exempt – police have been known to search cruise ship cabins after a whiff of cannabis has wafted through the air. First-time foreign offenders found with very small amounts of marijuana are commonly fined from $500 to $1000, while possession of larger amounts of marijuana or any hard drugs usually results in a prison sentence.

For emergency telephone numbers, see Emergency & Information under Post & Communications earlier in this chapter.

Flora & Fauna

There are no poisonous snakes or dangerous wild animals on Bermuda to worry about.

Hikers should be aware that poison ivy is abundant on some interior trails and nature reserves, so you may want to wear socks and long pants as a precaution. In addition, the pencil or milk-bush tree *(Euphorbia tirucalli)*, found in some coastal areas such as Great Head Park in St David's, has a poisonous milky latex and should not be touched.

Ocean Dangers

Drowning is a potential cause of accidental death for visitors. If you're not familiar with water conditions, ask someone. It's best not to swim alone in any unfamiliar place.

Rip Currents Rip currents are fast-flowing currents of water within the ocean, moving from shallow nearshore areas out to sea. They are most common in conditions of high surf, forming when water from incoming waves builds up near the shore. Essentially the waves are coming in faster than they can flow back out.

The water then runs along the shoreline until it finds an escape route out to sea, usually through a channel or out along a point. Swimmers caught up in the current can be ripped out to deeper water.

Although rip currents can be powerful, they usually dissipate 50 to 100 yards offshore. Anyone caught in one should either go with the flow until it loses power or swim parallel to shore to slip out of it. Trying to swim against a rip current can exhaust the strongest of swimmers.

Undertows Undertows are common along steeply sloped beaches when large waves backwash directly into incoming surf. The receding water picks up speed as it flows down the slopes. When it hits an incoming wave, it pulls under it, creating an undertow. Swimmers caught up in an undertow can be pulled beneath the surface. The most important thing is not to panic. Go with the current until you get beyond the wave.

Coral Most coral cuts occur when swimmers are pushed onto the coral by rough waves and surges. It's a good idea to wear diving gloves when snorkeling over shallow reefs. Avoid walking on coral, which can not only cut your feet, but is very damaging to the coral. For the treatment of coral cuts, see Cuts & Stings in the Health section earlier in this chapter.

Jellyfish Take a peek into the water before you plunge in to make sure it's not jellyfish territory. These gelatinous creatures, with saclike bodies and stinging tentacles, are

Deceptively beautiful, the Portuguese man-of-war's tentacles are studded with stinging cells.

cles can reach up to 50 feet in length. Even touching a Portuguese man-of-war a few hours after it's washed up on shore can result in burning stings.

For treatment of jellyfish and Portuguese man-of-war stings, see Cuts & Stings in the Health section earlier in this chapter.

Eels Moray eels are often spotted by snorkelers around reefs and coral heads. They're constantly opening and closing their mouths to pump water across their gills, which makes them look far more menacing than they actually are.

Eels don't attack, but they will protect themselves if they feel cornered by fingers jabbing into the reef holes or crevices they occupy. Eels have sharp teeth and strong jaws and may clamp down if someone sticks a hand in their door.

Sharks Sharks are sometimes found in Bermudian waters, with one of the more common varieties being the cub shark, which grows up to 12 feet in length.

Sharks are curious and will sometimes investigate divers, although they generally just check things out and continue on their way. If they start to hang around, however, it's probably time for you to go.

Should you come face to face with a shark, the best thing to do is move casually and quietly away. Don't panic, as sharks are attracted by things that thrash around in water.

Some aquatic officials suggest thumping an attacking shark on the nose or sticking your fingers into its eyes, which may confuse it long enough to give you time to escape. Indeed, it's not uncommon for divers who dive in shark-infested waters to carry a billy club or bang stick.

Sharks are attracted by blood. Some attacks on humans are related to spear fishing; when a shark is going after a diver's bloody catch, the diver sometimes gets in the way. Sharks are also attracted by shiny things and by anything bright red or yellow, which might influence your choice of swimsuit color.

sometimes found in Bermuda. The sting of a jellyfish varies from mild to severe, depending on the variety. Unless you have an allergic reaction to their venom, the stings are generally not dangerous.

The Portuguese man-of-war is by far the worst type to encounter. Not technically a jellyfish, the man-of-war is a colonial hydrozoan, or a colony of coelenterates, rather than a solitary coelenterate like the true jellyfish. Its body consists of a translucent, bluish, bladder-like float, which generally grows to be about five inches long. In the waters off Bermuda, the Portuguese man-of-war is most prevalent from March through July.

A man-of-war sting is very painful, similar to a bad bee sting except that you're likely to get stung more than once from clusters of long tentacles containing hundreds of stinging cells. These trailing tenta-

Getting Married in Bermuda

Many visitors come to Bermuda not only for their honeymoons but to take their wedding vows as well. While getting married in Bermuda requires some advance planning, there are both public offices and private wedding consultants that can help with the arrangements.

For those who want to take the public route, both the required paperwork and the ceremony can be handled by the Register General's office in the City of Hamilton. For a fee of $165, this government agency will put the mandatory 'Notice of Intended Marriage' in local newspapers. Provided no formal objection is raised to your marriage intention, the marriage certificate can be issued after a two-week waiting period. The registry maintains its own cozy little 'Marriage Room' where, for an additional fee of $160, a civil marriage ceremony can be performed.

Should you prefer something more tailored, there are a handful of wedding consultants that can arrange anything from a traditional church wedding to a seaside ceremony. Of course they can also arrange all of the incidentals as well, from a cake and flowers to bagpipe music and a horse and carriage.

For full details on arranging a wedding in Bermuda, contact the nearest Bermuda Department of Tourism office (see Tourist Offices earlier in this chapter) and request their four-page 'Marriage in Bermuda' brochure, which can be sent by mail or fax. It includes the 'Notice of Intended Marriage' form and all the nitty-gritty details and contact addresses you'll need. ■

While unpleasant encounters with sharks are extremely unlikely, it's helpful to have a healthy respect for them.

BUSINESS HOURS & HOLIDAYS

Normal banking hours are from 9:30 am to 3 pm Monday to Thursday and from 9:30 am to 5 pm on Friday. Government offices are open from 8:45 am to 5 pm Monday to Friday, except on public holidays.

On public holidays, most business offices and some shops and restaurants close, while buses and ferries run on a reduced schedule. Note that when a public holiday falls on a Saturday or Sunday, it is often observed on the following Monday. The following are Bermuda's public holidays.

New Year's Day	January 1
Good Friday	Friday before Easter
Bermuda Day	May 24
Queen's Birthday	3rd Monday in June
Cup Match	day before Somers Day
Somers Day	1st Friday in August
Labour Day	1st Monday in September
Remembrance Day	November 11
Christmas Day	December 25
Boxing Day	December 26

SPECIAL EVENTS

Bermuda offers visitors a wide variety of cultural and sporting events throughout the year. These vary with the season. For example, yachting events take place early in the summer before the hurricane season gets underway and golf tournaments are heaviest in the winter when the weather is cooler.

For some events, dates can vary a bit each year and the venues are not always the same; check with the tourist office, which maintains seasonally adjusted schedules, for the latest information.

January

New Year's Day features a variety of sporting events, as well as performances by costumed troupes of Gombey dancers.

The *Bermuda International Race Weekend*, held on the second weekend in January, includes a marathon, half marathon, 10K race, a fitness walk and the Bank of Butterfield Mile.

The *Bermuda Festival*, a six-week festival of the performing arts, takes place from mid-January to late February. International artists present dance, drama and musical performances.

The weeklong *Bermuda Senior Golf Classic*, open to golfers 50 years and older, is held in mid-January at the St George's Golf Club, the Port Royal Golf Course and the Ocean View Golf Course.

The *Regional Bridge Tournament* is sponsored this month by the Bermuda Unit of the American Contract Bridge League.

February

Golden Rendezvous Month, held Monday through Friday throughout the month of February, features special activities, such as ballroom dancing and island tours, geared specifically for visitors over age 50.

The *Bermuda Festival*, which begins in January and includes various dance, drama and musical performances, continues through late February.

The weeklong *Bermuda Valentine's*, a 54-hole mixed foursomes invitational golf tournament, is held annually during Valentine's Day week. The tournament takes place at St George's Golf Club and Port Royal Golf Course.

Spring Break

The Bermuda Department of Tourism sponsors a spring break program throughout the month of March. While college students have been encouraged to take their spring break in Bermuda for decades, in recent years the island has made a concerted effort to keep away from a free-for-all beach-party atmosphere and instead recruit college and university sports teams – both athletes and coaches.

Consequently, a new Spring Break Sports Programme has been introduced, with the tourism department coordinating sporting events between various visiting university teams. The tourism department makes playing fields available and sponsors group activities such as beach barbecues and boat cruises. Sporting events include lacrosse, field hockey, soccer, rugby, track and field, tennis and golf. While some of the activities are geared specifically for teams, individuals can participate in others.

For more information, contact the Bermuda Department of Tourism and ask for the Spring Break Sports brochure. ∎

The annual *Bermuda Rendezvous Bowling Tournament*, open to all ABC/WIBC sanctioned bowlers, is held in mid-February at the Warwick Lanes in Warwick.

The *Bermuda Mixed Foursomes Amateur Championship*, a 36-hole stroke play golf competition, is held for two days in mid-February at St George's Golf Club.

The *Lobster Pot Invitational Pro-Amateur Golf Tournament* at Castle Harbour Golf Club is held in late February.

The *Bermuda Amateur Golf Festival*, held on five island courses, takes place in late February and early March. There are men's, women's, juniors', seniors' and mixed-event categories.

March

Bermuda Spring Break is geared for visiting college students, with sports programs and beach activities throughout the month.

The weeklong *Bermuda Easter Lily Invitational Pro-Am Golf Tournament for Ladies*, with teams consisting of one professional and three amateur women, is held at Eastertime at the Port Royal Golf Course and St George's Golf Club.

The weeklong *Bermuda All Breed Championship Dog Shows* are held in early March at the Bermuda Botanical Gardens.

The *Annual Street Festival*, held on Front St in Hamilton in early March, features music, crafts, exhibitions, a fashion show and other entertainment.

The *Bermuda Men's Amateur Championship*, a five-day singles match for golfers, is held in mid-March at the Mid Ocean Club.

The *Bermuda Cat Fanciers Association Championship Cat Show* is held in mid-March at No 1 cruise ship passenger terminal on Front St in Hamilton.

Palm Sunday Walk is a guided annual walk put on by the Bermuda National Trust that takes place on Palm Sunday.

April

The *Peppercorn Ceremony*, held in the town of St George in mid-April, reenacts the ceremony in which the Masonic Lodge pays an annual rent of one peppercorn for the use of the Old State House.

The Garden Club of Bermuda hosts *Open Houses and Gardens* at distinctive island homes every Wednesday afternoon in April.

The *Agricultural Exhibition*, one of the oldest events in Bermuda, is a three-day exhibit of

Newport-Bermuda Race

The Newport-Bermuda Race, the premier sailing event between the US East Coast and Bermuda, began in 1906 and except for a few wartime pauses has been running biennially ever since. This historic race, held in late June on even-numbered years, attracts about 150 sailboats, ranging from clipper-shaped ketches that are nearly as old as the race itself, to state-of-the-art Maxis, the largest and fastest racing boats in the world.

The tricky and sometimes turbulent seas along the southeasterly route from Rhode Island to Bermuda make the crossing particularly challenging. Sailors invariably have to contend with the Gulf Stream, the powerful northeasterly current that flows between the US mainland and Bermuda. This warm ocean 'stream' not only generates unusual wave patterns, but can also bring about water temperature changes of nearly 30 degrees.

The seas can become even more turbulent if there's adverse weather, but the region's worst storms are generally not encountered since this race, like all US-Bermuda races, is scheduled early in summer to avoid the peak hurricane season. Still, there are enough hazards that all of the crews must attend special safety seminars and the boats must pass strict Level 1 standards set by the Offshore Racing Commission.

Being a speed race, it's not surprising that the hottest technology of the day often captures the top honors at the finish line. In 1982, the newly launched Maxi *Nirvana* became the first boat to break the 10-knot average speed, making the 630-mile crossing in just under 63 hours. In 1996, a fiery new 78-foot Frers-design sloop, the ILC Maxi *Boomerang*, crossed the finish off St David's Lighthouse in 57 hours and 31 minutes, slicing more than five hours off the former record! ■

produce, flowers and livestock, with equestrian shows and other activities held mid to late April at the Bermuda Botanical Gardens.

The *XL Bermuda Open Tennis Championship* is held in mid-April at the Coral Beach Tennis Club. This USTA-sanctioned event features international professional players.

The *Bermuda Ladies Amateur Championship* is a singles match play golf event held for four days in mid-April at Riddell's Bay Golf & Country Club.

May

During *Invitational International Race Week*, held early in the month, yachters from Bermuda, the UK and North America compete in various boat categories.

The Garden Club of Bermuda hosts *Open Houses and Gardens* at distinctive island homes every Wednesday afternoon in May.

The *Bermuda Senior Amateur Championships*, for men age 55 and older and women age 50 and older, is a 54-hole stroke play golf event held for three days in mid-May at the Belmont Golf Club.

The *TransAt Daytona-Bermuda Race* is a yacht race held in May on odd-numbered yearsfrom Ponce de Leon, Florida, to Bermuda.

Bermuda Day, a public holiday on May 24, began as a celebration of Queen Victoria's

birthday, but now kicks off the start of summer. It features a half-marathon that begins in Somerset; a colorful afternoon parade from Bernard Park, at the north side of the City of Hamilton; and fitted dinghy races in St George's Harbour.

Beating Retreat Ceremonies, historic military reenactments performed by the Bermuda Regiment Band, take place at various times of the month in St George and at the Royal Naval Dockyard.

June

The *Bermuda Amateur Stroke Play Championships* are held for four days in mid-June at the Port Royal Golf Course. Men play 72 holes, women 54 holes, in separate events.

The Bermuda Philharmonic Society performs the *President's Choice Open-Air Pops Concert* in early June at King's Square in St George and at the Royal Naval Dockyard.

The *Queen's Birthday*, a public holiday on the third Monday in June, features a military parade led by the Bermuda Regiment that marches down Hamilton's Front St.

The *Newport-Bermuda Race*, held in late June during even-numbered years, is one of the world's major ocean races, running from Newport, Rhode Island, to Bermuda. The

Royal Bermuda Yacht Club coordinates events at the Bermuda end.

Bermuda 1-2 Single-Handed Race, held in June in odd-numbered years, is a single-handed yacht race heading from Newport, Rhode Island, to Bermuda, and returning double handed to Newport.

The *Bermuda Cruising Rally* is a yacht race in mid-June heading from Norfolk, Virginia, to Bermuda. The host at the Bermuda end is the St George Dinghy & Sports Club.

The *Bermuda Ocean Race*, held in June in even-numbered years, is another yacht race, this one from Annapolis, Maryland, to Bermuda.

The *Marion-Bermuda Cruising Yacht Race*, held in mid-June in odd-numbered years, is an ocean race from Marion, Massachusetts, to Bermuda. The Royal Hamilton Amateur Dinghy Club is the host at the Bermuda end.

Beating Retreat Ceremonies, historic military reenactments performed by the Bermuda Regiment Band, take place at various times of the month in St George and at the Royal Naval Dockyard.

July

Bermuda Angler's Club International Light Tackle Tournament is held early this month.

Beating Retreat Ceremonies, historic military reenactments performed by the Bermuda Regiment Band, take place at various times of the month in St George and at the Royal Naval Dockyard.

SOCA, held at the end of July or in early August, is a Caribbean music festival that takes place at the Royal Naval Dockyard.

August

The *Cup Match Cricket Festival*, a two-day match between West End and East End cricket teams, is held on the first Thursday and Friday in August. Both days are public holidays, and numerous other activities occur on this long weekend.

The *Sea Horse Anglers Club Annual Bermuda Billfish Tournament* is a four-day event that begins on the first Saturday in August.

Bermuda Reggae Sunsplash, held mid-month, is a music festival of local and Jamaican bands.

September

Labour Day, a public holiday on the first Monday of September, features a small parade from Union Square in the City of Hamilton and speeches by union leaders and local politicians.

The *Bermuda Horse & Pony Association Fall Show* features various equestrian events at the Bermuda Botanical Gardens.

Beating Retreat Ceremonies, historic military reenactments performed by the Bermuda Regiment Band, take place at various times of the month in St George and at the Royal Naval Dockyard.

October

The *Bermuda Triathlon*, a swimming, bicycling and running competition, is held every year in early October.

At the *Omega Gold Cup International Match Racing Championship*, held in mid-October, Bermudians compete for prize money with international boaters, including America's Cup Match contenders.

The *Bermuda Open*, a golf tournament for men held for four days in mid-October at the Port Royal Golf Course, is open to professionals and amateurs with a handicap limit of 6. The professional purse is $50,000.

Beating Retreat Ceremonies, historic military reenactments performed by the Bermuda Regiment Band, take place at various times of the month in St George and at the Royal Naval Dockyard.

November

The *Bermuda Four Ball Stroke Play Amateur Championships*, a 72-hole golf event for men and a separate 54-hole event for women, is held for four days in early November at the Port Royal Golf Course.

The ceremonial *Convening of Parliament* takes place at Sessions House in the City of Hamilton this month.

The *Bermuda All Breed Championship Dog Shows & Obedience Trials* are held in mid-November within the Bermuda Botanical Gardens.

The *Bermuda Tattoo*, held during three evenings in early November at the National Stadium in Devonshire, is a beating retreat ceremony that takes its name from the 'tattoo', a type of nighttime military display. It features Bermudian, Jamaican and British military and pipe bands, skirling ceremonies and a grand finale of fireworks.

Remembrance Day, a public holiday on November 11, features a military parade along Front St in Hamilton and the laying of wreaths at the Cenotaph.

At the *World Rugby Classic* in mid-November, international and Bermudian teams compete

in rugby matches at the National Stadium in Devonshire.

The *Bermuda Lawn Tennis Club Invitational* hosts international and local players in two weeks of singles and doubles matches in early November at the Coral Beach Tennis Club.

The *Belmont Invitational Tournament*, a golf tournament for men, is held for four days in late November or early December at the Belmont Golf Club.

December

The *Bermuda Goodwill Tournament*, an annual golf event for men, is held for four days in early December at the Belmont, Castle Harbour, Mid Ocean and Port Royal golf courses.

There are various *Santa Claus parades* with floats and marching bands in the days leading up to Christmas.

On *Boxing Day*, a public holiday on December 26, colorful Gombey dancers take to the streets all around Bermuda.

WORK

Those interested in entering Bermuda for employment need to obtain a work permit in advance from Bermuda's immigration authorities. As employers on the island are required to give priority to local residents, it can be difficult for foreigners to get a job, unless they have a specialized skill for which there's not a suitable candidate.

ACCOMMODATIONS

Bermuda has no truly cheap accommodations – no youth hostels, no YMCAs, no family campgrounds and no economy-chain motels.

As a general rule, the most economical options are tourist apartments, which come completely furnished, as they not only provide you with a place to stay but also have cooking facilities. Considering that the average hotel charges a good $10 per person for breakfast, being able to prepare your own coffee and toast can represent a tidy savings! Small guesthouses, which generally include breakfast in their rates, also represent one of the more affordable options.

The term 'cottage colony' is generally used in Bermuda with more upmarket places that offer units in individual cottages, or in small clusters of buildings each of which contain a few units. The 'cottages' often have at least limited cooking facilities and generally have a more genteel setting with landscaped grounds, afternoon teas and the like.

Small hotels are by and large just that: smaller places that usually have a restaurant, lounge and swimming pool but don't necessarily offer the array of services found at the larger resort hotels. They range from unpretentious family-oriented places to some of the island's more prestigious and intimate spots, and accordingly rates vary widely.

Bermuda has seven resort hotels: the Belmont Hotel, Elbow Beach Hotel, Grotto Bay Beach Hotel, Marriott's Castle Harbour Resort, Hamilton Princess Hotel, Sonesta Beach Hotel and Southampton Princess. All have the usual resort facilities, including swimming pools, room service and restaurants. Three of them – the Bel-

---

Meal Plans

Most Bermuda accommodations offer meal-plan packages. At some places, a specific plan is mandatory, while at others you can select between plans. The following codes are used consistently in hotel literature throughout Bermuda to represent the various options.

EP (European Plan)	Room only
CP (Continental Plan)	Room and a light breakfast
BP (Breakfast Plan)	Room and a full breakfast
AP (American Plan)	Room and all three meals
MAP (Modified American Plan)	Room with breakfast and dinner ∎

mont Hotel, Southampton Princess and Marriott's Castle Harbour Resort – are on golf courses. All the resort hotels are either on the beach or provide a guest shuttle to a nearby sandy strand. Depending on which resort hotel you select, the rates can vary from moderate to expensive, though if you keep an eye out for special promotions or book a package deal you can sometimes find a bargain at any one of them.

On top of the rates given throughout this book, all places to stay add on a 7.25% hotel occupancy tax and almost all tack on a 10% service charge.

Long-Term Rentals

For long-term rentals a good place to look is in the classified ads section of the *Royal Gazette*. Generally, a small studio costs around $750 a month, while one-bedroom condos and apartments begin at around $1000.

If you're in Bermuda in the winter, and staying for a month or more, you can usually negotiate a reasonable monthly rate with one of the island's small hotels or apartment complexes. The best thing to do is call around and compare; three good places to start with are Sky Top Cottages and Salt Kettle House in Paget, and the Surf Side Beach Club in Warwick.

Booking Representatives

Many of Bermuda's small properties can be easily booked through a single reservation service. If you want to inquire about several properties at once, any one of the following room-booking services can help you:

Bermuda
Bermuda Small Properties
(☎ 236-1633, 800-582-4778, fax 236-1662)
Canada
RMR Group
(☎ 416-485-8724, fax 416-485-8256)
Germany
Eurep 92
(☎ 49-0-69-776012, fax 49-0-69-701007)
Sweden
Colibri Market & Travel Consultants
(☎ 46-8-80-62-85, fax 46-8-25-08-89)

UK
Morris-Kevan International
(☎ 0181-367-5175, fax 0181-367-9949)
USA & Canada
Bermuda Reservation Services
(☎ 508-822-8652, 800-637-4116,
fax 508-822-8649)
International Resort Services
(☎ 800-441-7087, fax 215-687-5018)

Camping

Although you may see Bermudians setting up tents, foreign visitors are not allowed to camp in Bermuda.

The only exception is for organized groups, who may apply for permits to camp at group sites run by the government on a handful of nearshore islands. Permits are issued to overseas groups between October and April only. The cost to book each campsite is a flat $790 per week plus a boat fee of $75 per trip – affordable if you're traveling with 70 people, which is the full contingent that the larger sites can hold, but a bit steep for small groups.

Information on group camping is available from the Camping Co-ordinator, Department of Youth and Sport, Old Fire Station Building, 81 Court St, Hamilton HM 12.

FOOD

Food, like everything else, tends to be expensive in Bermuda. On the plus side, Bermuda offers a good variety of dining options, from side-street delis in the capital to superb fine-dining seaside restaurants.

Restaurants

While the upmarket restaurants commonly focus on French-inspired fare, moderately priced eateries cover a wide gamut from English pub fare to Chinese, East Indian, Greek and Italian cuisine. Considering Bermuda's seclusion, most of the food is surprisingly authentic, and the island certainly has no shortage of recommendable dinner spots.

At the low end there are pizzerias, sandwich shops and fast-food outlets such as Kentucky Fried Chicken.

While 'smart casual' wear will get you a table at most restaurants, there are still a number of top-end restaurants that require jackets and ties, so it's always wise to inquire about dress codes when making a dinner reservation.

Bermudian Cuisine

The Bermudian dish most often tried by visitors is Bermuda fish chowder, a tasty reddish-brown chowder commonly made with rockfish or snapper and flavored with local black rum and sherry peppers sauce. The latter is a traditional Bermudian condiment made from sherry, peppers and spices.

Codfish cakes became a staple in Bermuda long ago and are still cooked on certain days of the year, particularly Good Friday. Popular everyday foods are johnny-cakes, which are cornmeal griddle cakes, and peas and rice. Of course, fresh fish is big in local diets as well. Fish sandwiches, made of a filet fried in a crisp batter, are as popular here as hamburgers are elsewhere.

The most traditional meal is the Sunday codfish breakfast, a huge affair to linger over, which consists of codfish, eggs, boiled Irish potatoes, bananas and avocado, with a sauce of onions and tomatoes. While it's most commonly served up in homes, there are a handful of restaurants on the island that offer this meal as well.

A Christmas tradition in Bermuda is cassava pie, made with a cake-like batter that contains the grated root of the cassava plant, stuffed with a meat filling and baked. The cassava bears special significance to Bermudians, as it's credited with having helped the early settlers get through periods of famine.

DRINKS
Nonalcoholic Drinks

Bottled water, both generic spring water and fancy carbonated brands, is readily available at grocery stores throughout the island, as are fruit juices and soft drinks. Being such a small island, it may come as a surprise that Bermuda has dairy cows and produces much of its own milk.

Bermuda Rum Swizzle

While every Bermudian bartender has his or her own twist, the basic rum swizzle starts out like this: Mix four ounces of dark rum with three ounces of pineapple juice, three ounces of orange juice, an ounce of grenadine or other sugar syrup, the juice of one fresh lemon and a couple of dashes of Angostura bitters. Add it all to a container with crushed ice, shake it until there's a head, pour into a pair of tall glasses and garnish them with slivers of orange. If you prefer, you can substitute a lime for the lemon. ■

Alcoholic Drinks

Bermuda Triangle Brewing (☎ 238-2430), a new microbrewery in Southampton Parish, boasts three kinds of fresh, locally made brew.

Wilde Hogge is a German-style amber ale with a full malty flavor, while Full Moon Pale Ale is a more traditional English bitter. For those more accustomed to lagers, there's Spinnaker Beer, a pale pilsner with a typical golden hue that resembles conventional North American beers. Bermuda Triangle brews can be found on tap at pubs and restaurants around the island – or you can tour the brewery and sample it straight from the tank (see the Southampton Parish chapter for details).

Gosling Brothers, one of Bermuda's oldest companies, has been blending and bottling spirits on the island since the 1860s. Their cornerstone product is Gosling's Black Seal Rum, a dark rum which until WWI was sold from the barrel using recycled wine and champagne bottles, the cork sealed with black sealing wax – hence the origins of the name. Take note if you pick up a bottle of Black Seal that these days it comes in standard 80 proof as well as a fire-breathing 151 proof.

The dark 'n' stormy, sometimes dubbed Bermuda's national drink, is a two-to-one mix of carbonated ginger beer with Black Seal Rum; it can be purchased premixed in cans at island liquor stores. Black Seal Rum is also the main ingredient in Bermuda's famous rum swizzle, which is far and away the most popular drink among island visitors.

Gosling produces three liqueurs as well: Bermuda Gold, Bermuda Banana Liqueur and Bermuda Coconut Rum. The one that gets the most attention is Bermuda Gold, which is made from loquats and comparable to an apricot brandy. It's commonly served straight on ice, with a twist of lemon (called a shipwreck) or with orange juice (a royal blossom).

ENTERTAINMENT

Bermuda has a number of venues with live music, ranging from ballroom dancing to rock and reggae. The main music scene is in the City of Hamilton, though many of the hotels also have entertainment. For specifics, see the Entertainment section in the individual parish chapters.

For the latest in what's happening, pick up the Friday edition of the *Bermuda Sun* or the *Royal Gazette*, both of which have complete entertainment listings.

There are four movie theaters in Bermuda: two in the City of Hamilton, one at the Royal Naval Dockyard and another in the Town of St George. All show first-run movies. Matinee showings generally cost about $5, evening shows $7.

The biggest entertainment event of the year is the six-week Bermuda Festival, held from mid-January to late February with dance, drama and musical performances by international artists. In recent years, there have been appearances by the Harlem Spiritual Ensemble, jazz trumpeter Wynton Marsalis and musicians from England's Royal College of Music. Tickets to individual events cost from $20 to $35. You can obtain a schedule and ticket information from the Bermuda Festival Office (☎ 295-1291, fax 295-7403) or get general information from any Bermuda Department of Tourism office.

SPECTATOR SPORTS

The main spectator sport that is played on Bermuda between April and September is cricket, with scheduled matches taking place at cricket fields around the island every Sunday.

From September to April, football (soccer) and rugby are the leading spectator sports; local competitions take place around the island every Sunday, while the biggest meets for both sports are held at the National Stadium in Devonshire.

Field hockey and sailing are two other popular spectator sports.

THINGS TO BUY

While luxury items in Bermuda are not as heavily taxed as many everyday items, Bermuda is not a duty-free port, and many things that you buy here may prove to be no cheaper than they would be at home.

Much of what attracts shoppers to Bermuda is the variety of high-quality items, including many top-name English and European imports. Generally the best selections and prices are found on items imported from the British Isles. These include English bone china, cashmere sweaters, Scottish tweeds and Irish wools and linens.

Other imports found in Bermudian shops include designer Italian leather and silk, Swiss watches, German silverware and French fashions. Two of the most extensively carried items are crystal, including Baccarat and Waterford, and china, including Bing Grondahl, Limoges, Lladro, Mikasa, Noritake, Royal Copenhagen, Royal Doulton, Spode and Wedgwood, as well as Goebel and Hummel figurines.

The main department stores in the City of Hamilton – Trimingham's, Smith's and AS Cooper & Sons – have the greater selection. Those stores also have branches in the Town of St George and outlets at many of the resort hotels.

Bermuda-Made Items

There are numerous Bermuda-made items that can make good souvenirs.

Duty-Free Allowances

US citizens who have been out of the USA for more than 48 hours may bring back $400 worth of goods duty free, as long as this allowance has not been used within the past 30 days. Within their duty-free allowance each adult can include one liter of spirits.

Canadian citizens can bring back $50 worth of goods duty free anytime they've been out of Canada for over 24 hours, $200 worth after 48 hours and $500 worth for trips of more than seven days. Within their duty-free allowance each adult can bring in 40 ounces of spirits.

UK citizens may bring back £136 worth of goods duty free. Within their duty-free allowance each adult can bring in one liter of spirits and two liters of wine.

For duty-free allowances for other countries, check with customs authorities before you leave home. ∎

The Bermuda Glassblowing Studio in Bailey's Bay creates a wide variety of hand-blown glass. Island Pottery at the Royal Naval Dockyard makes plates, vases and various other pottery items.

The Bermuda Perfumery in Bailey's Bay makes perfume, eau de toilette, after-shave colognes and soaps from locally grown Easter lilies, oleanders, jasmine flowers, passion flowers and frangipani blossoms.

There are other island-made fragrances for men. Bermuda's Royall Fragrances makes four varieties of men's colognes: Royall Bay Rhum, Royall Lyme, Royall Spyce and Royall Muske.

Jewelers on the island make earrings, charms and pendants utilizing island motifs, such as tree frogs, Bermuda onions, longtail tropicbirds, hog pennies – even mopeds. Any of the jewelry shops in Hamilton or St George should have a good variety of locally made items – there's also an extensive collection of jewelry at the Bermuda Craft Market in the Royal Naval Dockyard.

Bermuda designs show up on numerous other items, including silk-screened T-shirts, tea towels, refrigerator magnets, note cards and the like, any of which can make an inexpensive memento of a trip to Bermuda. Or bring home local flavor with Outerbridge's spicy sherry peppers sauce and island-made liqueurs and rums.

Stamp collectors can buy commemorative stamps from the General Post Office in Hamilton. Overseas, they can be ordered from Interpost, PO Box 378, Malverne, NY 11565, USA or CASB Ltd, 2 Carshalton Rd, Sutton, Surrey SM1 4RN, England.

Art Galleries

Bermuda inspires many artists. If you're interested in picking up a watercolor, oil painting or charcoal drawing of island scenes, some of the finer galleries are as follows.

Bermuda Society of Arts, City Hall, City of Hamilton (☎ 292-3824)

The Gallery, The Emporium, 69 Front St, City of Hamilton (☎ 295-8980)

Masterworks Foundation, Bermuda House Lane, 97 Front St, City of Hamilton (☎ 295-5580)

The Windjammer Gallery, 87 Reid St, City of Hamilton (☎ 292-7861)

Carole Holding galleries, on Front St in the City of Hamilton (☎ 296-3421), on King's Square in St George (☎ 297-1833) and at the Clocktower Mall in the Royal Naval Dockyard (☎ 234-3800)

Bridge House Gallery, 1 Bridge St, St George (☎ 297-8211)

Bermuda Arts Centre, Royal Naval Dockyard (☎ 234-2809)

Michael Swan Gallery, Clocktower Mall, Royal Naval Dockyard (☎ 234-3128)

Liquor

While Bermuda's ports of departure do not have duty-free shops selling liquor, leading Bermudian liquor stores, such as Gosling's and Frith's, still manage to offer an extensive selection of duty-free liquors to those heading off island.

The way it works is that you stop by one of their shops and pay the duty-free rate for the liquor. You can not walk out with the bottles; instead, the shop will deliver the liquor to the airport or your cruise ship prior to departure time. There's no extra charge for the delivery.

This system offers a hefty savings over standard island prices. A liter of Gosling's Black Seal Rum, for example, costs about $8 duty free, versus $20 in local shops.

Orders can be placed anytime before 9:30 am of your day of departure (2:30 pm the day before for Sunday and holiday departures), although it's wisest to make the arrangements a day or two in advance.

Gosling's has shops at Front St in Hamilton, at York and Queen Sts in St George and at some resort hotels. Frith's has shops on Front St in Hamilton, on York St in St George and at the Sonesta Beach Hotel.

Getting There & Away

AIR

There are regularly scheduled direct flights to Bermuda from the USA, Canada and the UK. Travelers arriving from other destinations will need to connect through one of these countries.

Airports & Airlines

Bermuda International Airport, located on the eastern side of the island, is Bermuda's only airport. It's a small, no-frills airport, but you will find gift shops selling Bermuda T-shirts and a few simple souvenirs in both the main lobby and the departure lounge. There are also pay phones and credit-card phones; an eatery selling ice cream, burgers and fries; and a bar and lounge.

Air Canada, American Airlines, British Airways, Continental, Delta and USAir have permanent, year-round counters.

Bermuda's arrival formalities and customs are generally efficient and straightforward. One unusual quirk is that if you're flying to the USA from Bermuda, you'll actually go through US Customs at the Bermuda airport before your departure.

Taxis meet all arriving flights. Taxi fares from the airport will cost about $9 to the Town of St George or the Marriott resort, $18 to the City of Hamilton or Elbow Beach and $25 to the Southampton Princess or the Sonesta Beach Hotel.

There is also a bus stop in front of the airport for the public bus that runs between Hamilton and St George, but this is practical only if you're traveling with very light luggage.

Travelers with Special Needs

If you have special needs of any sort – you require a special diet, you're traveling in a wheelchair or with a baby, or you have a medical condition that warrants special consideration – let the airline know as soon as possible so that they can make arrangements. Remind them when you reconfirm your booking (at least 72 hours before departure) and again when you check in at the airport. It may also be worth phoning several airlines before you make your booking to find out how each of them can handle your particular needs.

Most international airports will provide an escorted cart or wheelchair from the check-in desk to the plane, where needed, and there should be ramps, lifts and accessible toilets at your departure point. Aircraft toilets, on the other hand, are likely to present a problem for some disabled passengers; travelers should discuss this with the airline at an early stage and, if necessary, with their doctor. At the Bermuda end, there are no jetways, so wheelchair users are carried off the aircraft using a 'carry chair'.

Children under two travel for 10% of the standard fare (or free on some airlines) as long as they don't occupy a seat. They don't get a baggage allowance either. 'Skycots', baby food and diapers should be provided by the airline if requested in advance. Children between two and 12 can usually occupy a seat for half to two-thirds of the full fare, for which they do get a baggage allowance.

The USA

Most of Bermuda's air traffic arrives from the US East Coast, and that creates enough competition to occasionally set off a price war. It used to be that the best deals were found in the dead of winter, but in recent years some of the deepest cuts have occurred in spring and early summer when seasonal services by USAir and Kiwi International heat up the competition. At such time, fares can drop to as low as $200 roundtrip – often with no day-of-the-week restrictions.

Otherwise, expect the standard excursion fare from the US East Coast to begin around $350, with a 14-day advance purchase and a 21-day maximum stay.

The following airlines serve Bermuda from the USA.

American Airlines (☎ 800-433-7300) has daily nonstop flights from JFK airport in New York.

Continental Airlines (☎ 800-525-0280) has daily nonstop flights from Newark Airport.

Delta Air Lines (☎ 800-221-1212) has daily nonstop flights from Boston and Atlanta.

USAir (☎ 800-622-1015) has daily nonstop flights from Baltimore and Philadelphia all year round and from Boston and New York (La Guardia) from late April to mid-November.

Kiwi International (☎ 800-538-5494) has daily flights between May and September from Newark, Chicago and Atlanta.

Canada

Air Canada (☎ 800-776-3000) flies nonstop daily from Toronto. It also has a Saturday-only flight from Halifax from late April to the end of October. The cheapest excursion fare, with a two-week advance purchase, midweek travel and a 21-day maximum stay, is usually around C$325.

The UK

British Airways (☎ 0345-222-111) flies from London (Gatwick) to Bermuda on Tuesday, Thursday, Friday and Saturday. The excursion return fare, with a 14-day advance purchase and a maximum stay of two months, is £663 in summer and £490 in winter. Add another £30 if you're traveling on the weekend.

Continental Europe

There are occasionally charter services from Frankfurt, Germany. Check with a local travel agent for current information.

SEA
Cruise Ships

Some 170,000 cruise ship passengers sail to Bermuda each year. All arrive between April and October, as cruise ships suspend their operations to Bermuda during the winter season.

The typical cruise ship holiday is the ultimate package tour. Other than the effort involved in selecting a cruise, it requires minimal planning – just pay and show up – and for many people this is a large part of the appeal. Keep in mind that much of your time will be spent at sea, so you'll have notably less time on the island than someone with a comparable-length vacation who takes a flight.

Because cruises cover rooms, meals, entertainment and transportation in one all-inclusive price, they can be a relatively good value. While cruises cost more than lower-end independent travel, they will not necessarily cost more than a conventional package tour that covers airfare and expenses at a resort hotel.

Most travel agents have cruise ship brochures, complete with pictures of the ships and cabins, available for the taking. Brochures can also be obtained by contacting the cruise lines directly.

The following cruise lines all offer seven-day roundtrip cruises to Bermuda every week during the cruise ship season.

Celebrity Cruises Celebrity Cruises (☎ 800-437-3111), the only cruise line with two ships to Bermuda, sails to the island in the *Zenith* and the *Meridian*.

The *Zenith* departs from New York every Saturday between late April and mid-October, docking in Bermuda at both Hamilton and St George. The ship was built in 1992, has a crew of 670 and carries 1374 passengers. It weighs 47,255 tons, is 682 feet long, has a cruising speed of 21.4 knots.

The *Meridian* docks at the Royal Naval Dockyard. The ship, which was built in 1963 but refitted in 1992, weighs 30,400 tons, is 700 feet long and has a cruising speed of 24.5 knots. It carries 1106 passengers and a crew of 580. The boat departs from New York every Sunday from mid-June to early September. Prior to that, from early April to mid-June, it offers an alternating schedule of departures from the US East Coast cities of Philadelphia, Pennsylvania; Baltimore, Maryland; Newport News, Virginia; Wilmington, North Carolina; Charleston, South Carolina; and Fort Lauderdale, Florida.

Majesty Cruise Line The Majesty Cruise Line (☎ 800-532-7788) sails the *Royal Majesty* to Bermuda, departing from Boston every Sunday between mid-May and late October. It docks at the Town of St George. The ship weighs 32,400 tons, is 568 feet long and has a cruising speed of 21 knots. The ship, which was built in Finland in 1992, has a crew of 500 and carries 1056 passengers.

Norwegian Cruise Line The Norwegian Cruise Line (☎ 800-327-7030) sails the *Dreamward* to Bermuda, departing from New York every Saturday between late April and early October. It docks at both St George and Hamilton. The ship weighs 41,000 tons, is 624 feet long, has a cruising speed of 21 knots and carries 1242 passengers and a crew of 483. The maiden voyage was in 1992.

Royal Caribbean Cruise Line The Royal Caribbean Cruise Line (☎ 800-327-6700) sails the *Song of America* to Bermuda, departing from New York every Sunday from early May to mid-October. It docks at both St George and Hamilton.

In addition, in April and late October the *Song of America* makes 10-day cruises between New York and San Juan, Puerto Rico, with a stop in Bermuda. The ship had its inaugural cruise in 1982. It weighs 37,584 tons, is 705 feet long, has a cruising speed of 19 knots and carries 1402 passengers and a crew of 525.

Other Lines There are also a handful of other lines that periodically call on Bermuda, including Cunard's (☎ 800-528-6273 in the USA, 0171-839-141 in the UK) *Queen Elizabeth 2*, which occasionally includes a Bermuda stop on its transatlantic journey between the UK and the USA. Information on these cruises is available

from any good travel agent specializing in cruises.

Costs

Cruise lines do not divide passengers into class categories, but rather provide the same meals and amenities for all passengers on each ship.

Cruises are offered at a range of rates, however, depending mainly on the size, type and location of the cabin. Bottom-end cabins might well be small and poorly located, while top-end cabins are often spacious, luxurious suites. Price also depends on the dates of the cruise, the number of people in each cabin, transportation options between your home and the departure point and the cruise line you choose. In addition, discounts off the brochure rates are commonplace.

Standard rates, which for most cruises to Bermuda start between $1000 and $1500, are quoted per person, based on double occupancy. A third and fourth person (child' or adult) in the same cabin is often given a heavily discounted rate.

Provisions vary for single travelers who occupy a double cabin, but the single cost is commonly about 150% of the standard rate. Some cruise lines, such as the Royal Caribbean, also have a singles share program, in which they attempt to match up compatible (same-sex) cabin mates to share the double cabins.

Meals, which are typically elaborate affairs, are included in the cruise price. Alcoholic drinks are usually not included and are generally comparable in price to those in bars back home.

Entertainment shows and most on-board activities are included in the cruise price, but personal services such as hairstyling and laundry usually cost extra, as do most shoreside activities, such as diving or windsurfing.

Cruise lines generally suggest that each passenger tip, per day, $3 to the cabin steward, $3 to the dining room waiter and $1.50 each to the maitre d' and to the person who buses the tables, given in a lump sum on the last night of the cruise. For cocktail servers, a 15% tip is sometimes included in the drink price and, if not, is generally given on the spot.

Bermuda makes up for what it doesn't collect in hotel taxes by levying steep port charges. On most cruises, expect to pay between $120 to $170 in government taxes and fees; these are generally paid when you buy your ticket.

Before paying for your cruise, be sure to check the fine print about deposits, cancellation and refund policies and travel insurance.

Discounts When all is said and done, very few cruises are sold at the standard brochure rates.

Many cruise lines offer discounts for early reservations and also give last-minute discounts. Just a few years ago the cheapest rates were those obtained at the last minute – essentially standby rates for whatever cabins had not been booked – but the cruise lines have been largely successful in reversing this trend. These days, the general rule is the earlier the booking the greater the discount – and, of course, the better the cabin selection.

Still, cruise lines want to sail full, so if there are seats leftover at the end, there will be discounts available.

And then there are the occasional promotions: Some cruise lines offer a 50% discount for the second person on designated sailings, offer free cabin upgrades if certain qualifications are met, run two-for-one specials in selected markets, offer discounts to senior citizens etc.

Booking a Cruise

A good travel agent should be able to provide comparisons on cruise lines, facilities, rates and discounts. Be aware that the industry has also attracted the occasional fly-by-night company that advertises heavily, then takes the money and runs – be sure you're dealing with a reputable agent.

Those travel agents most knowledgeable about cruises are apt to belong to Cruise Lines International Association (CLIA), an organization of cruise lines that works in affiliation with about 20,000 North American travel agencies. You might also want to find a travel agent who subscribes to the *Official Cruise Guide*, which is a good source of information on cruise lines, listing schedules and facilities for virtually all ships.

Choosing a Cruise

In addition to finding a cruise that fits your budget, the following are some other things to consider.

Departure Point Most cruises leave from New York and Boston. However one company, Celebrity Cruises, alters its schedule so that there's at least one boat each season leaving from a series of other US East Coast ports, including Philadelphia, Baltimore, Wilmington, Newport News, Charleston and Fort Lauderdale.

The cost and ease of getting to the departure point should be taken into consideration when choosing a cruise.

Ship Facilities The conventional cruise ship is indeed a floating resort. Those sailing to Bermuda all hold more than 1000 passengers and have swimming pools, lavish entertainment, casinos, discos, multiple restaurants and lounges.

Ships can generally accommodate special diets with advance notice, but verify this before you book. Some ships are handicapped accessible, although details such as the measurement of bathroom clearance for wheelchairs should be checked carefully to make sure they are adequate for individual needs.

Cabin Outside cabins are best, as their view makes them the least claustrophobic, and higher decks are preferable, as are of course the largest and fanciest cabins. Prices will correspond accordingly. Although cruise ships have stabilizers to prevent roll, if you're prone to motion sickness, you might want to get a cabin in the center of the ship, which is more stable and rocks less in bad weather.

The inside cabins (with no portholes) on the lowest decks are the least desirable but also the cheapest. Bottom-end cabins sometimes have bunk-style beds and minuscule bathrooms, and they can be uncomfortably cramped. Avoid the cabins nearest the engine room, as they may be noisy.

Sanitation All cruise ships that arrive in US ports are subject to unannounced US sanitation inspections. The inspectors rate ships in four categories: potable water supply; food preparation and holding; potential contamination of food; and general cleanliness, storage and repair.

A summary sheet that lists ships, the latest date of inspection and their ratings is published weekly and may be obtained free by writing to: Chief, Vessel Sanitation Program, National Center for Environmental Health, 1015 N American Way, Room 107, Miami, FL 33132, USA.

Private Yacht

Most yachters who sail to Bermuda depart from the US East Coast. Bermuda is approximately 640 nautical miles southeast from Virginia, 670 nautical miles from New York City and 690 nautical miles from Boston. Of course, sailing time will vary with the weather and the boat, but the typical voyage time between Bermuda and the US East Coast is five to six days.

Approach Bermuda's two main entrances are at Town Cut channel and The Narrows channel, both at the eastern side of the island. Due to the vast reefs that lie as much as 10 miles offshore, the approach must be made cautiously, using updated charts. Bermuda has two lighthouses and numerous beacons, buoys and shore lights to aid navigation.

Bermuda Harbour Radio (call letters ZBM) broadcasts weather forecasts and navigational warnings at 2582 KHz; its working channel is VHF 27. All vessels approaching Bermuda are required to contact Bermuda Harbour Radio at 2182 KHz or VHF Channel 16 for entry and berthing instructions.

Arrival & Departure All visiting yachts are required to obtain customs, immigration and health clearance in the Port of St George before proceeding elsewhere in Bermuda. The clearance facility is at the east side of Ordnance Island and is open 24 hours a day. It can be reached at VHF Channel 68. Departure clearance at this facility is also required.

Anchorages & Facilities St George's Harbour offers anchorage for yachts at Somers Wharf, Hunters Wharf and the north side of Ordnance Island free of charge on a first-come, first-served basis.

Anchorage is available on a fee basis at the Dockyard Marina (☎ 234-0300) in the Royal Naval Dockyard. For information on berthing in Hamilton Harbour, contact the Royal Hamilton Amateur Dinghy Club (☎ 236-8372). Bermuda Harbour Radio can also provide information on anchorage options around the island.

Because there are several yacht races between Bermuda and the US East Coast in June, yachters who are not racing may find that to be a difficult time to secure a berth.

Bermuda has boat repair yards as well as shops selling marine accessories. If you're in need of service or repairs, the clearance authorities in St George can refer you to the appropriate facilities.

Books & Charts Anyone considering sailing to Bermuda should request a copy of *Yachts (Private) Sailing to Bermuda*, a 20-page pamphlet available from the Bermuda Department of Tourism. It has detailed information on everything from beacon locations and customs clearance to marina facilities and where to go to pick up ice.

In addition, two recommended books are *The Yachting Guide to Bermuda*, edited by the Bermuda Maritime Museum, and *Reed's Caribbean Almanac*.

Detailed charts are essential for sailing into Bermudian waters. In Bermuda, yachting books and charts are available at PW's Marine Centre (☎ 295-3232), at Waterloo, Pitts Bay Rd, City of Hamilton.

In the USA, books and charts can be ordered from the following companies.

Armchair Sailor World-Wide Navigation
      543 Thames St, Newport, RI 02840
      (☎ 401-847-4252)
LJ Harri, Nautical Books & Charts
      120 Lewis Wharf, Boston, MA 02110
      (☎ 800-242-3352)
New York Nautical Instrument & Service
      140 W Broadway, New York, NY 10013
      (☎ 212-962-4522)
Blue Water Books & Charts
      1481 SE 17th St Causeway,
      Fort Lauderdale, FL 33316
      (☎ 800-942-2583)

DEPARTURE TAXES

Anyone leaving Bermuda by air must pay a $20 departure tax, which is collected at the airport; you can purchase a voucher for the tax at your hotel or from the airline counter on your day of departure.

Cruise ship passengers are assessed a $60 departure tax, but it's generally added on to the ticket price when paying for the cruise.

Children under age two are exempt from the tax.

ORGANIZED TOURS
Package Tours

Conventional package tours to Bermuda that include airfare and accommodations

---

US Customs in Bermuda

Because of a special arrangement in which US customs officers are stationed at the Bermuda International Airport, Americans who depart from Bermuda by air clear customs in Bermuda, rather than in the USA. Their flight home is then treated like a domestic flight, with no re-entry formalities upon arriving in the USA. ■

---

are available from the USA, Canada and England. Most tours are between three nights and one week in duration, though they often can be tailored for longer stays.

As tour consolidators get steeply discounted rates on both airfare and hotels, a package tour typically works out cheaper than if you were to book the same hotel and flight separately. Particularly if you are going to Bermuda for a short getaway vacation, package tours can be very economical – at times the cheapest three-day tour can be little more than what the airfare alone would cost.

From the USA, where most flights to Bermuda originate, package tours are highly competitive. Three-day tours that include accommodations in a guesthouse or small hotel and airfare from the US East Coast commonly begin as low as $400. The ads found in the travel sections of big-city Sunday newspapers, such as the *New York Times* or the *Boston Globe*, are a good source of information. Package tours in general represent a substantial part of the bookings for most travel agents, and they can usually pile you high with tour brochures to Bermuda.

Specialized Tours

Elderhostel (☎ 617-426-8056), 75 Federal St, Boston, MA 02110, is a nonprofit organization offering educational programs for those age 55 and older. The organization, which has its origins in the youth hostels of Europe and the folk schools of Scandinavia, generally focuses on the environment and natural history. The Bermuda program is operated in conjunction with the Bermuda Biological Station for Research (BBSR) in St George's Parish and includes marine ecology courses at the BBSR. The one-week programs run throughout the year and cost about $700, including meals, classes, field trips and hotel accommodations. Airfare to and from Bermuda is not included.

National Audubon Society Nature Odysseys (☎ 212-979-3066), 700 Broadway, New York, NY 10003, periodically

Summer School In Bermuda

The Bermuda Biological Station for Research (BBSR) in St George's Parish offers intensive three- and four-week summer courses in marine zoology, ecology and oceanography. The staff includes BBSR researchers and visiting professors from prestigious US and Canadian institutes such as Harvard University, the Smithsonian Institution and the Royal Ontario Museum. The courses are geared to graduate students and upper-level undergraduates.

Tuition and accommodations for the programs costs from $2100 to $2600, but scholarships are available to assist students accepted into the program. As class space is limited and admission competitive, it's best to apply as far in advance as possible.

For more information on these summer programs, as well as details on volunteer programs and graduate internships, contact the Bermuda Biological Station for Research (☎ 297-1880, fax 297-1839), Ferry Reach, St George's GE 01. ■

offers five-day birdwatching tours to Bermuda. The tour cost of $1895 includes hotel accommodations, meals and field trips and lectures by local birdwatching authorities. The price does not include airfare to and from Bermuda.

PADI Travel Network International (☎ 800-729-7234, fax 714-540-2983) can arrange customized dive tours to Bermuda, packaging together accommodations and diving outings. Rates vary depending upon the length of stay and the type of accommodations you select, but they begin at around $300 for a three-night stay with two days of diving. Airfare to and from Bermuda is not included.

WARNING

The information in this chapter is particularly vulnerable to change: Prices for international travel are volatile, routes are introduced and canceled, schedules change and special deals come and go.

At times it seems that airlines and cruise companies make price structures and regulations as complicated as possible. You should check directly with the airline, cruise operator or travel agent to make sure you understand how a fare works and what sort of restrictions your ticket will have.

The details given in this chapter should be regarded as pointers and are not a substitute for your own up-to-date research.

Getting Around

There are no car rentals in Bermuda. Visitors can ride public buses and ferries, rent a moped or motorscooter, use taxis – or even hire a horse and carriage.

BUS

Bermuda has a good islandwide public bus system that you can use to reach most sights and beaches. The buses are reliable and generally run on time. Pick up a free copy of the bus and ferry schedule at any of the tourist offices or at the bus terminal on Washington St in the City of Hamilton.

Buses are quite busy on weekdays between 3:30 and 5:30 pm, when schoolchildren and office workers make the commute home, but at most other times getting a seat isn't a challenge. Frequencies vary with the route and the time of travel, but during the day the busier routes generally have a bus operating every 15 to 30 minutes. Sundays and holidays have substantially reduced schedules.

Of the dozen bus routes, all of them, with the exception of the St George's-St David's route, leave from the Hamilton bus terminal. Consequently, if you use buses often, you'll find yourself transferring there frequently.

Bus stops are marked with striped pink-and-blue posts; the top stripe is pink for buses heading into Hamilton, blue if the direction is away from Hamilton.

Fares & Passes

To ride the bus you must have the exact fare *in coins* or have a token, ticket or transportation pass. Paper money is not accepted and change is not given.

Bermuda is divided into 14 bus zones. Fares are based either on three zones (meaning the trip covers one to three zones) or 14 zones (for a trip covering four to 14 zones).

From the City of Hamilton it's a three-zone fare to the Bermuda Aquarium, Museum & Zoo (bus No 10 or 11); the Bermuda Botanical Gardens (bus No 1, 2 or 7); Elbow Beach or Horseshoe Bay (bus No 7); or Spittal Pond (bus No 1). From Hamilton, it's a 14-zone fare to the Royal Naval Dockyard (bus No 7 or 8) and to the airport, Bailey's Bay or St George – all of which can be reached by bus No 1, 3, 10 or 11.

The regular adult fare is $2.50 in coins or $2 in tokens for up to three zones and $4 in coins or $3.50 in tokens for more than three zones. Children ages three to 13 may ride for $1 in coins for any number of zones, and those under age three ride for free.

Bus transfers are free as long as they are made with the next scheduled connecting bus. If you need a transfer, request it from the driver when you get on the first bus.

Tickets, which are valid on buses but not on ferries, offer a handsome discount compared to the cash fare. The cost for adults is $13 for 15 tickets valid for up to three zones and $22 for 15 tickets valid for all zones. The cost for children is $6 for 15 tickets valid for all zones.

Transportation passes are handy if you're going to do a lot of exploring, as they allow unlimited use of both buses and ferries. Passes valid for three consecutive days cost $20 and those valid for seven consecutive days cost $32.50. In addition, there's a monthly pass for $37 that is valid for the calendar month in which it is purchased.

Ticket books, tokens and transportation passes are sold at the bus terminal in Hamilton every day of the week. Ticket books and tokens are also sold at most sub-post offices, but not at the main post office in Hamilton. Shorter transportation passes are sold at some hotels and guesthouses, as well as at tourist offices.

If you have any inquiries regarding public bus service, contact the Public Transportation Board (☎ 292-3851) between 8:45 am and 5 pm Monday to Friday.

Minibus Service

In addition to the islandwide public bus service, there are two private regional minibus services.

The West End Mini-Bus Service (☎ 234-2344) operates from the Royal Naval Dockyard south to Somerset Bridge. Minibuses generally run from 8:30 am (from 10 am on Saturdays and Sundays) to 4:30 pm in winter and to 5:30 pm in summer. The cost from the Royal Naval Dockyard is $2.50 to Somerset Village, $3 to the Somerset Bridge.

The St George's Mini-Bus Service operates in the greater St George's area from 7 am to 10 pm (to 11 pm in summer) Monday to Saturday, and until 6 pm on Sundays. You can call ☎ 297-8199 to arrange to be picked up anywhere in their service area. The cost is $1.75 around the Town of St George, $2.50 to the Bermuda Biological Station and $5 to St David's. The minibus office is in the St George Town Hall, opposite the tourist office.

For information on minibus tours of St George's, see Organized Tours later in this chapter.

MOPED & MOTORSCOOTER

Mopeds, which are called 'cycles' in Bermuda, are the main mode of transport for touring the island independently. They can be a fun way of getting around, but Bermuda's narrow winding roads present challenges for drivers who aren't used to these conditions – or who don't have moped experience.

In fact, enough visitors spill their cycles that the term 'road rash' is part of the island vernacular. If you're not used to riding, make sure you're comfortable with the moped before taking to the road. All moped rental shops are required to have an instructor show you how to use the bike and to provide you with an opportunity to practice. If you're not satisfied with your ability to handle the moped after your instruction, feel free to cancel the contract.

Automobile Ban

Bermudians managed to do without automobiles for some four decades after most of the rest of the Western world had become accustomed to driving around in 'horseless carriages'.

In 1906, Bermudians passed a law forbidding automobiles on the island after somebody imported a car with no mufflers and ended up creating a ruckus by spooking the horses.

It wasn't until WWII, when the US military insisted on importing motor vehicles for their own use, that Bermudians began to take to the idea of motorized transportation. In 1946, private ownership of automobiles was legalized.

There's still a strict regulation that limits the number of cars to one per household; today there are about 21,000 private cars on Bermuda and an additional 23,000 mopeds, scooters and motorcycles. ■

Road Rules

In Bermuda, as in Britain, driving is on the left. The maximum speed limit throughout Bermuda is 35 km (20 miles) per hour, except in a few municipal areas like central St George, where it drops to 25 km per hour.

Bermuda has a handful of roundabouts (also known as rotaries or traffic circles) – you must give way to traffic already on the roundabout, but once you enter you have the right of way.

To drive a moped you must be at least 16 years old, but if the bike's engine is 50 cc or less – as most of them are – you don't need to have a driver's license.

Helmets are provided by the cycle livery you rent from, and most mopeds come equipped with locks and carrying baskets. Bringing a short bungee cord from home will prove convenient for securing small packages in the basket.

Helmets are required of both drivers and passengers. Be cautious if you stop to do a lot of sightseeing, as it's easy to place the helmet in the moped's carrying basket and then forget to put it back on when you resume traveling – a situation that can draw a stern lecture from a police officer . . . or even from a passing citizen!

Parking

Cycle parking is clearly marked and easy to find in the City of Hamilton and other built-up areas. Parking a moped or motorcycle in car bays is forbidden.

Rentals

Moped rates are competitive and the longer you keep the bike the cheaper the per-day cost gets. You may find that you'll do just as well renting from the shop connected with your hotel or guesthouse, but if you want to seek out the best price, many cycle liveries will either pick you up and take you to their office or will deliver the cycle to you.

When comparing rates, take note of the add-ons that pad up the bill – a mandatory 'repair waiver' of $12 to $15 is the most common one. Insurance is included in the rates posted by some companies and treated as an add-on by others.

Whichever cycle livery you rent from, and regardless of the insurance offered, you'll likely have either a large deduction for theft or find that it will not be covered at all. Because of a rash of stolen cycles (one out of every 10 motorbikes is stolen each year), mopeds have become virtually impossible to insure against theft. Incidentally, it's not just a problem for rental bikes – most islanders have had theft coverage dropped from their own insurance policies in the past year or two.

Rates for a one-person moped average $25 to $30 for a one-day rental, $40 to $50 for two days, $50 to $70 for three days and $80 to $100 for a week – plus the one-time repair waiver charge. For about $10 more a day you can rent a larger cycle, commonly referred to as a scooter, that's capable of carrying a passenger. Carrying a passenger isn't recommended, however, unless you are an experienced motorbike driver.

The mopeds come with a full tank of gas and most have a small reserve tank. If you need to refill on the road, there are gas stations throughout the island from St George to Somerset.

Moped rental is available from the following companies.

Astwood Cycles (☎ 292-2245) has rates on the high side, but it has the advantage of nine locations, including the Sonesta Beach Hotel in Southampton; Belmont Hotel in Warwick; Coral Beach Club and Horizons in Paget; Hamilton Princess Hotel in Pembroke; and on North Shore Rd in Flatts Village.

Bermuda Cycles (☎ 292-5457) is a 10-minute walk north of the Hamilton city center on Serpentine Rd.

Dowling's Cycles (☎ 297-1614) is at 21 York St in St George.

Elbow Beach Cycle Livery (☎ 236-3535) is at Elbow Beach Hotel in Paget.

Eve Cycles (☎ 236-6247) is at 114 Middle Rd in Paget, 91 Reid St in the City of Hamilton and 1 Water St in St George.

Grotto Bay Cycles (☎ 293-2378) is at 17 Blue Hole Hill, near the Grotto Bay Beach Hotel in Hamilton Parish.

Oleander Cycles (☎ 236-5235), a large reputable operation with its main office on Valley Rd in Paget, has other locations, including the Royal Naval Dockyard and Middle Rd in Southampton.

Rockford Cycle Livery (☎ 292-1534), at Glebe Rd in Pembroke, boasts low rates.

Smatt's Cycle Livery (☎ 295-1180) is on Pitts Bay Rd, next to the Hamilton Princess Hotel in Pembroke.

Wheels Cycles (☎ 295-0112) is at 13 Dundonald St opposite Victoria Park in the City of Hamilton, at the Southampton Princess Hotel in Southampton and at Marriott's Castle Harbour Hotel.

BICYCLE

Bicycling is not overwhelmingly popular in Bermuda, but it is an option for getting around. However, Bermuda's roads are narrow, curving and often hilly, so people planning on bicycling need to be cautious of traffic and expect to work up a sweat. Using the Railway Trail, when it's going your way, is a good way of avoiding traffic.

Some of the moped rental shops, including Elbow Beach Cycle Livery, rent bicycles for around $15 a day or $45 a week.

Rental bicycles vary, but most are mountain bikes; helmets are included in rental fees.

FERRY
Public ferries, which operate daily in the Great Sound and Hamilton Harbour, offer a scenic alternative to the bus. As the distances across water are often shorter than comparable land routes, the ferries can also be quicker. The shortest ferry from the City of Hamilton to the Royal Naval Dockyard, for example, takes just 30 minutes, while the bus ride takes a full hour.

There are three different ferry routes connecting Hamilton with Paget, Warwick and the Somerset/Dockyard area. Each route leaves from the Hamilton terminal, which is conveniently located on Front St at the end of Queen St, just a stone's throw from the tourist office.

All fares are collected at the Hamilton terminal for both departing and arriving passengers. If you happen to be taking a ferry on intermediate stops – from the Dockyard to Somerset, for instance – there are no provisions for paying, so it's a free ride.

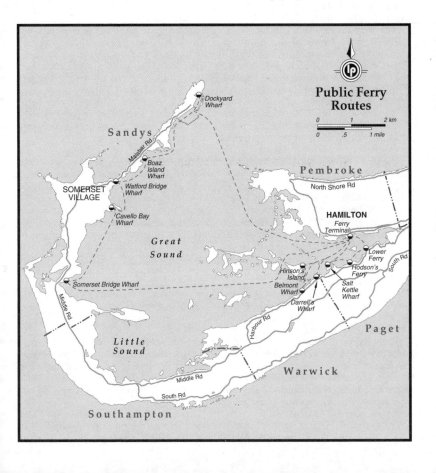

For details on transportation passes and tokens, which are valid on both public buses and ferries, see Fares & Passes in the earlier Bus section. If you have questions regarding ferries, contact the Marine and Ports Services Department (☎ 295-6575).

Paget & Warwick Routes
The Paget ferry connects the City of Hamilton with the north side of Paget Parish, making a 20-minute roundtrip loop from Hamilton that stops at Lower Ferry, Hodson's Ferry and Salt Kettle Wharf along the way. An exception is in the evening, when some sailings skip the Lower Ferry and Hodson's Ferry stops.

The Warwick ferry makes a 30-minute loop, connecting Hamilton with Darrell's Wharf, near the intersection of Harbour Rd and Cobb Hill Rd; Belmont Wharf, near the Belmont Golf Club; and Hinson's Island.

Note that the order of the stops on both the Paget and Warwick routes varies throughout the day, as some sailings make clockwise loops, while others are counter-clockwise.

The cost on either route is $2 one way. The boats, which operate from 7:15 am to 11 pm, leave Hamilton about once every 30 minutes. On Saturdays, the first ferry leaves Hamilton at 8:45 am. On Sundays and holidays, the Warwick and Paget routes are merged and served by a single ferry that operates every 40 minutes from 10:10 am to 7 pm.

Somerset/Dockyard Route
The Somerset/Dockyard route provides service between the City of Hamilton and the West End, with stops at the Royal Naval Dockyard, Boaz Island, Watford Bridge, Cavello Bay and Somerset Bridge. The order of stops varies with the sailing – so it can take as little as 30 minutes to get to the Dockyard from Hamilton or as long as 1¼ hours depending on the course of the boat you catch. The whole loop route takes about one hour and 45 minutes.

The one-way fare is $3.50. You can also take a moped on the Somerset/Dockyard

boat for an additional $3.50, which gives you the option of sailing one way and driving back.

From Monday to Friday, the boats leave Hamilton at 6:25, 7:30, 9, 10 and 11 am; at noon; and at 1, 2, 3, 4 and 5:20 pm. Saturday departures are the same, except that the first boat is at 9 am. On Sundays and public holidays, the boats depart from Hamilton at 9 and 11 am and at 1, 3 and 5 pm. Every day of the week, both the 9 am and 1 pm boats make a direct 30-minute sailing to the Dockyard.

HITCHHIKING
Hitchhiking is not illegal in Bermuda, but it's just not done. As one police officer told us: 'I don't know if people would know what you're doing. They might stick their thumb back up at you, thinking you're just having a good time'.

And of course, as with everywhere else in the world, hitchhiking is never entirely safe and Lonely Planet does not recommend it.

WALKING
Walking is a good way to get around towns, such as St George and Hamilton. Outside of town centers, few of Bermuda's narrow roads have sidewalks, which makes walking a less-than-ideal way to get between villages. The main exception is when the villages happen to be connected by the old railroad route, as most of that route has been turned into a trail system geared for walkers and cyclists. For more information, see Hiking in the Outdoor Activities chapter.

TAXI
Taxis are readily available from the airport at flight times, and most larger hotels have taxis at the waiting. In addition, there are taxi stands in heavily touristed areas, such as Front St in Hamilton and King's Square in St George.

All taxis are equipped with meters. The standard rate, for up to six passengers, is $4.60 for the first mile plus $1.60 for each additional mile. A 25% surcharge is charged between midnight and 6 am and all day on Sundays and public holidays.

There's an additional charge of 25¢ for each package or piece of luggage placed in the trunk.

If you need to call for a taxi, Radio Cabs (☎ 295-4141) has numerous cabs and 24-hour service. Other taxi companies include BIU Taxi Co-op Transportation (☎ 292-4476) and Bermuda Taxi Operators Company (☎ 292-4175).

HORSE & CARRIAGE

Although it's more of a romantic ride than a practical means of transportation, horse-and-carriage rides are available in the City of Hamilton from along Front St. They usually take a seaside route west along Pitts Bay Rd or make a circular route north on Bermudiana Rd, west on Richmond Rd and back to Front St via Serpentine and Par-la-Ville Rds.

The cost per carriage, for one to four passengers, is $20 for the first 30 minutes (the minimum charge) and $20 for each additional 30-minute increment. If the carriage is drawn by two horses, as some of them are, they are allowed to carry more than four passengers, in which case the cost for the fifth and additional passengers is $5 per person per 30 minutes.

ORGANIZED TOURS

If you want to piece together your own private sightseeing tour, taxis can double as tour operators, catering a tour to your interests. The drivers are generally knowledgeable and their commentary can add plenty of local color as you explore. The cost is $30 per hour for one to four passengers, $42 per hour for five to six passengers.

In addition, the St George's Mini-Bus Service offers one-hour tours of the Town of St George, mainly on weekdays during the cruise ship season. At the height of summer there are commonly two tours in the morning and two in the afternoon. The cost is $12.50. Inquiries can be made at the minibus office in the St George Town Hall or by calling ☎ 297-8492.

Ferry rides (see the Ferry section, above) provide an inexpensive harbor cruise, and there are plenty of other sightseeing cruises (see the Outdoor Activities chapter) around Bermuda as well.

Outdoor Activities

HIKING

Bermuda's numerous parks and nature reserves provide opportunities for short hikes. Some of the best walking destinations are the areas with the greatest acreage, such as Spittal Pond Nature Reserve in Smith's Parish and South Shore Park in Warwick and Southampton parishes.

Bermuda's Railway Trail

The longest walking trails on the island aren't to be found in parks and nature reserves but are along the now covered-over tracks that once carried Bermuda's narrow-gauge railway. The railway, which began operations in 1931, never gained in popularity and the last train was taken off the tracks in 1947. The government, which had acquired the railway in its final days, sold the engines and cars to British Guiana and shipped them off to Georgetown in 1948. After that, most of the track was simply forgotten, though a few sections were lost to modernization, most notably a three-mile stretch around the City of Hamilton that was widened into new roads.

In 1984, the government set aside the remaining sections of the old railway route for foot and bridal paths. In all, this encompasses some 21 miles of trail from Somerset Village at the West End of Bermuda to St George's at the East End. The Railway Trail is not a single continuous route; there is a significant break between Paget and Devonshire parishes, as well as many shorter breaks here and there where hikers must – at least briefly – walk along a vehicle road until the Railway Trail starts up again. Some sections are open only to hikers, bicyclists and horseback riders, while others are open to motorbikes and limited local car traffic.

The government publishes a nifty pocket-size booklet, *The Bermuda Railway Trail Walking Guide*, which details all

seven sections of the trail, complete with a map and tidbits about the nature and history of sights you'll encounter along each section. The free booklet can be picked up at tourist offices on Bermuda after you arrive.

Organized Walks

The Walking Club of Bermuda meets regularly at 7 am on Sundays for walks of about six miles; visitors are welcome to participate. The location changes each week; look for the schedule in the current *This Week in Bermuda* tourist magazine.

Creative Fitness (☎ 238-8545) offers 1½-hour guided walks along the Railway Trail on most Tuesdays and Thursdays in the summer, leaving at 8 am from the entrance of the Belmont Hotel in Warwick. The cost is $2.

BIRDWATCHING

With only 22 species of birds nesting on Bermuda, it's not surprising that the peak birdwatching season is during the spring and fall migrations. During those periods birdwatching can be excellent, with more than 200 species of migratory birds – from warblers and thrushes to shorebirds and seabirds – visiting the island.

One of the finest all-around birdwatching sites is Spittal Pond, Bermuda's largest nature reserve. For sighting land birds, easily accessible areas include the Heydon Trust Estate in Sandys Parish, the Bermuda Botanical Gardens in Paget Parish and the Arboretum in Devonshire Parish. Good places for spotting shorebirds and wading birds include Warwick Pond in Warwick Parish and Somerset Long Bay Nature Reserve in Sandys Parish.

A good companion for birdwatchers is *A Guide to the Birds of Bermuda* by Eric Amos, which describes virtually every species of bird that has been seen on the island and gives detailed information on

Bermuda International Race Weekend

The big running event of the year is the Bermuda International Race Weekend, held annually on the second weekend of January. It centers around Sunday's running of the Bermuda International Marathon, a 13-mile, two-loop route that begins on Front St in Hamilton, and the Bermuda International Half-Marathon, held concurrently but covering only one loop of the course. Record holders for the full marathon are Moises Requena of Mexico (2:24.22; in 1995) and Sally Eastall of England (2:42.47; in 1990).

Activities begin Friday evening in Hamilton with the Bank of Butterfield Mile, a series of mile-long invitational races by elite runners, children and local celebrities. The evening is capped off with music by the Bermuda Regiment Band.

Saturday's event is the Bermuda International 10K & Fitness Walk, a 10-km race and a concurrent noncompetitive fitness walk along the north shore starting at the National Sports Centre in Devonshire.

Entry fees are $20 for the marathon, less for the other races. Total prize money for the marathon is more than $20,000, plus up to an additional $30,000 in the event of new marathon records.

Information and an entry form can be obtained from the Bermuda Department of Tourism, or contact the Race Committee (☎/fax 297-8045). Special hotel and air packages are offered by Marathon Tours (☎ 617-242-7845), 108 Main St, Charlestown, Boston, MA 02129, and USAir, two of the event sponsors. ∎

good birding areas. Also recommended is *A Checklist and Guide to the Birds of Bermuda* by David B Wingate, which has some species descriptions as well as charts on the seasonal distribution and abundance of birds.

For more information on birdlife in Bermuda, see Birds in the Flora & Fauna section of the Facts about Bermuda chapter.

RUNNING

The Railway Trail (see the Hiking section) makes a good, traffic-safe route for joggers. Use caution when running in other areas, as many Bermuda roads are narrow with heavy traffic, no sidewalks and the occasional blind curve.

TENNIS

Numerous places in Bermuda have tennis courts open to the general public. Fees are charged on a per-hour, per-court basis. If you plan on playing much tennis, it's a good idea to bring your own equipment; however, most places rent racquets and sell tennis balls.

The Government Tennis Stadium (☎ 292-0105) at Bernard Park on Marsh Folly Rd in Pembroke Parish, at the north side of the City of Hamilton, has three clay and five plexicushion courts. The cost is $8 for adults, $4 for children. Racquets can be rented for $5 an hour, lessons are available for $40 an hour, and at night there's an additional $8 fee to light the courts. Proper tennis attire is required.

The following also have tennis courts open to the public.

Belmont Hotel (☎ 236-1301), Warwick; three courts; $15 for visitors, free for hotel guests; night lighting $5

Elbow Beach Hotel (☎ 236-3535), Paget; five courts; $12 for visitors, $8 for hotel guests; lessons available

Grotto Bay Beach Hotel (☎ 293-8333), Hamilton Parish; four courts; $12 for visitors, $8 for hotel guests; night lighting $15; lessons available

Hamiltonian (☎ 295-5608), Pembroke; three courts; $10 for visitors, free for hotel guests; night lighting $5; lessons available

Horizons (☎ 236-0048), Paget; three courts; $10 for visitors, $3.50 for hotel guests; Horizons guests may also use the courts at Coral Beach

Marriott's Castle Harbour Resort (☎ 293-2040), Hamilton Parish; six courts; $14 for visitors, $12 for hotel guests; lessons available

Newstead (☎ 236-6060), Paget; two clay courts; $14 for visitors, $3.50 for hotel guests; Newstead guests may also use the courts at Coral Beach

Palm Reef Hotel (☎ 236-1000), Paget; one court; $10 for visitors, free to hotel guests

Port Royal Tennis Club (☎ 234-0974), Southampton; four courts; $8; night lighting $4

The Reefs (☎ 238-0222), Southampton; two courts; $10 for visitors, free to hotel guests

Sonesta Beach Hotel (☎ 238-8122), Southampton; six courts; $10 for visitors, $8 for hotel guests; night lighting $2; lessons available

· Southampton Princess (☎ 238-1005), Southampton; 11 courts; $12 for visitors, $10 for hotel guests; night lighting $2; lessons available

Stonington Beach Hotel (☎ 236-5416), Paget; two courts; $10 for visitors, free for hotel guests; lessons available

Willowbank (☎ 234-1616), Sandys; two courts; $6 for visitors, free for hotel guests

Ariel Sands in Devonshire, Pompano Beach Club and Lantana in Sandys, and Cambridge Beaches and Pink Beach Club in Smith's have tennis courts free for their guests, but they are not open to the public.

The tennis courts at the private Coral Beach & Tennis Club in Paget, which is considered the island's top tennis club, and at the exclusive Mid Ocean Club in Tucker's Town are open only to members or by introduction from a member.

Information on tennis tournaments is available from the Bermuda Lawn Tennis Association (☎ 296-0834), PO Box HM 341, Hamilton HM BX.

Tennis Anyone?

The game of tennis, which originated in England in 1872, was played for the first time in the Western Hemisphere in 1873 at the Bermuda home of Sir Brownlow Gray, the island's chief justice.

Mary Outerbridge, a guest at the Gray home, was so enthralled by the game that she carried a pair of racquets with her on a trip from Bermuda to New York. She is credited with introducing tennis to the USA in 1874. ■

SQUASH

The Bermuda Squash Racquets Club (☎ 292-6881), on Middle Rd in Devonshire, has four courts available on a reservation basis. The cost is about $6 per court, plus a per-person fee of $5 for 40 minutes. Balls and racquets can be rented.

The Coral Beach & Tennis Club in Paget has squash courts too, but only for their guests or by introduction from a club member.

GOLF

There are eight golf courses on Bermuda, six open to the public and two that require introduction by members.

All courses require 'proper golf attire', which means shirts must have collars and shorts must be Bermuda-shorts length; jeans, cut-offs and sleeveless shirts are not allowed.

Reservations for tee times for the Ocean View, Port Royal and St George's golf courses can be made through an automated reservation system by calling ☎ 295-6500. Tee times for the other courses are made directly.

Lessons are available at all courses for $30 to $45 per half-hour. Golf shoes can be rented at some courses for $6 to $10. Prices given for club rentals are for full sets; left-handed and right-handed sets for both men and women should be available at each course.

Courses open to the general public include the following.

Belmont Golf Club (☎ 236-6400), Warwick; 18 holes, par 70, 5769 yards; free to hotel guests, $57 for others; mandatory use of gas carts at $18 per nine holes; club rentals $25

Castle Harbour Golf Club (☎ 293-2040, extension 6670), Tucker's Town, St George's Parish; 18 holes, par 71, 6440 yards; $60 in winter, $100 in summer (sunset rate of $55 after 4:30 pm); mandatory use of gas carts at $42 for 18 holes; club rentals $26

Ocean View Golf Course (☎ 295-9093), Devonshire; nine holes, par 35, 2940 yards; $20 for nine holes (sunset rate of $14 after 4 pm); optional pull carts $6 or gas carts $16; club rentals $16

Port Royal Golf Course (☎ 234-0974), Southampton; 18 holes, par 71, 6565 yards; $65, with cheaper rates after 4 pm and five-day weekday packages available; optional pull carts for $8, or gas carts for $16 per nine holes; club rentals $20

Southampton Princess Golf Club (☎ 238-0446), Southampton; 18 holes, par 54, 2684 yards; hotel guests $34, others $38, with sunset and multiround rates available; mandatory use of gas carts for $34; club rentals $15

St George's Golf Club (☎ 297-8353), St George's; 18 holes, par 62, 4043 yards; $40, with cheaper rates after 4 pm and five-day weekday packages available; pull carts for $6 or gas carts for $32; club rentals $17

The following golf courses require introduction by a member.

Mid Ocean Club (☎ 293-0330), Tucker's Town, St George's; 18 holes, par 71, 6547 yards; $120, or $50 if playing with a member; caddies available at $25 per bag; club rentals $12

Riddell's Bay Golf & Country Club (☎ 238-1060), Warwick; 18 holes, par 70, 5588 yards; $50 on weekdays, $70 on weekends and holidays, discounts if playing with a member; optional pull carts for $5 or gas carts for $35; club rentals $13

Golf Tournaments

Bermuda's golf tournaments, which are held from October to June, are open to both islanders and visiting golfers. Tournaments are listed under Special Events in the Facts for the Visitor chapter.

More information on tournaments can be obtained by contacting the Bermuda Golf Association (☎ 238-1367, fax 238-0983), PO Box HM 433, Hamilton HM BX.

HORSEBACK RIDING

Spicelands Riding Centre (☎ 238-8212), on Middle Rd in Warwick, has 1½-hour guided rides along south shore trails and beaches at 6:45 am daily, followed by a continental breakfast; one-hour trail rides at 10 and 11:30 am and 3 pm; and, from May to September, evening rides at 6 pm weekdays. The cost is $45 for the morning

rides, $35 for the others. All rides are at a walking pace and all ages and experience levels are welcome. Reservations are required in advance.

Lee Bow Riding Centre (☎ 236-4181), on Tribe Rd No 1 in Devonshire, caters mainly to junior riders (up to age 18), offering lessons as well as $35 one-hour guided trail rides by appointment. Beginners are welcome.

For information on horse shows, contact the Bermuda Equestrian Federation, PO Box DV 583, Devonshire DV BX.

BEACHES & SWIMMING

There are pleasant beaches all around Bermuda, but one singularly outstanding area is South Shore Park, a 1½-mile-long coastal park that encompasses many of the island's finest beaches. Its eastern boundary begins in Warwick Parish with the expansive Warwick Long Bay, a half-mile-long unbroken stretch of pink sand, while the western boundary runs just beyond picturesque Horseshoe Bay in Southampton Parish. In between are nearly a dozen coves and bays of various sizes that offer protected swimming and a bit of seclusion. Coastal trails link the beaches and make exploring fun and easy. No matter where you're staying on Bermuda, be sure to include an outing here.

Other notable beaches include Elbow Beach (Paget Parish), a mile-long strand that's a favorite with beachgoers from the City of Hamilton; John Smith's Bay (Smith's Parish), which often has calm waters when westerly winds kick up the surf elsewhere around the island; and Shelly Bay Beach (Hamilton Parish), which is a favorite with families because of its shallow waters and playground facilities.

In the tourist season, lifeguards are stationed at Horseshoe Bay in Southampton Parish and John Smith's Bay in Smith's Parish.

Bermuda does not have beaches designated for nude or seminude sunbathing. Note that the stinging Portuguese man-of-war is sometimes found in Bermuda's

Who's in the Water?

Islanders say that in the off-season it's easy to tell the nationality of the people splashing in the waves. Bermudians don't swim after September, they say, Americans won't swim much after November, but British visitors will swim year round.

Most Bermudians take their first swim of the year on Bermuda Day, May 24, though the more timid wait until the Queen's Birthday in mid-June. ■

waters from March to July (see Dangers & Annoyances in the Facts for the Visitor chapter).

DIVING

Despite the fact that Bermuda's coral reefs are the most northerly in the Atlantic, diving in Bermuda is quite similar to diving in Florida or the Bahamas.

The combination of shallow water and warm ocean currents has allowed Bermuda's reefs to thrive even though they are separated by hundreds of miles of cool ocean water from other coral reefs. In all, waters surrounding Bermuda harbor some 24 species of hard coral, including brain coral and tree coral, and another two dozen species of soft coral, including sea fans and sea whips.

Many of the same species of tropical fish that are common to Caribbean waters can be found feeding on the corals in Bermuda as well. Some of the more colorful fish include the clown wrasse, queen angelfish, rainbow parrotfish, rock beauty, spotted puffer, blue chromis, foureye butterflyfish, blue tang, triggerfish, orange spotted filefish, small squirrelfish and large green moray eels.

Bermuda waters also hold brittle stars, sea horses, sea spiders, sea hares, sea cucumbers, sea anemones, sea urchins, squids, conchs, slipper lobsters and spiny lobsters.

The main diving season in Bermuda is from April through October, although it

can stretch a bit longer in either direction. The warmest conditions are during the summer months, when the water temperature reaches about 85°F. In spring and autumn, the average water temperature is only in the 60s. Visibility is generally 75 to 100 feet.

King Edward VII Memorial Hospital in Paget has a decompression chamber for divers who get the bends.

Wreck Dives

Scores of shipwrecks still lie scattered along Bermuda's treacherous reefs. Because the reefs are relatively shallow, there are many wreck dives suitable for both novice and intermediate-level divers. Since most wrecks are on the reef, a wreck dive in Bermuda commonly doubles as a reef dive.

The *Constellation*, a four-masted schooner that provided the inspiration for the *Goliath* in Peter Benchley's novel *The Deep*, is a favorite among wreck divers. The ship, which is now widely scattered along the ocean floor at a depth of only 30 feet, was en route from New York to Venezuela when it diverted to Bermuda for mechanical repairs in July 1942. On the approach to the island, just seven miles northwest of the Royal Naval Dockyard, a current carried the 200-foot schooner into the reef where – laden with a cargo of cement – it sank into a watery grave.

Less than 20 yards from the *Constellation* is the wreck of the *Montana*, a 236-foot paddle steamer that was built in England to be used as a blockade runner during the US Civil War. Launched in 1863, it made it only as far as Bermuda, where it sank on the reef during its maiden voyage to the Confederate South. Some sections of the ship, including the paddle wheels, remain intact.

The *Cristobal Colon*, a 500-foot Spanish liner that went aground in 1936, is the largest ship ever to wreck in Bermudian waters. The ship, which lies eight miles north of the island, was traveling with only its crew, who, due to the outbreak of civil war in Spain, were unable to return to their home port. Because the cruise ship grounded on the reef, rather than sinking, it was an easy target for pilfers. While the authorities salvaged items during the day, scores of other islanders came aboard after nightfall and stole off with everything from chandeliers and silverware to plumbing fixtures.

In 1937, the 250-foot Norwegian cargo ship *Aristo* sighted the still-intact *Cristobal Colon* in a position that appeared to be sailing straight up through the reef, and

Brittle stars move by waving their arms in a rowing action.

the captain set his course to follow. By the time he recognized his error, the *Aristo* had a lethal gash in its hull.

During WWII, the US military decided to use the *Cristobal Colon* as a target ship, literally blowing the ship in two, with one half settling on either side of the reef. The *Aristo* on the other hand stands intact, its forward deck still holding a fire truck and other cargo that it was carrying to Bermuda. Both boats sit in about 50 feet of water.

In the same general area is the *Taunton*, a 228-foot freighter that sank, weighed down with a load of American coal, as it arrived in Bermuda in 1920. This a good wreck dive for novices, as it's just 20 feet beneath the surface.

The newest and most intact of the shipwrecks is the *Hermes*, a 160-foot freighter that was built during WWII. In the early 1980s, after the *Hermes* was abandoned in Bermuda, the government decided to scuttle the boat and turn it into a dive site. They first stripped the hatches and other potential hazards so that it could be used safely for penetration dives and then towed it out to sea. The boat sits upright in 75 feet of water about a mile south of Warwick Long Bay and Bermuda's south shore.

Dive Operations

There are a handful of dive operations on Bermuda. In addition to dives for certified divers, most also offer a half-day introductory program for first-time divers that includes a condensed basic scuba lesson and a supervised shallow dive.

If you're interested in a full certification course, PADI programs are offered by all of Bermuda's dive operators. Two of the companies, Fantasea Diving and Nautilus Diving, have a PADI 5-star rating; Nautilus also has a PADI five-star Instructor Development Center. In addition to PADI programs, Blue Water Divers also handles NAUI and SSI certification.

Prices are competitive, but you should inquire as to what gear is included in the dive price, as it can vary depending upon the dive program and operation. If you need gear, expect to pay an extra $6 to $10 each for rental of a regulator and gauge, a BCD, a wet suit, or a set of mask, fins and snorkel.

Underwater cameras can be rented from most dive shops, but if you're planning on this, you should call in advance to get information on what equipment is available. Night dives can be arranged for around $60 from Blue Water Divers, Fantasea Diving and South Side Scuba Watersports.

Fantasea Diving (☎ 236-6339, fax 236-8926), Darrell's Wharf, Harbour Rd, Paget PG 01, offers an $85 'discover scuba' course for beginners, which includes an hour-long introductory lesson at either a hotel pool or the beach and a supervised shallow wreck or reef dive. The price includes all equipment – just bring a bathing suit. Fantasea does a one-tank afternoon wreck dive for $45 and a morning two-tank dive for $65; both are geared for experienced divers and include tanks and weights.

Blue Water Divers (☎ 234-1034, fax 234-3561), Robinson's Marina, PO Box SN 165, Southampton SN BX, offers an $88 introductory scuba course similar to Fantasea's, as well as a $75 follow-up beginner's dive. One-tank dives, which vary from 30 to 80 feet depending on the diver's experience, cost $45, while two-tank dives are $65, weights and tanks included. Nondiving friends are welcome to ride along on the 42-foot dive boat to the

dive site for $12.

Nautilus Diving (☎ 238-2332, fax 236-4284), PO Box HM 237, Hamilton HM AX, has locations at both the Southampton Princess hotel in Southampton Parish and the Hamilton Princess Hotel in Pembroke Parish. They offer a $95 scuba introduction course that includes a lesson in the pool followed by a shallow reef dive, and the standard one-tank and two-tank dives for $50/70 respectively.

South Side Scuba Watersports (☎ 238-1833, fax 236-0394), PO Box PG-38, Paget PG BX, is at the Sonesta Beach Hotel in Southampton Parish. They have a $95 pool-and-shallow-dive scuba introduction course and $45 one-tank dives that are geared to the diver's level of experience. In addition, there are discounted dive packages for those interested in a minimum of six dives.

HELMET DIVING

Helmet diving offers visitors a chance to jump beneath the surface of the water without having to master diving skills. Participants don a headpiece, called a helmet, which has a clear face plate and works on a similar premise to a glass held upside-down in water. The helmet rests atop one's shoulders and is connected to a hose that pumps in fresh air. The 'dive', which lasts about 30 minutes, occurs at the sandy edge of the reef in about 10 feet of water, allowing fish and coral to be viewed up close.

There are two companies in Bermuda offering helmet diving from May through October. Greg Hartley's Under Sea Adventure (☎ /fax 234-2861) departs from the Watford Bridge dock in Sandys Parish. Bronson Hartley's Underwater Wonderland (☎ 292-4434, fax 292-7488) departs from Flatts Inlet in Smith's Parish. Both charge $44 for adults, $33 for children.

SNORKELING

Snorkeling, like swimming and diving, is far more popular in the summer months, when the waters are at their warmest.

Two of the best places for snorkeling right from the beach are Church Bay, in Southampton Parish on the south shore, and Tobacco Bay, north of the Town of St George. There are also a number of other lesser beaches where you'll find coastal outcrops that harbor colorful fish – essentially, any rocky shoreline in calm waters is a potential snorkeling site.

Some of the best and most pristine snorkeling spots are too far offshore to be reached without a boat. Among the advantages of joining a snorkeling cruise are that they often include a visit to a shipwreck, an easy task since most wrecks are found along coral reefs.

Equipment Rentals

You can save money by bringing your own snorkeling equipment, but snorkel sets (mask, snorkel and fins) can be rented at several locations around Bermuda. Some places give discounts for rentals of more than one day. If you're not using a credit card, a deposit of about $30 will be required.

Blue Hole Water Sports (☎ 293-2915) at Grotto Bay Beach Hotel in Hamilton Parish rents snorkel sets for $6 an hour, $18 a day.

Blue Water Divers (☎ 234-1034) at Robinson's Marina in Sandys rents snorkel sets for $14 a day.

Fantasea Diving (☎ 236-6339) at Darrell's Wharf in Warwick rents snorkel sets for $15 a day.

Mangrove Marina Ltd (☎ 234-0914) at Somerset Bridge in Sandys rents snorkel sets for $3 an hour, $10 a day.

Nautilus Diving, at both the Southampton Princess (☎ 238-2332) in Southampton and the Hamilton Princess Hotel (☎ 295-9485) in Pembroke, rents snorkel sets for $7 an hour or $21 a day. They can provide masks with prescription lenses.

South Side Scuba Watersports rents snorkel sets for $6 an hour or $18 a day at Marriott's Castle Harbour Resort (☎ 293-2543) in Hamilton Parish and at the Sonesta Beach Hotel (☎ 238-1833) in Southampton.

Snorkeling Cruises

All four of the dive companies (see Diving) take snorkelers out on their boats to snorkel above the reefs while the divers are beneath the surface. The cost ranges from $30 with Fantasea Diving to $38 with Nautilus Diving, snorkeling gear included.

However, most snorkelers will be better off going on a cruise designed specifically for snorkelers. As a rule, these snorkeler-designated tours will take you to shallow reefs where you can better view the fish from the surface, rather than peering down at the coral through 20 to 40 feet of water, which happens often when you go out with divers.

Most of the snorkeling cruises are combination sightseeing tours; some use glass-bottom boats. All include complimentary use of snorkeling equipment and a bit of instruction for first-time snorkelers. A few offer complimentary drinks, while others have a cash bar.

The main season is from May through October, although some tours begin as early as April and continue as late as November. Children's prices are usually half the adult fare.

Cruise time is generally from 3½ to four hours. However, if you're going along primarily for the snorkeling, it's a good idea to inquire about the length of time that will be spent in the water, as it can vary significantly between tour companies.

As the different boats leave from different piers around the island, it's usually possible to pick one up close to where you're staying.

Bermuda Barefoot Cruises (☎ 236-3498), which departs from Darrell's Wharf in Warwick, uses a 32-foot powerboat, goes out at 9:30 am and 1:30 pm and costs $45.

Bermuda Watersports (☎ 293-2640), which departs from the Grotto Bay Beach Hotel in Hamilton Parish, has a 60-foot motorized catamaran and charges $35.

Bermuda Water Tours (☎ 236-1500), which departs near the ferry terminal in the City of Hamilton, uses a 65-foot glass-bottom boat. There are both morning and afternoon snorkeling tours and the cost is $39.

Elusive Cruises (☎ 234-8042), which departs from Albuoy Point in the City of Hamilton and also picks up at Darrell's Wharf in Warwick, uses a 44-foot motorboat and charges $36. The morning cruise goes to a coral reef, the afternoon one features shipwrecks.

Hat Trick Sailing & Snorkelling (☎ 234-1434) has a 38-foot trimaran, with morning and afternoon departures from the Royal Naval Dockyard. The cost is $40.

Hayward's Snorkelling & Glass Bottom Boat Cruises (☎ 292-8652) departs near the ferry terminal in the City of Hamilton for both morning and afternoon cruises on a 54-foot motorboat and charges $40.

Jessie James Cruises (☎ 236-4804) departs from Albuoy Point in the City of Hamilton and also picks up passengers at Darrell's Wharf and Belmont Wharf in Warwick. It has both 48-foot and 57-foot boats and charges $40.

Pitman's Snorkelling (☎ 234-0700) departs from Robinson's Marina at Somerset Bridge in Sandys for morning and afternoon cruises in a 44-foot motorboat.

Sand Dollar Cruises (☎ 236-1967), which departs from the Marriott's Castle Harbour Resort in Hamilton Parish, has a 40-foot sailboat that offers morning and afternoon snorkeling trips for $35.

Salt Kettle Boat Rentals (☎ 236-4863) departs from Salt Kettle in Paget both mornings and afternoons aboard a 35-foot motorboat. It charges $42 and sometimes snorkels the *Constellation* and *Montana* wrecks.

Snorkel Park

The Bermuda Snorkel Park (☎ 292-8652), at the north side of the Royal Naval Dockyard, has a shallow lagoon with a little beach that's suitable for children. This seasonal site is open from 10 am to 5 pm from mid-April through October. There's a shallow reef that can be snorkeled; for $2 you can go in and use the beach or for $17.50 rent a snorkel, mask, fins and buoyancy vest. There are showers and changing rooms.

WINDSURFING

Windsurfing has not taken off in a big way in Bermuda, but it does have its enthusiasts. Conditions tend to be best in the winter. The Great Sound sees the most windsurfing action, but the best locations change with the wind. When winds come from the south, the south shore can have decent waves for wave sailing.

Pompano Beach Club (☎ 234-0222) in Southampton rents beginner and intermediate boards from May to October. The cost is $12 an hour or $36 for four hours.

Blue Hole Water Sports (☎ 293-2915) at the Grotto Bay Beach Hotel rents windsurfing equipment for $20 an hour, $45 for four hours and $75 for eight hours.

FISHING

Ocean fishing is possible at any time of the year, but the best conditions are from about May to November.

Game fish in Bermuda's waters include Atlantic blue marlin, white marlin, blackfin tuna, yellowfin tuna, bluefin tuna, skipjack tuna, dolphinfish (not the marine mammal), wahoo, great barracuda, greater amberjack, almaco jack, Atlantic sailfish, gray snapper, yellowtail snapper, Bermuda chub, bonefish, palometa, African pompano and rainbow runner.

In the interest of Bermuda's conservation efforts, sport fishers are encouraged to release game fish, particularly marlin and other billfish, unless they're being taken for food. Of the approximately 150 billfish caught annually aboard charter boats, some 80% are released.

Shore Fishing

Catches from shore include gray snapper, great barracuda, bonefish and pompano. Rods, reels and tackle can be rented from Mangrove Marina Ltd (☎ 234-0914) at Somerset Bridge in Sandys for $15 a day. Licenses are not required.

Deep-Sea Fishing

Boat charters are available for deep-sea fishing, either by the half day or full day. Rates vary according to the size of the boat, trip location, number of people on board etc; all fishing equipment is included with the rental.

Charter boats can be booked through the following offices.

Bermuda Charter Fishing Boat Association, PO Box SB 145, Sandys SB BX (☎ 292-6246)

Bermuda Sports Fishing Association, Creek View House, 8 Tulo Lane, Pembroke HM 02 (☎ 295-2370)

St George Game Fishing & Cruising Association, PO Box GE 107, St George's GE BX (☎ 297-8093)

WATER SKIING

Water skiing is allowed at Harrington Sound, Hamilton Harbour, Great Sound, Spanish Point, Ferry Reach, Castle Harbour, Ely's Harbour, Riddell's Bay and Mangrove Bay.

The following two companies offer water skiing for all levels, from beginner to advanced. Rates vary according to the location and the number of skiers, but are around $60 for a half-hour, $95 for an hour, instruction included.

The Bermuda Waterski Centre (☎ 234-3354), at Somerset Bridge in Sandys, is open from 8 am to 7:30 pm daily from May through September, and sporadically the rest of the year. They also offer slalom, knee-boarding, barefoot skiing and trick skiing.

Island Water Ski (☎ 293-2915), at the Grotto Bay Beach Hotel in Hamilton Parish, operates from April to August, from 6 to 8 pm on weekdays and from 8 am to 8 pm on weekends. They offer slalom, knee-boarding and tubes, and also have wet suits and children's skis.

KAYAKING & CANOEING

Kayaks and canoes can be rented for leisurely paddling, or to get to the nearshore islands for snorkeling outings.

Mangrove Marina Ltd (☎ 234-0914) at Somerset Bridge in Sandys rents one-person kayaks for $15 for one hour, $40 for four hours, $60 for eight hours. Two-person kayaks or canoes cost $20/50/70 for one/four/eight hours.

South Side Scuba Water Sports (☎ 293-2543) at Marriott's Castle Harbour Resort in Hamilton Parish rents one-person kayaks for $18 an hour.

Pompano Beach Club (☎ 234-0222) in Southampton rents one-person kayaks for $10 an hour, $30 for four hours.

Marine Life Protections

The following marine life is protected and may not be killed or otherwise taken: sea turtles, all types of corals (including sea fans), scallops, helmet shells, bonnet shells, netted olive shells, Bermuda cone shells, Atlantic pearl oysters, calico clams and West Indian top shells. Lobsters may only be taken by licensed residents, and only from September to March.

Spear guns are banned. Spear fishing is not allowed within one mile of shore and no more than two fish of a single species may be speared within a 24-hour period. ■

SAILING

Bermuda has no shortage of sailing locales, with the greatest abundance to be found in the protected waters of the Great Sound and Little Sound.

Salt Kettle Boat Rentals (☎ 236-4863), at Salt Kettle in Paget, offers two-hour sailing lessons for beginners for $90 and one-hour refresher lessons for $60 on a 17-foot O'Day Sailer. They also rent Sunfish for $40/85 for two/eight hours and O'Day Sailers for $65/135.

Other places that rent sailboats include the following.

Mangrove Marina Ltd, Somerset Bridge, Sandys (☎ 234-0914)
Pompano Beach Club, Pompano Beach Rd, Southampton (☎ 234-0222)
Rance's Boatyard, Crow Lane, Paget (☎ 292-1843)
South Side Scuba Water Sports, Marriott's Castle Harbour Resort, Hamilton Parish (☎ 293-2543)

Rates vary with the company, depending on the type and size of sailboat; costs range from $18 to $35 for one hour, $35 to $75 for two hours and $70 to $160 for eight hours.

SAILING CRUISES

It's possible to charter a skippered yacht for day cruises once you're on Bermuda. A listing of more than a dozen boats can be found in the main activities brochures distributed by the tourist office.

Prices vary depending upon the boat. Near the low end is Starlight Sailing Cruises (☎ 292-1834), which has the 31-foot sloop *Starlight* and charges $180 for up to six people on a three-hour sail, $375 for a six-hour sail. At the high end is Salt Kettle Boat Rentals (☎ 236-4863), which charges $435 for up to eight people for a three-hour sail or $760 for six hours on its 55-foot sloop *Bright Star*. These two companies, as well as most of the other yachts, can include a swimming and snorkeling stop during the cruise.

See also the previous Snorkeling Cruises, Deep-Sea Fishing and Sailing sections.

Unfinished Church, Town of St George

NED FRIARY

CATHI BELOW

Heydon Trust chapel, Sandys Parish

NED FRIARY

Bermuda Cathedral, Pembroke Parish

CATHI BELOW

AME Church, St George's Parish

Typical Bermudian moongates

Bermudian stepped-roof cottage

Newstead, a manor-house inn.

Colonial thoroughfare, Town of St George

To Admiralty
House Park

To Bernard Park,
Blackwatch Pass,
North Shore Rd

Serpentine Rd

Par-la-Ville Rd

Bulls Head Hill

W2

Washington St

Dundonald St

Park Rd

Victoria
Park

Wesley St

Brunswick St

Victoria St

Victoria St

4 ▼

T 5

Richmond Rd

2 ▼ 3 ●

City
Hall

Washington St

Bus Terminal

Cedar Ave

Bermuda
Cathedral

♿ 1

6 ●

Church St

Church St

▼ 13

● 16

7 ▼

9 ●

▼ 12

▼ 14

Windsor
Place

Washington Lane

8 ●

10 ●

▼ 11

▼ 15

Burnaby St

21 ●

22 ▼

Gorham Rd

23 ▼

25 ▼

Washington
Mall

Reid St

The
Emporium

32 ▼ 33 ●

Chancery Lane

Par-la-Ville
Park

26

28 ●

29 ▼

▼ 30

31 ▼

55 ● 56 57 58 ● 60 ▼

27 ▼

Queen St

Walker
Arcade

Walkway Arcade

53 ●

54 ●

51 ●

59 ●

Bermudiana Rd

24 ▼

45 ●

47 ● 48 ●

50 ●

52 ●

44 ●

46 ●

43

Begin
Walking
Tour

End
Walking
Tour

49 ●

To Hamilton
Princess Hotel

Pitts Bay Rd

40 ● 42
41

ℹ

Pt Pleasant Rd

S

T

Ferry
Terminal

67 ●

Park

Albuoy
Point

Hamilton Harbour

HAMILTON

City of Hamilton

The City of Hamilton is the hub of Bermuda, serving as both its capital and commercial center. While it's not a large city, it has a surprising amount of hustle and bustle – at least in comparison to the rest of the island.

Hamilton has the main government offices, a handful of interesting sightseeing spots and the island's largest collection of shops. In addition, Hamilton rates as the best dining locale in Bermuda, in terms of both selection and price.

Hamilton's pulse is Front St, a harbor-front road lined with turn-of-the-century Victorian buildings in bright pastels of lemon, lime, apricot and sky blue. Many of them have overhanging verandas, where you can linger over lunch and watch the boats ferry across the harbor.

Hamilton serves as a central terminus and transfer point for island buses, so you can expect to be visiting the city frequently if you use the public bus system. Note that

Hamilton is commonly called 'town' by Bermudians – 'going to town' means, without a doubt, going to Hamilton.

The City of Hamilton is in Pembroke Parish; sights and accommodations outside of the city boundaries are described in the Pembroke Parish chapter.

History
The city is named for Sir Henry Hamilton, the Bermuda governor (1788-94) who encouraged the building of a town in the central part of Bermuda in order to have a settlement convenient to all islanders. The new town adopted the motto *Hamilton Sparsa Collegit*, meaning 'Hamilton has brought together the scattered', which can still be found on the town's coat-of-arms.

In 1790, the grand design of Hamilton was laid out, with 50-foot-wide streets in a neat grid pattern that covered an area of about 150 acres, spreading north half a dozen blocks from a new commercial harbor. By 1795, the town had taken shape and the first municipal elections were held in the new town hall.

Hamilton prospered and grew so quickly that in just two decades it had become the biggest town in Bermuda. In 1815, the capital was moved from St George to Hamilton. In 1897, Hamilton's status was changed from that of a town to a city.

While little more than 1000 people live in the narrow boundaries of the city itself, nearly a quarter of the island's population lives within a two-mile radius of the city.

Information
Tourist Offices The Visitors Service Bureau (☎ 295-1480) at 8 Front St, next to the ferry terminal, is open Monday to Saturday from 9 am to 4 pm in summer, from 9:30 am to 2 pm in winter. It's a good place to pick up islandwide tourist brochures, as well as get specific information on current happenings in Hamilton.

NED FRIARY
Joseph Stockdale's house, Town of St George

CATHI BELOW
Somerset Village, Sandys Parish

CATHI BELOW
Turkey Hill, Town of St George

NED FRIARY
Sessions House, Bermuda's parliament meeting house, City of Hamilton

NED FRIARY

Stalwart Fort St Catherine and St Catherine's Beach, St George's Parish

CATHI BELOW

Eyebrows on City Hall, City of Hamilton

CATHI BELOW

NED FRIARY

Gable and shutters, Bermudian house

Queen Street, Town of St George

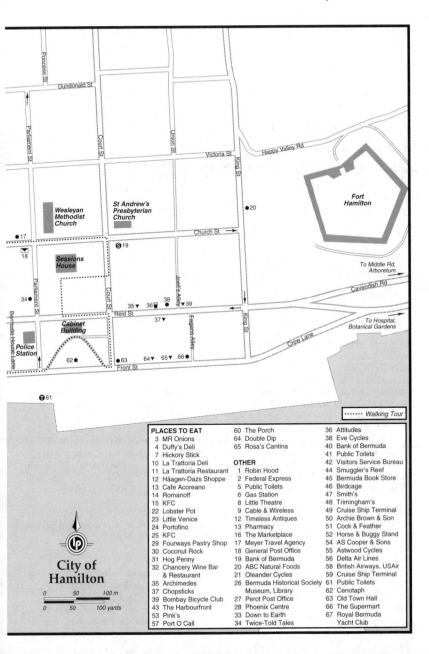

City of Hamilton

0   50   100 m
0   50   100 yards

PLACES TO EAT
3 MR Onions
4 Duffy's Deli
7 Hickory Stick
10 La Trattoria Deli
11 La Trattoria Restaurant
12 Häagen-Dazs Shoppe
13 Cafe Acoreano
14 Romanoff
15 KFC
22 Lobster Pot
23 Little Venice
24 Portofino
25 KFC
29 Fourways Pastry Shop
30 Coconut Rock
31 Hog Penny
32 Chancery Wine Bar
     & Restaurant
35 Archimedes
37 Chopsticks
39 Bombay Bicycle Club
43 The Harbourfront
53 Pink's
57 Port O Call

60 The Porch
64 Double Dip
65 Rosa's Cantina

OTHER
1 Robin Hood
2 Federal Express
5 Public Toilets
6 Gas Station
8 Little Theatre
9 Cable & Wireless
12 Timeless Antiques
13 Pharmacy
16 The Marketplace
17 Meyer Travel Agency
18 General Post Office
19 Bank of Bermuda
20 ABC Natural Foods
21 Oleander Cycles
26 Bermuda Historical Society
     Museum, Library
27 Perot Post Office
28 Phoenix Centre
33 Down to Earth
34 Twice-Told Tales

36 Attitudes
38 Eve Cycles
40 Bank of Bermuda
41 Public Toilets
42 Visitors Service Bureau
44 Smuggler's Reef
45 Bermuda Book Store
46 Birdcage
47 Smith's
48 Trimingham's
49 Cruise Ship Terminal
50 Archie Brown & Son
51 Cock & Feather
52 Horse & Buggy Stand
54 AS Cooper & Sons
55 Astwood Cycles
56 Delta Air Lines
58 British Airways, USAir
59 Cruise Ship Terminal
61 Public Toilets
62 Cenotaph
63 Old Town Hall
66 The Supermart
67 Royal Bermuda
     Yacht Club

Money The Bank of Bermuda, with offices on Front St beside the ferry terminal and on the corner of Court and Church Sts, is open Monday to Thursday from 9:30 am to 3 pm and Friday from 9:30 am to 4:30 pm. If you have a major credit card or a Cirrus or Plus system banking card, you can get cash withdrawals outside banking hours from sidewalk ATMs at either branch.

Post & Communications The General Post Office, at the corner of Church and Parliament Sts, is open Monday to Friday from 8 am to 5 pm and Saturday from 8 am to noon. The branch Perot Post Office on Queen St, opposite Reid St, is open Monday to Friday from 9 am to 5 pm.

Federal Express, United Parcel Service and DHL operate express delivery services on Bermuda. The main Federal Express office at Par-la-Ville Place, 14 Par-la-Ville Rd, is open weekdays from 8:30 am to 6 pm and Saturdays from 9 am to 3 pm; a more central branch in the Washington Mall is open Monday to Friday from 9 am to 3 pm.

You can buy phone cards or send and receive faxes, telegrams and telexes at the Cable & Wireless office, 20 Church St. It's open Monday to Saturday from 9 am to 5 pm. There are also fax machines that accept credit cards at the harborside tourist office and at the General Post Office. See the Facts for the Visitor chapter for rate information.

Travel Agencies There are a number of travel agents in the city center, including Meyer Travel Agency (☎ 295-4176) at 35 Church St, opposite the General Post Office.

Library The public library, on Queen St, is open Monday to Friday from 9:30 am to 6 pm and Saturday from 9:30 am to 5 pm. The downstairs reference room has a good collection of Bermuda books, while the 2nd floor has a reading room where you'll find local and international newspapers, including the *Boston Globe*, the *New York Times*, the *Globe & Mail*, the *Guardian* and London's *Sunday Times*.

Newsstands The Phoenix Centre, 3 Reid St, sells a wide variety of US, Canadian and British newspapers, including most of the UK tabloids. Washington Mall Magazines, on Reid St in the Washington Mall, carries the most international selection of newspapers and magazines, with a far-flung range that includes Italy's *La Stampa* and the *New Zealand Herald*. See the Things to Buy section later in this chapter for bookstore information.

Photo Shop Bermuda Photo Craftsmen in the Walker Arcade carries print and slide film at reasonable prices. They also develop film, with a roll of 24-exposure prints costing around $15.

Airline Offices British Airways (☎ 295-4422) and USAir are together at 89 Front St; Delta Air Lines (☎ 293-1024) is nearby at 85 Front St. Air Canada (☎ 293-2121) and American Airlines (☎ 293-1420) are on the 2nd floor of Windsor Place on Queen St. All of these city ticket offices are open Monday to Friday from 9 am to 5 pm.

Laundry Quickie Lickie Laundromat (☎ 295-6097), at 74 Serpentine Rd, northwest of the city center, has coin-operated washing machines and dryers. It's open Monday to Saturday from 6 am to 10 pm and Sunday from 6 am to 6 pm.

Pharmacies There's a pharmacy above the Cafe Acoreano bakery on Washington St, opposite the bus station, and another in the Phoenix Centre, 3 Reid St.

Emergency The police headquarters (☎ 295-0011) is at 42 Parliament St. Dial ☎ 911 for emergencies.

Walking Tour

Sights marked with an asterisk (*) are given more detail in separate headings at the end of this Walking Tour section.

The tourist office on Front St is a good place to begin an enjoyable half-day walking tour that takes in the main sights of central Hamilton. You can explore this area before beginning. Behind the Bank of Bermuda you'll find the picturesque building that quarters the **Royal Bermuda Yacht Club** and a little grassy **park** with benches and water views. The Bank of Bermuda itself has the island's most notable **coin collection***.

At the intersection of Queen and Front Sts, there's a colorful box used by a bobby for directing traffic. With its supporting posts and little roof, it's easy to see why it's nicknamed the **birdcage**.

If you head north on Queen St, you'll shortly come to the **Perot Post Office**, which occupies a classic Bermudian building, whitewashed with black shutters, that was erected by Postmaster William Perot on his own property in 1842. As is duly noted on the sign fronting the building, it was here in 1848 that Perot issued the first Bermudian postage stamps. While the main post office has long since moved to larger quarters, this historic building still functions as a neighborhood post office.

Next to the post office is **Par-la-Ville**, a graceful Georgian-style house built in 1814 by William Perot, father of the aforementioned Hamilton postmaster. This building now houses the public **library** and the **Bermuda Historical Society Museum***, while the family gardens have been turned into **Par-la-Ville Park**. The little public park offers a pleasant respite of birdsong in the city center and has lawns, flowers and a variety of trees including Bermuda cedar and a huge Indian rubber tree, both found at the east side of the grounds.

The **rubber tree** that shades the library, was planted by postmaster Perot in 1847 using a seed sent from British Guiana by his son Adolphus. As is often the case with exotics, the tree hasn't fit its environment as well as it may appear – its extensive root system not only extends beyond the library and post office, but has spread clear down to the waterfront, eating its way through cement en route! Still, the tree's historic significance has thus far saved it from the ax.

If you continue north on Queen St, and bear right on Church St, you'll arrive at **city hall***, which houses two art galleries and has a number of other interesting features both inside and out.

At Washington St, the site of the main bus terminal, you can make a detour one block north to **Victoria Park**, which has shaded lawns, a sunken garden and a Victorian-style gazebo that was suitably built in 1887 in Queen Victoria's honor.

If you make your way back to Church St, you'll almost immediately come to the Anglican **Bermuda Cathedral**, a weighty neo-Gothic building that is one of the city's most dominant landmarks. Built of limestone block in 1911, after an arsonist burned down the original church, the cathedral has some stained glass, but lacks the historic interest found in Bermuda's older churches. Entry to the cathedral is free. For $3 you can climb the 157 steps to the top of the church tower for a sweeping 360° view of greater Hamilton.

As you continue on Church St, it's easy to see how the street got its name, as there's a church on every block. First up is the **Wesleyan Methodist Church**, followed by the pretty pink **St Andrew's Presbyterian Church**, which dates to 1846, making it the oldest church still standing in the city.

If you now head south on Court St, you'll pass Bermuda's two 19th-century government buildings, **Sessions House*** and the **Cabinet Building***, both of which are open to the public.

At the east corner of Court and Front Sts, is the **old town hall**, a building with one of the longest histories in Hamilton. It was erected in 1794 as a warehouse for customs, served as a meeting place for the House of Assembly from 1815 to 1822 and in the late 19th century was converted into Hamilton's city hall. It is currently used as the Registry of the Supreme Court.

Continue west on Front St to view the **Cenotaph**, a war remembrance monument built of Bermuda limestone. The cornerstone was laid in 1920 by the Prince of

Wales. The monument is a replica of the cenotaph that stands in Whitehall, London.

As you walk west on Front St, back towards the tourist office, you'll pass Hamilton's cruise ship docks on the left and the city's most fanciful Victorian buildings on the right.

Coin Collection

A fascinating coin collection, displayed in half a dozen glass cases, can be viewed on the 2nd floor mezzanine of the Bank of Bermuda on Front St.

Many of the coins were collected by the late E Rodovan Bell, who focused on acquiring coins that over the years would have been accepted as a currency of trade in Bermuda. These include British coins from 1603 to the present; coins and tokens of the English-American colonies; early US coins; Central and South American coins; and other foreign coins, many of gold or silver.

Of greatest interest is the complete set of 'hog money', Bermuda's original currency and the first British colonial coins ever made. These were rough-stamped on the island from around 1614, and show a colonial sailing ship on one side and the imprint of a hog on the other. This rare collection include twopence, threepence, sixpence and shilling coins.

The hog, incidentally, takes its lofty status for having been a significant food source for the earliest British settlers, who shipwrecked on the island in 1609. Although hog money hasn't been minted for two centuries, it continues in a modified form, with the hog appearing on the back side of Bermudian pennies.

The bank is open from 9:30 am to 3 pm on weekdays, until 4:30 pm on Fridays.

Bermuda Historical Society Museum

The Bermuda Historical Society Museum occupies the front rooms of Par-la-Ville, the Queen St building that also houses the public library.

In the lobby you'll find models of the ill-fated *Sea Venture* and the two ships that Admiral George Somers built to replace it. In the same room is Somers' sea chest, made of Italian cypress, flanked by portraits of Somers and his wife.

The museum also contains the lodestone that Somers used to magnetize his compass, a rare 1615 'hog money' shilling and a map of Bermuda drawn in 1622. There are also portraits of the Perots, who built the house, pieces of period china painted by Josiah Wedgwood and two rooms of 18th-century furniture built of Bermuda cedar. The museum has a few quirky items as well, including a Confederate officer's sword that was made in London and items made by Boer prisoners of war during their stay on Bermuda at the turn of the century.

Although it's not on display, the museum also has a letter written by George Washington in 1775 requesting the support of the people of Bermuda in the American struggle for independence.

The Bermuda Historical Society Museum is open Monday to Friday from 9:30 am to 3:30 pm. Admission is free, but donations are welcomed.

City Hall

The whitewashed city hall on Church St, a handsome building of limestone block construction, was designed by Bermudian architect Wilfred Onions and completed in 1960.

Exterior features include a prominent 91-foot-high tower; a colorful insignia of the city crest; and pointy 'eyebrows,' a type of decorative detail crowning the windows on the building's right side. If you step back a bit and stare up to the top of the tower, you'll be able to see a weathervane topped with a bronze replica of the *Sea Venture*, the boat that brought Bermuda's first settlers. The water fountain fronting city hall contains two life-like statues of playful children created by renowned local sculptor Desmond Fountain.

Inside, the foyer walls are decorated with the portraits of the former mayors of Hamilton, some painted by Antoine Verpilleux, a French artist who retired here in the 1930s. The foyer also contains an oil painting of Queen Elizabeth; another contemporary statue by Desmond Fountain; and heavy chandeliers of Canadian pine, which rather oddly resemble cement. The most attractive woodwork, the staircase and doors, are made of native cedar.

At the left side of the foyer is a 378-seat theater that is used for local theater and concerts, as well as for international performances, which in the past have included the English Chamber Orchestra, the Royal Danish Ballet and Irish flutist James Galway.

If you're interested in postage stamps, you can find one of the island's best collections in the city office at the right side of the foyer. Known as the Benbow Stamp Collection, the stamps were donated by Colin Benbow, a former member of parliament and the current curator of the Bermuda Historical Society Museum.

The city hall is open Monday to Friday from 9 am to 5 pm, though the foyer is usually open on weekends as well.

Bermuda National Gallery At the east side of the 2nd floor of city hall, the national gallery has three sections.

The Hereward T Watlington Room contains the gallery's initial collection, some 18 European paintings spanning the 15th to 19th centuries. These include a portrait of American patriot Thomas Paine by George Romney and works by Thomas Gainsborough, Joshua Reynolds and Bartolomé Murillo.

The Ondaatje Wing contains changing exhibits that have ranged from printmaking techniques and African art to works by individual artists.

A Pretty Penny

William Benet Perot, Hamilton's first postmaster, was a colorful character best known in posterity for the postage stamps he created.

After the Post Office Act of 1842 established the cost of mailing a domestic letter at one penny, Perot set up two boxes in his post office, one where customers dropped the letter to be mailed and the other where they dropped a penny coin to cover the postage. Over time, Perot discovered that he was collecting more letters than pennies.

To stem his losses, in 1848 Perot decided to drop the honor system and create his own stamps. He stamped them 12 to a sheet, using a cancellation seal – so that each circular imprint read 'Hamilton, Bermuda' along with the year. Perot then wrote 'one penny' where the date would normally appear and signed each 'WB Perot'.

Not only did the stamps generate enough money for Perot to keep the postal system solvent, but a century later they've become prized collector's items, one having recently fetched £185,000 at a Christie's auction in London. Of the thousands of stamps Perot created, only 11 are still known to exist, and seven of these are in the royal stamp collection of Queen Elizabeth II. ■

In the Upper Mezzanine Gallery, the ambitious Masterworks Foundation displays changing exhibits of fine art specific to Bermuda. This nonprofit organization focuses on acquiring major artworks created on the island by foreign and Bermudian artists. Among the works they've obtained are two of the 21 paintings that Winslow Homer created while on Bermuda and pieces by Americans E Ambrose Webster and Charles Demuth, and French cubist painter Albert Gleizes, all of whom spent time in Bermuda during the early 20th century. In addition, the gallery sometimes displays pieces on loan, such as the 12 drawings created by Georgia O'Keeffe during her stays in Bermuda in the 1930s.

The gallery's (☎ 295-9428) hours are Monday to Saturday from 10 am to 4 pm and Sunday from 12:30 to 4 pm. Admission is $3 for adults, free for children under 16.

Bermuda Society of Arts Gallery At the west side of the 2nd floor of city hall, the Bermuda Society of Arts displays and sells works by resident and visiting artists. Many of these quality pieces, both abstract and realistic, depict scenes of Bermuda through the media of watercolors, pastels, oils and stained glass. The gallery is open Monday to Saturday from 10 am to 4 pm, and admission is free.

Sessions House

Hamilton's centerpiece building, the Sessions House, dates to 1817, though it owes much of its grand appearance, including the landmark clock tower, Italianate ornamentation and terra-cotta colonnade, to additions made in 1887 marking Queen Victoria's golden jubilee.

Bermuda's parliamentary meeting house for the 40-member House of Assembly, Sessions House also serves as the chambers of the Supreme Court. The assembly meetings take place on the 2nd floor, where the speaker of the house, outfitted in the typical British wig and robes and flanked by paintings of King George III and Queen Charlotte, presides over parliamentary debate.

The desk of the speaker's clerk, which stands between the speaker and the assembly, is inset with the coat-of-arms of the Virginia Company and topped by a silver mace that symbolizes the speaker's authority and without which parliamentary sessions cannot be held. The members of the House, in typical Westminster style, are arranged in rows on either side of the chamber, with the two major parties facing each other.

House sessions, which are open to the public, are held from late October through July on Fridays at 10 am. If you happen to be around at budget time (February and March), the House often convenes on Mondays and Wednesdays as well. In addi-

tion, Sessions House is open Monday to Friday from 9 am to 12:30 pm and from 2 to 5 pm. Photography is only allowed when the House is not in session.

Cabinet Building

The 19th-century Cabinet Building, a stately two-story limestone structure, contains the meeting chamber of Bermuda's senate. On weekdays from 9 am to 5 pm, visitors are free to climb the steps to the 2nd-floor chamber, which holds the round table where the 11 members of the senate conduct their Wednesday morning sessions.

The Cabinet's round table, although not its chamber, has also been used for meetings between international heads of state. The table was dismantled and removed to a private location for a conference that was held in 1953 between Sir Winston Churchill and President Dwight Eisenhower. In 1971, the table was again moved, this time to Government House, for a meeting between Prime Minister Edward Heath and President Richard Nixon.

Fort Hamilton

This substantial hilltop fort, just a 15-minute walk from Hamilton center, was one of a series of island fortifications erected in the mid-19th century during a period of rising tensions between Great Britain and the USA.

The fort remains intact, its ramparts still mounted with 10-inch rifled muzzleloader guns that were capable of firing a 400-pound cannonball through an 11-inch-thick iron plate – more than enough penetration force to have sliced any iron-hulled vessel that sailed the seas. But as history would have it, no enemy ships ever appeared.

Today the carefully renovated fort is as much park as historic site and makes an enjoyable place to explore. The south-facing ramparts offer an unsurpassed bird's-eye view of Hamilton Harbour. You can also scurry about in the fortification's dungeons, where you'll find gun embrasures, shell hoists, munitions storage rooms and the like.

Don't miss taking a stroll through the fort's narrow moat, which has been turned into one of Hamilton's more unusual gardens. Sandwiched by the steep walls of the fort's inner and outer ramparts, this dry moat is cool and shady with a luxuriant growth of ferns and other tropical vegetation; many of the plants are identified with name plaques.

The somewhat inconspicuous entrances to the dungeon and moat are both to the left of the main fort entrance immediately after you cross the bridge over the moat. Fort Hamilton is open from 9:30 am to 5 pm daily. Entry is free and there's a little tea room selling inexpensive coffee, tea and scones.

If you're in Bermuda during the winter season (November through March), try to plan your visit to coincide with the colorful skirling performance held on Mondays at noon by the kilted bagpipers and drummers of the Bermuda Islands Pipe Band.

To get to the fort from the city center, walk east on Church St, which terminates at King St where you'll turn left. Continue north up King St for a block; at the top of the hill make a sharp right onto Happy Valley Rd – the fort is about 150 yards farther east.

Places to Stay

There are no places to stay within the strict boundaries of the City of Hamilton, but there are numerous places within walking distance of town; these are detailed in the following Pembroke Parish chapter.

'November to March' Activities

To lure more people to the island in the off-season, the Bermuda Department of Tourism offers visitors a special series of activities during the months of November to March. All are free.

On Mondays at 10 am a guided walking tour of the City of Hamilton begins at the waterfront tourist office. At 11 am there's a tour of Sessions House and at noon there's a colorful skirling ceremony at Fort Hamilton; both are included in the walking tour or can be taken in separately. At 3 pm there's a Tea & Fashion Show at the No 1 cruise ship passenger terminal on Hamilton's Front St.

On Tuesdays at 10:30 am in Hamilton there's a hour-long Heritage & Cultural Trail Walk that covers the city's history and starts at the Cabinet Building. At 3 pm in Hamilton, a performance by a troupe of costumed Gombey dancers takes place at the No 1 cruise ship passenger terminal, complete with fruit punch and cookies. If you prefer to do your own dancing, there's ballroom dancing at the Hamilton Princess Hotel from 8 to 11 pm.

On Wednesdays the Town of St George offers an hour-long walking tour from King's Square at 10:30 am and a noontime re-enactment of the ducking-stool punishment that was once meted out to gossipers. If you miss the first walking tour, there's another one at 2 pm. For those who want to learn about Bermudian cuisine, a cooking demonstration is given at 2:30 pm at the No 1 cruise ship passenger terminal in Hamilton.

Thursdays feature Bermuda's West End, beginning with a walking tour of Somerset departing at 10 am from the Somerset County Squire restaurant on Mangrove Bay. At 2:15 pm a 45-minute tour of the Royal Naval Dockyard begins in front of the Clocktower Mall.

Friday is for nature lovers. At 10:30 am there's a tour of the Bermuda Botanical Gardens in Paget and at 1 pm there's a tour of Spittal Pond Nature Reserve in Smith's Parish, beginning at the east end parking lot.

Saturdays again feature a walking tour of the Town of St George, starting at King's Square at 10:30 am. As with the Tuesday tour, this includes a greeting from the mayor in Town Hall.

The main Sunday events are at the Royal Naval Dockyard, where a walking tour with a focus on nature begins at the Clocktower Mall at 11:15 am. At 2:15 pm a more conventional walking tour of the Dockyard begins at the entrance to the craft market. ■

Places to Eat

Markets On Church St near the Bermuda Cathedral, *The Marketplace* is open Monday to Thursday from 7 am to 6:30 pm and on Fridays and Saturdays from 7 am to 8 pm. This modern, well-stocked grocery store has a good produce section; a selection of wines, beer and spirits; a bakery with tasty pecan rolls and almond-poppy muffins (75¢); a deli with salads and meat pies at reasonable prices; and a salad bar with fruit, veggies and fried chicken for $5 per pound.

The Supermart, on the east end of Front St, is another large grocery store with a decent produce section and a salad bar good for a light takeout meal. It's open Monday to Saturday from 7:30 am to 7 pm.

Hamilton has three little health food stores. The biggest is *Down to Earth*, on Reid St near Bermuda House Lane; open Monday to Saturday until 5:30 pm, it sells yogurt, bulk foods, granola, teas, vitamins and a few deli items. Also centrally located is *The Health Store* at the Washington Mall, open Monday to Saturday from 9 am to 5 pm; try the healthy homemade cookies (25¢). The Seventh-Day Adventist church, on the east side of the city at 41 King St, operates the *ABC Natural Foods* shop, which has dried fruits, nuts, grains and vitamins; it's open Monday to Thursday from 9 am to 5:15 pm and on Fridays from 9 am to 1:15 pm.

Cafes, Delis & Fast Food Hamilton has two *KFC* eateries with the colonel's standard menu; at either place two pieces of chicken and a roll will set you back just $4.70. The KFC on Queen St is open daily from 11 am to at least 10 pm, while the one on Burnaby St is open Monday to Saturday from 11 am to 6:30 pm.

There's a *Häagen-Dazs Shoppe* on Church St opposite the bus terminal. A small scoop of Häagen-Dazs ice cream costs $2, a large scoop $3.80. It's open from 11 am to 8 pm on weekdays, until 10 pm on weekends.

The *Double Dip* at 119 Front St has ice cream and cheap fast-food items including $3 burgers, hot dogs and pizza.

Cafe Acoreano, across from the bus terminal at the corner of Church and Washington Sts, has good inexpensive Portuguese pastries and coffee.

For gourmet coffee, the place to go is *Caffe Latte*, upstairs in the Washington Mall. This tiny cafe makes a pleasant respite from the mall's bustle and has a wide range of coffee drinks, both hot and cold, including espresso. They also have muffins and $5 sandwiches. It's open daily except Sundays from 7 am (8 am on Saturdays) to 5 pm.

If you enjoy lingering over the newspaper with a cup of fresh brew, *Twice-Told Tales*, 34 Parliament St, a bookstore with a handful of cafe tables, sells the *Royal Gazette* along with reasonably priced coffee and muffins. It's open Monday to Friday from 8 am to 5 pm and on Saturdays from 11 am to 4 pm.

Kathy's Kaffee, a simple little cafe in the back of The Emporium at 69 Front St, sells inexpensive breakfast fare, sandwiches, gyros and carrot cake. It's open daily except on Sundays from 7:30 am (from 8:30 am on Saturdays) to 4 am.

Take Five, upstairs at the Washington Mall, is a locally popular cafe with French toast, fish chowder and burgers for around $5, and various salads for a few dollars more. On Saturdays, a traditional Bermuda codfish breakfast will set you back $11.75. It's open Monday to Saturday from 7 am to 4 pm.

Pink's, a delicatessen at 55 Front St in the Walkway Arcade, is modern and inviting with good food and a harborview balcony. A variety of generous sandwiches (including ham, turkey and crab with cream cheese) cost around $5, as do healthy pasta, fruit and green salads. At breakfast there are Danish pastries, scones, bagels and various coffees, including cappuccino, at reasonable prices. Expect a crowd around noon. It's open in summer from 7:30 am to 10 pm on weekdays, from 8:30 am on Saturdays; in winter it closes at 5 pm.

La Trattoria Deli, opposite the La Trattoria Restaurant on Washington Lane, sells lasagna, pasta with meatballs and other Italian items for around $5, all for takeout only. Open weekdays for lunch, it attracts long queues of office workers. This little hole-in-the-wall also sells authentic Italian gelato.

Duffy's Deli, a little basement shop at 5 Wesley St, has good takeout sandwiches for around $5, including standard meat sandwiches, BLTs, crab sandwiches and more exotic items like avocado and tabbouleh in pita bread. The *Hickory Stick* deli at 2 Church St also has generous takeout sandwiches at similar prices.

Fourways Pastry Shop, at the Reid St end of the Washington Mall, is operated by the upmarket Fourways Inn. At this pleasant deli-style cafe you can get a fresh fruit salad or a slice of quiche for $3.75, a nice salad platter for $6. Lasagna, the hot special of the day or bagels with lox and cream cheese are all under $8. There are also luscious cakes and pastries and reasonably priced teas and coffees.

Although not quite as fancy, there's a second deli-style cafe, *The Gourmet Shop*, tucked back in the Washington Mall. It has good salads, stuffed baked potatoes, lasagna and sandwiches for around $5 at lunch, served from 11:30 am to 3:30 pm. Breakfast, from 7 to 10:30 am, includes inexpensive muffins and bagels, or a meal of eggs, bacon, hash browns and coffee for $6.50.

Restaurants – middle *Chopsticks* (☎ 292-0791), 88 Reid St, has a pleasant, understated Asian decor and makes a good choice for a reasonably priced dinner. It not only has the best Chinese food in Hamilton, but as one of the cooks is Thai, you'll also find Thai items on the menu. There's a nice spicy hot and sour soup ($3.75) and a full dinner menu of pork, beef, poultry, vegetarian and seafood dishes for $12 to $18, including a recommendable chicken plum dum gai. All dishes come with rice. At lunch, from noon to 2:30 pm on weekdays,

the price of the main courses drops to around $8. Dinner is from 6 to 11 pm nightly. There's also a popular takeout service at the side of the restaurant.

Archimedes (☎ 295-1580), 63 Reid St, has checkered tablecloths and the authentically simple decor of a neighborhood Greek tavern. The extensive menu includes Greek wines, vegetarian dishes, squid, baklava and many other Greek mainstays. At lunch, from noon to 2 pm on weekdays, there are pita sandwiches and gyros for around $8 and a moussaka and salad meal for $12. At dinner, from 6:30 to 10 pm nightly, salads and starters begin around $8, while main dishes, such as a souvlaki plate, begin around $15.

La Trattoria Restaurant (☎ 295-9499), on Washington Lane, is a large Italian restaurant that packs in a crowd each noon with its inexpensive lunch menu that includes sub sandwiches for $6, a good vegetarian pizza loaded with artichokes, mushrooms and olives for $7.50 and numerous other hot dishes for under $10. At dinner, pizzas begin around $10, pastas are a few dollars more and most meat and fish dishes are around $20. They also sell 10-inch takeout pizzas from $6.

The *Bombay Bicycle Club* (☎ 292-0048), on the 3rd floor at 75 Reid St, has a pleasant East Indian atmosphere with rattan peacock chairs, sitar music and good food. Weekdays from noon to 2:30 pm there's a recommendable all-you-can-eat lunch buffet that includes basmati rice, lentils, potato curry, a fine puffy nan and a few meat dishes for $12 (or $10 if you select only the vegetarian dishes). At dinner, from 6:30 to 11 pm Monday to Saturday, the menu features dishes such as lamb curry, tandoori chicken and prawn masala, priced from $14 to $22. In the off-season, there are also a couple of good-value four-course dinner specials from $20.

The *Hog Penny* (☎ 292-2534), at 5 Burnaby St, has a dark, pub-like interior and good British, Bermudian and East Indian fare. There's an excellent fish chowder at $5 a bowl and caesar and spinach salads for the same price. Appetizers include a curried seafood crepe or escargot for $9, while entrees, priced from $15 to $19, include fettuccine Alfredo, chicken provencale or catch of the day. There's also a simple pub-fare menu with traditional English dishes such as shepherd's pie or bangers and mash (sausage with mashed potatoes) for around $13, or a burger-and-fries plate for half that. It's open for lunch from 11:30 am to 4 pm and for dinner from 5:30 to 11 pm. The bar stays open until 1 am.

The popular *Rosa's Cantina* (☎ 295-1912) on Front St is Hamilton's Tex-Mex restaurant. At lunch, salads, sandwiches and combination plates with rice and beans cost around $10. At dinner you can get various vegetarian offerings (using organic black beans and olive oil) or a two-item combo plate for a reasonable $12. Mexican dishes can be ordered from mild to hot. The menu also includes barbecued chicken and ribs, steaks and sizzling fajitas – all priced under $20. For starters, try the cheese-stuffed jalapeño peppers, called Iguana Eggs ($5.50), and wash them down with a Dos Equis or any of a variety of margaritas. Rosa's is open for lunch Monday to Saturday from noon to 2:30 pm and for dinner daily from 5:30 pm to midnight.

Coconut Rock (☎ 292-1043), at 20 Reid St, is a trendy meeting place with music videos and some creative sandwiches, including a blue-cheese burger, a lentil burger with guacamole and the C-Rock Sandwich of grilled chicken breast with bacon and Swiss cheese, all for under $10. There are also salads, pastas, fish and curry dishes. Lunch is from 11:30 am to 2:30 pm Monday to Saturday, dinner from 6 to 10:30 pm nightly.

Flanagan's (☎ 295-8299), upstairs in The Emporium at 69 Front St, is a pleasant Irish pub with traditional Irish fare and Murphy's beer by the pint. At any time of day you can get a breakfast of eggs, Irish sausage, grilled tomato and home fries for $10. For the same price at lunch you can order bangers and mash, a burger topped with mushrooms and bacon, or a ploughman's lunch of meat pie and cheeses. At dinner there are some more substantial offerings for around $15, including baby back ribs, an eight-ounce sirloin or shepherd's pie. The kitchen is open from 11:30 am to 9:30 pm daily, the bar to 1 am.

MR Onions (☎ 292-5012) on Par-la-Ville Rd is a popular restaurant with casual dining and family-style fare. The $15 early-bird specials, available from 5 to 6:30 pm, include dessert, a house salad of fresh mixed greens and a choice of main dishes such as ribs, chicken teriyaki and pan-fried catch of the day. Otherwise, dinner entrees are priced from $12 for vegetable lasagna to $30 for surf-and-turf combinations. At lunch, there are sandwiches, salads and barbecued chicken for under $10. Lunch is from noon to 2:30 pm on weekdays, dinner from 5 to 10 pm nightly.

The often jam-packed *Portofino* (☎ 292-2375) on Bermudiana Rd has good Italian food, a bright upbeat setting and attentive service, at least when it's not overly busy. Soups, salads and starters such as calamari fritti in a spicy tomato sauce are reasonably priced. There are a dozen varieties of nine-inch pizzas for $10, numerous creative pasta dishes for $10 to $15 and chicken, fish and steak dishes for around $20. It's open from 11:30 am to 4 pm on weekdays and from 6 pm to around midnight daily. Portofino also has an espresso bar where you can get an afternoon caffe latte and a scoop of gelato.

Little Venice (☎ 295-3503), on Bermudiana Rd just north of Portofino, also has good authentic Italian food but a less bustling atmosphere. It offers various pastas, including vegetarian and seafood versions, from around $15 and fish and meat dishes from around $20. There's also a full menu of hot and cold antipasti and some good-value early-bird specials. It's open from 11:45 am to 2:15 pm for lunch on weekdays and for dinner daily from 6 to 10 pm.

The Porch (☎ 292-4737) at 93 Front St, opposite the cruise ship terminal, has a

2nd-floor balcony overlooking the harbor. At lunch you'll find dishes such as calamari, Cajun chicken on greens and fishcakes on a bun for around $10, while at dinner the menu includes the likes of rack of lamb, pan-seared scallops and tenderloin tournedos for around $23. It's open from 11 am to 1 am daily and makes a nice place for a late-night drink.

Restaurants – top end The *Lobster Pot* (☎ 292-6898), on the corner of Bermudiana and Gorham Rds, has a good reputation for its fresh lobsters and other seafood. Main dishes range from a curried fish crepe with mango chutney or lobster ravioli in a vermouth sauce for $19 to a seafood lover's plate that includes clams, mussels, shrimp, crab claws and half a Maine lobster for $29. There are also sandwiches and steaks. At lunch, which is served until 4:30 pm on weekdays, there's a three-course special for $15. Dinner hours are from 6 to 11 pm Monday to Saturday.

The Harbourfront (☎ 295-4207), on Front St opposite the ferry terminal, is a cozy bar and restaurant with harborview dining. Its contemporary menu includes chicken satay or rockfish ravioli for around $20 and duck breast in Napoleon sauce or various fresh fish dishes for $25. There's also a sushi bar with sashimi, nigiri and norimaki priced around $5 an order – a bit cheaper during happy hour, which is from 4:30 to 6 pm Monday to Saturday. Casual dress is fine at lunch, served from 11:30 am, while at dinner, served from 6:30 pm, jackets are preferred. If you arrive before 7:30 pm, ask about the early dinner specials.

Port O Call (☎ 295-5373), at 87 Front St, has an upmarket nautical decor and good seafood, if perhaps a bit pricey. Chowder and lobster bisque are $5.75, while catch of the day or shrimp and scallops on linguine are around $25. It's open for lunch on weekdays from noon to 3 pm and for dinner Monday to Saturday from 5 pm.

The *Chancery Wine Bar & Restaurant* (☎ 295-5058), on Chancery Lane off Front St, is an atmospheric wine bar with good

food. The menu changes monthly but contains the likes of grilled quail salad with smoked fruit, local fish in a pine-nut butter sauce, venison and rack of lamb. At dinner, most main dishes are $20 to $30. Desserts are also creative, with offerings such as prickly pear mousse, and there's a good selection of international wines by the glass. At lunch there's usually a table d'hôte menu with a choice of starter, main course, dessert and coffee for $25, but if you prefer to eat light, you could order from the menu for about half that. The kitchen is open on weekdays from noon to 2:30 pm and nightly from 6 to 10 pm (from 7 pm on Sunday), while the bar closes at 1 am.

Romanoff (☎ 295-0333), on Church St just west of Burnaby St, is a formal restaurant with burgundy velvet chairs and old-fashioned decor. The award-winning à la carte dinner menu features traditional continental fare, with main dishes such as stroganoff, veal and chateaubriand in the $30 to $40 range. Dinner is served from 7 to 10 pm Monday to Saturday. From noon to 2:30 pm on weekdays, Romanoff offers a full three-course 'business lunch' with coffee for $17.75.

Entertainment
Oasis (☎ 292-4978), on the 3rd floor of The Emporium at 69 Front St, is the city's top dancing spot and a popular place for singles. The music is loud, ranging from disco to live rock and pop.

Flanagan's (☎ 295-8299), an Irish pub and sports bar in The Emporium, often has live music, ranging from reggae to oldies. It's another meeting place for singles.

Cock & Feather (☎ 295-2263) on Front St is a popular 2nd-floor pub with live entertainment nightly. Just around the corner at 5 Burnaby St is the *Hog Penny* (☎ 292-2534), an atmospheric pub that has good grub and nightly entertainment.

Robin Hood (☎ 295-3314), on Richmond Rd at the north side of town, is a fun pub with an English flavor that carries European soccer games on big-screen TV.

Coconut Rock (☎ 292-1043), a combination restaurant and bar at 20 Reid St, is a gathering place that packs in a crowd. There's no dancing, but music videos play continuously.

Attitudes, on Reid St between King and Court Sts, has a bar, music and dancing and attracts a predominantly gay and lesbian crowd, but is open to all.

Sunday open-air concerts are periodically held in the *gazebo bandstand* at Victoria Park; for the latest, ask at your hotel or check the listings in the *Bermuda Sun*.

The *City Hall Theater* in the city hall has plays, concerts and other performances throughout the year, including those by international artists during the Bermuda Festival in January and February. Call the ticket office (☎ 292-2313) for schedule and ticket information.

The *Little Theater* (☎ 292-2135), at 30 Queen St, and the *Liberty Theater* (☎ 291-2035), 49 Union Square, both show first-run Hollywood movies.

Things to Buy

Hamilton offers shoppers the greatest selection of both goods and shops found in Bermuda.

The island's largest department stores – Trimingham's, Smith's and AS Cooper & Sons – all have their main shops on Front St, in the block between Queen and Burnaby Sts. These are good places to get an idea of selection and costs, as they carry everything from Waterford crystal, Wedgwood china and international designer clothing to Bermuda shorts, Royall Bay Rhum cologne and miniature replicas of Bermuda cottages and moongates.

Archie Brown & Son, 51 Front St, has a high-quality selection of Scottish cashmere, tartan kilts, Donegal tweed suits and Irish woolens.

For more casual clothing needs, Smuggler's Reef, 29 Front St, has lots of T-shirts with Bermuda slogans. The Bermuda Sunglass Centre, inside the Smuggler's Reef store, carries the island's best selection of brand-name sunglasses.

Jewelry Jewelry stores abound. Walker Christopher, 9 Front St, has one of the best Bermuda-related collections, including charms, pendants and earrings in the shape of tree frogs, longtail birds and hog pennies. They also have some fine antique jewelry, gold doubloons recovered from a 1715 Spanish ship and rare gems.

The Gem Cellar, in the Walker Arcade on Front St, and Personalized Jewelry, at 69 Front St, both carry affordable charms and pendants with Bermuda motifs. Astwood Dickinson, 85 Front St, has watches ranging from inexpensive souvenir versions with Bermuda logos to pricey Omega models. Crisson, 16 Front St, carries exclusive items such as Rolex watches, international designer jewelry and diamonds.

Arts & Crafts The Bermuda Society of Arts, which has a gallery and showroom on the 2nd floor of city hall, sells quality artwork, most with local themes. You can buy watercolors, pastels, acrylics, oils, gouaches and sculptures, with prices in most mediums beginning from around $150, although the finest pieces go for many times that.

Another good gallery is the nonprofit Masterworks Foundation, on Bermuda House Lane between Reid and Front Sts, which sells prints of many of the works of art shown at the Bermuda National Gallery. They also carry vintage travel posters.

The Windjammer Gallery, on the corner of Reid and King Sts, sells original watercolors, oils and bronzes, including those of Bermuda's best-known sculptor, Desmond Fountain. They also sell Bermuda-theme posters, prints and cards.

Queen Street Glass, on Queen St at the entrance to the Windsor Place mall, sells island-made hand-blown glass items, including colorful plates, vases and decorative figurines such as tropical fish, tree frogs and Christmas tree ornaments.

Stamps, Antiques & Collectibles Stamp collectors can buy commemorative stamps at the Bermuda Philatelic Bureau window inside the General Post Office on Parliament and Church Sts.

Pegasus Prints and Maps, a small shop at 63 Pitts Bay Rd, on the west side of town, has maps and prints, including some antique ones.

Heritage House, in the York House building on the ocean side of Front St, opposite Bermudiana Rd, carries British antiques, including paperweights and china. If interested in grandfather clocks and antique furniture, the best collection is at Timeless Antiques, 26 Church St.

Books & Music The Bookmart, upstairs in the Phoenix Centre at 3 Reid St, is Bermuda's best and biggest bookstore, with a good selection of books about Bermuda and international best-sellers at US cover prices. The Bermuda Book Store, on Queen St just north of Front St, also has a good collection of island books. Washington Mall Magazines, on Reid St in the Washington Mall, has magazines and books, including a good selection of travel books.

Twice-Told Tales, 34 Parliament St, sells used general-interest books at reasonable prices, and also has rare first-edition books that relate to Bermuda. Nature Aroma Ecology, 61 Reid St, carries metaphysical books as well as meditative tapes, massage oils and crystals.

The Music Box, on Reid St at the east side of Bermuda House Lane, has a good selection of CDs and cassettes by local musicians, such as the Clay House Inn Steel Band, the Bermuda Strollers and Hubert Smith, who wrote one of the island's best-known songs, *Bermuda is Another World*. For something more offbeat, the Music Box even sells recordings of Bermuda's tree frogs.

Getting Around
All public buses and ferries terminate in Hamilton. You can pick up a bus to anywhere on the island at the open-air bus terminal on Washington St. Note that if you are traveling by bus from the east side of Bermuda to the west (or vice versa), you'll have to transfer buses at the Washington St terminal. Ferries leave from the terminal adjacent to the tourist information office on Front St.

The are a number of shops in the greater Hamilton area that arrange moped rentals. Three that are centrally located are Oleander Cycles (☎ 295-0919), on Gorham Rd just off Bermudiana Rd; Astwood Cycles (☎ 292-2245), 77 Front St; and Eve Cycles (☎ 236-6247), 91 Reid St.

The cruise ship wharves are conveniently located along Front St, just minutes from the tourist office and all central city sights.

For information on horse-and-carriage rides around the City of Hamilton and more on other public transportation, see the Getting Around chapter in the front of the book.

Pembroke Parish

With 11,500 residents, Pembroke is the most heavily populated of Bermuda's nine parishes. It encompasses the island's capital, the City of Hamilton, and that – combined with its central location – makes Pembroke the busiest and most frequently visited place in Bermuda.

The parish's primary sightseeing attractions are in the City of Hamilton, but there are a handful of less significant sights outside the city that can be explored as well, most found along the parish's north shore.

Pembroke offers plenty of places to stay, but they're not on sandy beaches and thus are best suited for those who value being within easy reach of the capital with its restaurants, shops and other conveniences.

For information on Fort Hamilton and sights within Hamilton, see the City of Hamilton chapter.

Spanish Point Park

In 1603, a Spanish galleon passing by Bermuda struck a rock on the reef, forcing its captain, Diego Ramirez, to come ashore at Stovel Bay, where the crew stayed for three weeks to repair the ship to a seaworthy condition. Six years later, when the first English settlers came ashore on Bermuda, they discovered remnants of the camp here, at the northwest tip of Pembroke Parish, hence the name Spanish Point.

Today, the north side of Stovel Bay has been turned into the seven-acre Spanish Point Park. The bay is a mooring area for small boats, while the park consists mainly of grassy lawns dotted with casuarina trees. A short, paved footpath leads from the bay to the tip of the point, from where there's a clear-on view of the Royal Naval Dockyard's twin towers, which sit two miles across the Great Sound to the northwest.

You'll also see what looks like a shipwreck off the west side of the point; actually, it's an old drydock that sank here in 1902. Windsurfers sometimes launch from the park, but the main activity is picnicking.

Admiralty House Park

Once home to the admiral who served as the regional commander-in-chief of British naval forces, Admiralty House Park is now a 16-acre recreational area. A network of short trails lead through shaded woods filled with birdsong and along low cliffs with coastal views.

Admiralty House, built in 1812 as a naval hospital, was turned into the admiral's residence in 1816 and served that function until the late 1950s, when the navy withdrew and turned the property over to the island government. In 1974, the house had fallen into such poor disrepair that the government decided to raze it and convert the grounds into a new park. Some other less significant buildings that had been used by the navy now house the offices of various community groups, such as the Boy Scouts and other youth organizations.

The park encompasses **Clarence Cove**, a sheltered cove with shallow waters and a tiny sandy beach, making it a popular destination for families on weekend outings.

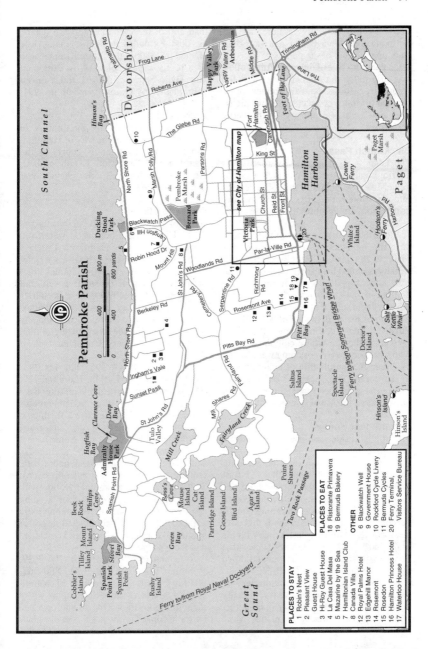

Pembroke Parish

South Channel

Great Sound

Hamilton Harbour

Paget

Devonshire

PLACES TO STAY
1 Robin's Nest
2 Pleasant View Guest House
3 Hi-Roy Guest House
4 La Casa Del Masa
5 Mazarine by the Sea
7 Hamiltonian Island Club
8 Canada Villa
12 Royal Palms Hotel
13 Edgehill Manor
14 Rosemont
15 Rosedon
16 Hamilton Princess Hotel
17 Waterloo House

PLACES TO EAT
18 Ristorante Primavera
19 Bermuda Bakery

OTHER
6 Blackwatch Well
9 Government House
10 Rockford Cycle Livery
11 Bermuda Cycles
20 Ferry Terminal, Visitors Service Bureau

You may also see divers here, as the Bermuda Sub-Aqua Club, a private dive club, operates out of the park.

On the south side of the road, **Tulo Valley** was originally the vegetable garden for Admiralty House, and a tunnel, now blocked off, once connected the two areas. It is now used as a nursery by the parks department.

Blackwatch Pass

The island's most impressive road engineering feat is the Blackwatch Pass, a tunnel-like pass cut more than 50 feet deep into the limestone cliffs separating the north shore of Pembroke from the City of Hamilton.

Along the north side of Blackwatch Pass, near the intersection with Langton Hill road, is the site of **Blackwatch Well**, which is marked by a small enclosure. The well, now capped, was dug during a severe drought in 1849 to provide the area with a more reliable source of water.

North of the well site is **Ducking Stool Park**, a small coastal park. It's most notable as the site where colonial women who were accused of gossiping were forced to endure the humiliation of being dunked in the ocean. The ducking stool used for that purpose has been moved to the Town of St George for use as a tourist attraction.

Government House

The official residence of Bermuda's governor, Government House is not open to the public, but can be seen from neighboring roads. Built in 1892 atop the 112-foot Langton Hill, this stately stone house has more than 30 rooms, as well as extensive verandas and an outdoor swimming pool. It was on the 33-acre estate grounds that governor Sir Richard Sharples, along with his bodyguard and the Great Dane that Sharples was walking, were gunned down by an assassin on March 10, 1973.

For more than a century, dignitaries visiting Government House have traditionally been invited to ceremoniously plant a tree, which is then endowed with a plaque. More than 100 of these commemorative plantings dot the grounds, including a mango tree planted in 1880 by the future King George V, a princess palm planted by Ethiopian king Haile Selassie in 1963 and a queen palm planted by Queen Elizabeth in 1994.

Activities

The Government Tennis Stadium is in Bernard Park north of the City of Hamilton and there are also tennis courts at the Hamiltonian Island Club. Details on both are in the Outdoor Activities chapter near the front of the book.

Places to Stay

West of Hamilton The western outskirts of the City of Hamilton has a waterfront dominated by the Hamilton Princess Hotel. Inland from the Princess is a quiet neighborhood of wealthy homes that includes a handful of small hotels and guesthouses. Collectively, these hostelries offer a nice variety of accommodations, ranging from moderate to upscale, and any one of them could be an appealing option. All are within an easy 10-minute walk of the city center.

Edgehill Manor (☎ 295-7124, fax 295-3850), PO Box HM 1048, Hamilton HM EX, is the most affordable of the west Hamilton accommodations. All nine rooms in this small guesthouse have a fresh coat of paint, TV, private bath and either air-conditioning or a ceiling fan. Some have a pair of twin beds, others have a king-size bed, and many contain a desk and a sofa. Double rooms without balconies cost $82/108 in the winter/summer. Rooms with balconies cost $92/124, as does a small apartment with a full kitchen and an extra sofabed. Rates are about $10 less for singles. A continental breakfast is included and there's a pool.

Rosemont (☎ 292-1055, fax 295-3913, ☎ 800-367-0040 in the USA, 800-267-0040 in Canada), PO Box HM 37, Hamilton HM AX, is a suite-style complex with a nice hilltop location. Owned and operated by the Cooper family, it's a friendly place with complimentary coffee and newspapers, free local phone calls and provisions for late check-outs. All 37 units are modern and equipped with kitchenettes that sport full ovens and a refrigerator. The rooms, which can hold up to four people, also have air-conditioning and cable TV. You can choose between poolside rooms in a motel-like three-story building or smaller garden-side cottages. Rates for up to two people are $100/134 in the winter/summer; add another $15/25 for each additional guest.

Royal Palms Hotel (☎ 292-1854, fax 292-1946, ☎ 800-678-0783 in the USA, 800-799-0824 in Canada), PO Box HM 499, Hamilton HM CX, is an intimate family-run hotel in a turn-of-the-century home. There are 13 rooms, all individually decorated but each with tasteful Victorian furnishings, private bath, TV, air-conditioning and coffeemaker. There are lots of pleasant personal touches throughout, and the hotel is a cut above others in this price range. Rates, which include continental breakfast, are $105/130 in the winter/summer for singles, $125/150 for doubles. The well-regarded Ascots restaurant is located on site, so lunch and dinner can also be taken at the hotel.

Rosedon (☎ 295-1640, fax 295-5904, ☎ 800-742-5008 in the USA), PO Box HM 290, Hamilton HM AX, directly opposite the Hamilton Princess Hotel, is a small hotel with the character of a genteel guesthouse. The historic main house has a cozy fireplaced living room where afternoon tea is served and a couple of atmospheric 2nd-floor guestrooms with Victorian furnishings. However, most of the hotel's 42 rooms are in two modern two-story wings that flank the heated pool and garden-like grounds behind the main house. All rooms have private bath, TV, phone, ceiling fan, air-conditioning, coffeemaker, refrigerator and wall safe. Standard rooms – including No 42, a nicely appointed room in the main house – cost $144/188 double in the winter/summer, breakfast included. A complimentary taxi service is provided to Elbow Beach.

Waterloo House (☎ 295-4480, fax 295-2585, ☎ 800-468-4100 in the USA), PO Box HM 333, Hamilton HM BX, is a small upmarket hotel that's a member of the Relais et Chateaux chain. Located in a restored 19th-century townhouse, Waterloo has a quiet harborside location just a few minutes west of central Hamilton. The inn's fireplaced sitting room is furnished with antiques, as are the 30 guestrooms and suites. No two guestrooms are the same, but all are spacious and have air-conditioning and twin beds that can be made up as a king. In winter, the double rates are from $180 to $280; in summer, from $240 to $380; single rates are $40 to $60 less. All rooms are essentially of the same standard, with the lower prices for city views and the highest for views of the harbor. There are also suites, which cost $300/410 in the winter/summer. Rates include a full breakfast. For an additional $30 per person, dinner can be added on and taken at the restaurant here or at either of the hotel's sister properties, Horizons and Newstead.

Hamilton's only large hotel is the *Hamilton Princess Hotel* (☎ 295-3000, fax 295-1914, ☎ 800-223-1818 in the USA, 800-268-7176 in Canada, 0171-407-1010 in the UK), PO Box HM 837, Hamilton HM CX. It is a five-minute walk west of the city center. As Bermuda's oldest 1st-class hotel, opened in 1884, it has hosted presidents, princes and luminary travelers such as Mark Twain; these days it's a favorite among business travelers. The 447 rooms are modern and comfortable, all with air-conditioning, cable TV, mini-safes and phones. Rates without breakfast start at $150 in winter and $210 in summer for both singles and doubles. There's a heated swimming pool, a fitness club, a putting green, a nightclub, a pub, banquet halls and numerous shops and restaurants. The harborside locale is not well-suited for swimming, but there's free transportation to its sister hotel, the Southampton Princess, where there's an appealing beach and other recreational offerings.

North Pembroke The following places are in residential neighborhoods north of Hamilton.

Closest to town is *Canada Villa* (☎ 292-0419, fax 296-1128), PO Box HM 1864, Hamilton HM HX, a small guesthouse run by Christine Barritt, an amiable host who coincidentally is half-Canadian, though the house was named long before her family moved in. It's an informal place with a shared kitchen and TV lounge. There are three guestrooms, each with a private bath, air-conditioning, ceiling fan and clock radio. Singles/doubles cost $63/80 in the winter and $70/90 in the summer, continental breakfast included. There's also a separate apartment with two bedrooms and a kitchen that costs $135/150 in the winter/summer for up to four people. The minimum stay is two nights. There's a pool. Canada Villa is about a 10-minute walk north of central Hamilton.

Another friendly little place is *Hi-Roy Guest House* (☎ 292-0808) at 22 Princess Estate Rd, Pembroke HM 04, about a mile northwest of Hamilton center. 'Soul spoken here' reads a sign in the back room, above a wall of musicians' photos. Everard 'Jonesy' Jones, DJ for a local radio jazz show, runs the place. No two rooms are decorated the same – expect bright colors, shag carpeting and a homey ambiance. Each of the six guestrooms has a private bath, air-conditioning and TV; most have ceiling fans. There's a large lounge, an outdoor patio, a refrigerator and a phone that guests can use. Rates are the same year round and include home-cooked meals: Singles/doubles cost $56/96 with breakfast, $70/124 with breakfast and dinner.

Just two houses away on Princess Estate Rd is the *Pleasant View Guest House* (☎ 292-4520), PO Box HM 1998, Hamilton HM HX. The six guestrooms are simply furnished, but each has a private bath, phone, cable TV, ceiling fan and air-conditioning. The winter/summer rate is $50/60 for singles and from $80/100 for doubles. Breakfast is available for $5 per

person. There's also a room set up as a studio, with a hot plate, toaster-oven, sink and refrigerator, which costs $100/120 for two people. Guests have use of a lounge, dining room, refrigerator and coin-operated washer and dryer.

Another nearby place is *La Casa Del Masa* (☎ 292-8726, fax 295-4447), PO Box HM 2494, Hamilton HM GX, which has three units, each with a bedroom with two double beds, private bath, a kitchen, TV, phone, ceiling fan and air-conditioning. There's a patio, barbecue grill and whirlpool for guests' use. An apartment for one or two people costs $80/90 in the winter/summer; add $10 for an upper-floor unit and $30 more for a third person. La Casa Del Masa is atop a little hill, making it a somewhat hefty climb for walking home but also affording a panoramic view of the north shore.

In the same north shore neighborhood is *Robin's Nest* (☎ /fax 292-4347, ☎ 800-223-6510 in the USA, 800-424-5500 in Canada), 10 Vale Close, Pembroke HM 04, which has three modern rental units: a studio, a one-bedroom apartment and a two-bedroom apartment. Each has a bathroom with both shower and tub, a kitchen, cable TV, air-conditioning, ceiling fans and phones with free local calls. Year-round rates are $95 for two people, $125 for three and $150 for four; add $10 for children ages six to 12, those under six are free. This is a quiet, somewhat secluded place, with a pleasant swimming pool. Owners Milt and Terri Robinson also have a nearby house to rent.

Mazarine by the Sea (☎ 292-1659, fax 292-6891, ☎ 800-441-7087 in the USA), PO Box HM 91, Hamilton HM AX, has seven units in a two-story building perched above the water's edge on North Shore Rd. There's no sandy beach, but there's a small pool. The units have kitchens, private baths, TV and phones. The cost is $110 for doubles, $150 for a studio for three. Two units that don't have ocean views are $5 less.

The *Hamiltonian Island Club* (☎ 295-5608, fax 295-7481, ☎ 800-441-7087 in the

USA and Canada), PO Box HM 1738, Hamilton HM GX, on a knoll about a 15-minute walk north of Hamilton, is a two-story timeshare complex that's a member of Resort Condominiums International. There are 32 contemporary, one-bedroom condo units, each with a TV, phone, oceanview balcony, air-conditioning, toaster, microwave, coffeemaker and mini-refrigerator. Those units that have not been booked by timeshare members can be rented by the general public and are a particularly good deal in winter. Winter/summer rates are $74/130 for singles, $88/170 for doubles. There's a large pool and three tennis courts, two lit for night play.

Places to Eat

There are a handful of places to eat in the section of Pembroke Parish just west of Hamilton. You can also take advantage of the full array of restaurants in Hamilton, which is within walking distance of most Pembroke accommodations. (See Places to Eat in the City of Hamilton chapter.)

You can pick up pastries and bread at *Bermuda Bakery*, on Pitts Bay Rd opposite Waterloo House.

Ristorante Primavera (☎ 295-2167) is an Italian restaurant on Pitts Bay Rd between Front St and the Hamilton Princess Hotel. Pasta main dishes are priced from $15, chicken dishes average $20 and fish and steak dishes are around $25. It's open for lunch on weekdays from 11:45 am to 2:30 pm and for dinner daily from 6:30 pm. Call to ask about early-bird specials.

Ascots (☎ 295-9644), at 24 Rosemont Ave in the Royal Palms Hotel, a 10-minute walk west of Hamilton center, has a Victorian setting, both indoor and al fresco dining, and excellent continental fare. The varied menu includes starters such as curried fish cakes or a delicious warm duck salad for $11, vegetarian crepe and pasta main dishes for around $20 and seared Cajun wahoo, grilled shrimp in ginger sauce or chicken with mango chutney for around $25. For dessert, crepes garibaldi

($7), topped with hazelnuts and chocolate sauce, is a treat big enough for two. The lunch menu includes some creative meat, fish and pasta dishes, served with salad, for only $10.50 – certainly one of the area's best dining deals. Ascots also has an extensive wine list. Lunch is from noon to 2:30 pm on weekdays, dinner from 6:30 to 10:30 pm daily.

There are a handful of restaurants at the Hamilton Princess Hotel (☎ 295-3000), including the trattoria-style *Harley's Bistro*, which has pizzas for $10, pastas for a few dollars more and meat and fish dishes from $20. The hotel's *Colony Pub* is a New York-style steakhouse restaurant featuring cuts of Angus beef priced from $20 to $30. Both are open daily for lunch and dinner. There's also an expensive fine-dining dinner restaurant, the *Tiara Room*, which specializes in seafood dishes with a French influence.

Waterloo House (☎ 295-4480), an upmarket restaurant at the Waterloo House hotel on Pitts Bay Rd, has a formal English-style dining room, a well-regarded chef and an international menu. Starters such as escargot or Thai noodles cost $10, and main dishes like salmon in champagne sauce, saffron grilled rockfish or duck breast with pear chutney are around $25. Jackets and ties are required at dinner, which is served daily from 7:30 to 9:30 pm. There's a less-expensive lunch menu from noon until 2:30 pm that is served on the harborside terrace.

Entertainment

The *Hamilton Princess Hotel* often features a cocktail theater in its main lounge. Performances range from Caribbean-style musicals and the music of Billie Holiday to island comedies and British farces. Tickets cost $25 for the show, $54 for a dinner and show package. Reservations and show information can be obtained by calling ☎ 295-3000.

For other entertainment in the area, see the Entertainment section in the City of Hamilton chapter.

Getting Around

Bus No 4 runs west from the City of Hamilton along St John's Rd to Spanish Point Park and returns to Hamilton along the North Shore Rd; the route direction is occasionally reversed at rush hour. Monday to Saturday the bus runs at least hourly from 8 am to 6 pm, but on Sundays there are only half a dozen runs.

Bus No 11, which terminates in the Town of St George, connects the City of Hamilton with the northeast coast of Pembroke via Blackwatch Pass.

For moped rentals, contact Astwood Cycles at the Hamilton Princess Hotel, Smatt's Cycle Livery on Pitts Bay Rd or Rockford Cycle Livery on Glebe Rd.

St George's Parish

St George's, Bermuda's easternmost parish, is the site of the historic Town of St George. This unspoiled town, which overlooks St George's Harbour, was Bermuda's first capital and remains its most fascinating sightseeing area.

St George's Parish also includes the remainder of St George's Island, which boasts forts and beaches; St David's Island, with the airport and a couple of historic sites; and ritzy Tucker's Town, which is located – somewhat confusingly – on the southwest side of Castle Harbour with no land connection to the rest of the parish.

The best spots for hiking are along the Railway Trail at the westernmost part of St George's Island and on the footpaths at Great Head Park in St David's. Ferry Point and Great Head Park also happen to be two of the parish's most promising bird-watching venues.

The area's best swimming and snorkeling beaches can be found north of the Town of St George and are described in the Around St George's Island section.

For information on St George's Golf Club in the Town of St George, and on snorkeling cruises departing from St George's Harbour, see the Outdoor Activities chapter near the front of the book.

The parish population is 4623.

Town of St George

Befitting its history as Bermuda's original capital and Britain's second oldest settlement in the New World, St George is seeped in period charm. Many of its original twisting alleyways and colonial-era buildings remain intact. Some of these centuries-old structures have been set aside as museums, while others continue to function as public meeting places, churches and shops. Even the names of the public ways – King's Square, Old Maid's Lane and Featherbed Alley, to name a few – conjure up images of the past.

St George has a pleasantly slow pace that sets it aside from the bustle of Hamilton, Bermuda's present-day capital. With the exception of outlying forts and beaches, all of the main sights are within easy walking distance of the town center and are best explored on foot.

If you enjoy shopping as much as historic sights, you'll find a run of quality shops along the west side of the waterfront. There are also a handful of waterfront restaurants that can make for atmospheric dining.

Wednesday is a particularly good day to visit St George, as it's the one day of the week when the Old State House and the Old Rectory are open to the public and the nearby Bermuda Biological Station gives guided tours of its facility.

Information
Tourist Offices The Visitors Service Bureau (☎ 295-1480), at the south side of King's Square, has brochures covering all of Bermuda and provides sightseeing information. The office is open from 9 am to 4 pm Monday to Saturday.

Money There are branches of the Bank of Butterfield and the Bank of Bermuda on King's Square.

Post & Communications The post office, on Water St a block west of King's Square, is open from 8 am to 5 pm Monday to Friday.

There's a pay phone on King's Square and a public fax terminal inside the tourist office.

Laundry There's a coin laundry, Tic-O-Matic Laundromat, on Shinbone Alley just north of York St.

Emergency The St George Police Station (☎ 297-1122) is located in the town center at 22 York St.

Walking Tour

A walking tour that includes the town's main sights and a ramble along some of its old alleys and backstreets can be done in a leisurely half-day.

A good place to begin your walking tour is on tiny Ordnance Island, which once served as a British arsenal. Today it has a cruise ship dock and two sights commemorating earlier visitors.

On the west side of Ordnance Island is a **statue** of Bermuda's shipwrecked founder, Sir George Somers, created by local sculptor Desmond Fountain. On the east side of the island is a replica of *Deliverance*, the **wooden ship** that Somers built in 1610 in order to continue his journey to the Virginia colony of Jamestown. For a $3 admission fee, you can walk through the boat's holds, where interesting exhibits using mannequins and an audio presentation give a glimpse of what life was like in these cramped quarters.

A short bridge leads from Ordnance Island to historic King's Square, the heart of St George. **Town Hall**, erected in 1782 and decorated with the parish's colorful seal, forms the square's eastern flank. This attractive building, where the mayor and council still meet, retains its original period character, with walls of Bermuda cedar and portraits of former mayors. Visitors are welcome from 10 am to 4 pm Monday to Saturday; admission is free. For information on an audio-visual show presented in the Town Hall Theatre at midday, check with the nearby tourist office.

On the north side of the square are replicas of the **pillory and stocks** once used to publicly chastise those who offended colonial mores. On the south side of the square are a couple of old cannons and the **ducking stool**, which has a seat at the end

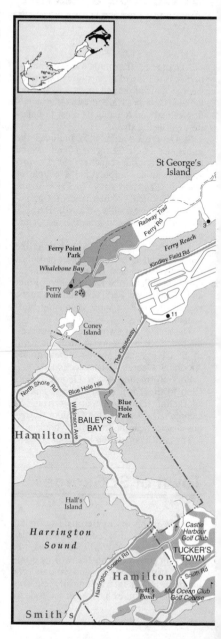

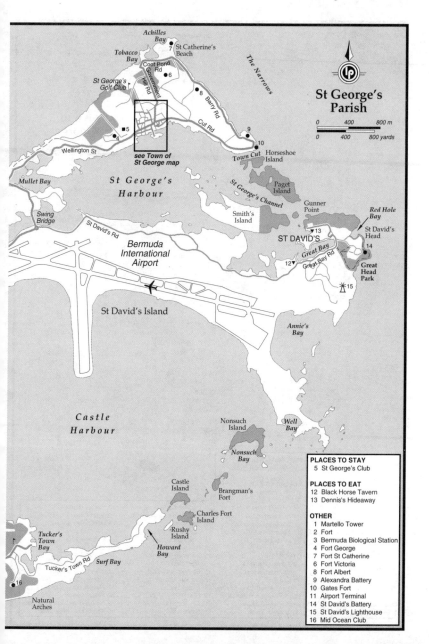

St George's Parish

0   400   800 m
0   400   800 yards

PLACES TO STAY
5 St George's Club

PLACES TO EAT
12 Black Horse Tavern
13 Dennis's Hideaway

OTHER
1   Martello Tower
2   Fort
3   Bermuda Biological Station
4   Fort George
7   Fort St Catherine
6   Fort Victoria
8   Fort Albert
9   Alexandra Battery
10 Gates Fort
11 Airport Terminal
14 St David's Battery
15 St David's Lighthouse
16 Mid Ocean Club

Town of
St George

St George's
Golf Club

Unfinished
Church

To Tobacco Bay

Church Folly Lane

Slippery Hill

Governor's Alley

Queen St

Turkey Hill

Chapel Lane

Clarence St

Kent St

Blockade Alley

Somers
Garden

Shinbone Alley

To East
Coast
Forts

Needle and Thread Alley

Printers Alley

Broad
Alley

Old Maid's Lane

Nea's Alley

Church Lane

Featherbed
Alley

York St

One Gun Alley

Water St

Aunt Peggy's Lane

Cemetery

Cemetery

St Peter's
Church

Clarence St

Princess St

Pound Alley

Silk Alley

Queen St

Bridge St

King St

Barbers Alley

To Fort George

Water St

End
Walking
Tour

Town
Hall

King's
Square

Market
Wharf

Begin
Walking
Tour

Ordnance
Island

St George's
Harbour

Cruise Ship
Terminal

······· Walking Tour

PLACES TO STAY
1 Hillcrest Guest House

PLACES TO EAT
10 Pasta Pasta
14 Temptations
22 Wharf Tavern
23 San Giorgio Ristorante
29 Carriage House
32 Robinson's Coffee Shop
34 White Horse Tavern

OTHER
2 Former Home of
   Joseph Stockdale
3 Old Rectory
4 Featherbed Alley Printery
5 St George's Historical
   Society Museum
6 Somers' Tomb

7 Commemorative Monument
8 Tic-O-Matic Laundromat
9 Bus Stop
11 Smiths
12 Dowling's Cycles
13 Police Station
15 Bermuda National
   Trust Museum
16 Bank of Butterfield
17 Somers Market
18 Bridge House
19 Bust of Tom Moore
20 Old State House
21 Eve Cycles

24 Tucker House
25 Book Cellar
26 AS Cooper & Sons
27 Trimingham's
28 Carriage Museum
30 Post Office
31 Frangipani
33 Bank of Bermuda
35 Pillory and Stocks
36 Ducking Stool
37 Visitors Service Bureau
38 Public Toilets
39 Statue of Sir George Somers
40 Replica of Deliverance

of a long seesaw-like plank that's hung over the water's edge. In times past, women accused of gossiping or other petty offenses were forced to endure the humiliation of being dunked into the harbor; these days, costumed actors reenact the scene.

Head east from King's Square and make a short detour north on Bridge St to **Bridge House**, a nearly 300-year-old house maintained by the Bermuda National Trust; it was once home to island governors and now contains a gift shop and the studio of watercolorist Jill Amos Raine.

Return to King St and proceed east, where you'll come to a little green space containing the **bust** of Irish poet Tom Moore, who sojourned in Bermuda in 1804.

The **Old State House**, at the east end of King St, dates to 1620 and is the oldest building in Bermuda. Although modest in size, the building incorporates Italianate features and has a stately appearance apropos to its former role as colonial Bermuda's parliamentary house. After the capital was moved to Hamilton in 1815, the Freemasons were granted the building as a meeting hall in exchange for the nominal rent of a single peppercorn. Prince Charles officiated at the reopening of the building in 1970 after it had gone through an extensive restoration. The ornate chamber, where island lawmakers met for nearly 200 years, can be entered on Wednesdays from 10 am to 4 pm. Admission is free.

Go north on Princess St and then cross York St to get to **Somers Garden**, a little park with tall royal palms and a monument erected in 1909 to commemorate the 300th anniversary of the founding of Bermuda by Sir George Somers. Admiral Somers, as islanders like to note, left his heart in Bermuda – and they mean this quite literally. Somers' heart, along with his entrails, are contained in a modest tomb at the southwest corner of the park. As was customary at the time, the rest of his body was shipped back to England.

From the garden, head north along Kent St to Featherbed Alley to where the **St George's Historical Society Museum** is found. This museum, which is in an early 18th-century house, is decorated with period furnishings, including four-poster beds, a wood-fired oven, a 1644 Bible, an 1813 rifle, a collection of old bottles and the like. The friendly volunteers who staff the museum will gladly point out intriguing little oddities, and admission is a mere $2. The museum is open from 10 am to 4 pm Monday to Saturday.

In the basement of the same building, but with a separate entrance, is the **Featherbed Alley Printery**, where broadsheets are still imprinted on a working centuries-old press. A cell at the side of the printery once served as the town jail; it was here in 1801 that the Reverend John Stephenson, a Methodist missionary, was incarcerated for six months for the 'crime' of preaching to slaves. The printery is open from 10 am to 4 pm Monday to Saturday. Admission is free.

From Featherbed Alley head west on Church Lane, which passes the backside of **St Peter's Church**, and turn north up Broad Alley to the **Old Rectory**, which is open only on Wednesdays but can be viewed from the gate on any day. Both the church and the Old Rectory are detailed below.

The winding streets and alleys west of the Old Rectory have picturesque houses and are fun to wander. A plaque on the corner of Printers Alley and Needle and Thread Alley marks the former home of Joseph Stockdale, who in 1783 brought the first printing press to the island and founded the *Bermuda Gazette* newspaper, the forerunner of the current *Royal Gazette*. Stockdale, incidentally, also started Bermuda's first postal service, a horseback operation in St George's that began in 1784.

If you continue south on Old Maid's Lane and Barbers Alley to Water St, you can visit the Tucker House and the Carriage Museum on your return to King's Square.

Tucker House

Built in the early 18th century, the Tucker House on Water St has been well preserved, with rooms that maintain a period look. The house is named for the family of Henry

Tucker, the Colonial Treasurer and Governor's Council President who purchased it in 1775. The Tuckers were one of the most prestigious families in Bermuda, and many of the furnishings, silver and china that are displayed here come from their estate.

The collection includes numerous portraits of the Tuckers, as well as many fine pieces of furniture, some of local cedar and others of imported mahogany. In a side room beyond the courtyard, there's a little archeological exhibit that details the history of the property.

Tucker House, which is owned by the Bermuda National Trust, is open Monday to Saturday, from 9:30 am to 4:30 pm during the months of April to October, and from 10 am to 4 pm the rest of the year. Admission is $4.

Carriage Museum

The Carriage Museum on Water St contains a collection of 20 horse-drawn carriages. The majority were made in the USA, although there are also a few European models. The carriages include a tub cart, pony carts, wicker carriages, an Irish jaunting cart and a couple of hearses that belonged to parish churches. All are well-preserved, as they were still highly valued and kept in use until 1946, when the importation of motor vehicles for private use was finally introduced.

The museum is open from 10 am to 5 pm Monday to Friday (and on some Saturdays). Admission is free, but donations are appreciated.

Old Rectory

The Old Rectory on Broad Alley was built by the notorious pirate George Dew, who left the American colonies, came to Bermuda and converted to the good life, becoming a church warden and lawyer. Although the exact date of construction is not known, the house was standing by 1705. It was one of the first houses in Bermuda to have a stone roof, rather than palmetto thatch. The walls were made of limestone quarried from beneath the house

foundation, a technique which also created a cellar in the process.

The Old Rectory takes its name from a later owner, Alexander Richardson, a minister who was given the property in the mid-18th century as a wedding gift from the father of his Bermuda-born bride.

The building is now owned by the Bermuda National Trust and is lived in by local historian Brendan Hollis, who graciously opens the property to visitors on Wednesdays from noon to 5 pm. It's a charming little house inside with period furnishings, cedar ceilings and a solidly colonial character. There's no admission charge.

Bermuda National Trust Museum

This museum, on the corner of York St just north of King's Square, occupies a well-preserved colonial structure that was erected in 1700 by Bermuda governor Samuel Day. In the mid-1800s it was turned into a hotel called The Globe, and in 1863 the hotel became the base for Major Norman Walker, an agent for the Confederate government.

During the US Civil War, Bermuda was an important transshipment center for Southern cotton headed for England. Because of the Union blockade, swift steamships were employed as blockade-runners by the Confederacy to get the cotton as far as Bermuda, where it was then transferred to more seaworthy cargo vessels for the transatlantic passage. During this period, St George enjoyed unprecedented economic activity, its harbor bustling with North American ships and its waterfront warehouses piled high with cotton.

The museum focuses on the role Bermuda played during the US Civil War. It contains period furnishings, a map of blockade-running routes and various exhibits. These include displays on an attempted Union blockade of Bermuda; Confederacy money; Major Walker; and Joseph Hayne Rainey, a black American who escaped to Bermuda and then in 1866 returned to South Carolina to become the first black member of the US Congress.

There's also an audio-visual presentation about the Civil War days and an antique press where you can get a replica imprint of the Great Seal of the Confederacy.

The museum is open year round every day except Sunday. From April to October the hours are from 9:30 am to 4:30 pm and from November to March it's open from 10 am to 4 pm. Admission is $4 for adults, $3 for senior citizens and $1 for students.

St Peter's Church

One of the oldest Anglican churches in the Western Hemisphere, the original St Peter's Church was built of wood and thatch in 1612. A more permanent structure followed a few years later, while much of the present church was built in the early 1700s.

It's a thoroughly historic building with open timber beams, hanging chandeliers and a wall of marble memorial stones whose epitaphs honor early governors, business leaders and clergy. The oldest piece of Bermudian furniture on the island, an altar made of mahogany under the direction of the first governor, can be seen in the east wing.

Don't miss the vestibule behind the main altar, where there's a glass-doored vault containing a number of notable items, including a 1594 Bible and a few old Bermudian coins found during church restorations. The prized piece in the vault is a silver chalice given to the church in 1625 by the Bermuda Company, engraved with the company's coat-of-arms and a scene of the *Sea Venture* grounding on a rock. There's also a second 17th-century chalice, this one presented by King William III.

The **churchyard**, like St Peter's Church itself, once had segregated areas for black and white parishioners, with the graves for slaves confined to the west side of the yard in the walled area closest to Queen St. On the church's east side is the grave of Sir Richard Sharples, the Bermudian governor who was gunned down in March 1973. The governor is buried alongside his bodyguard, Captain Hugh Sayers of the Welsh Guards, who was murdered by the same assassins on the grounds of Government House.

> ### The Tempest
> When the first English castaways washed up on Bermuda's shores in July 1609, they may well have set the stage for William Shakespeare's final work, *The Tempest*. Shakespeare is thought to have begun work on that play in 1610, after the first reports of the *Sea Venture*'s wreck in a tempestuous storm appeared in England.
>
> It seems that Shakespeare, who knew several of the shareholders of the Virginia expedition, probably had a copy of the account entitled 'A Discovery of the Bermudas, otherwise called the Isle of Devils' at his disposal when he wrote the play. While the plot of *The Tempest* is not set in Bermuda, the description of the storm and shipwreck bear a close resemblance to the events surrounding the ill-fated *Sea Venture*. Indeed, in Act 1, Scene II, Shakespeare appears to make a direct reference to the islands with a mention of the 'still-vex'd Bermoothes'. ∎

The church is open daily from 9:30 am to 5 pm. Admission is free.

Unfinished Church

Although it looks like the ruins of a once-grandiose church, the Unfinished Church at the north end of Kent St is in fact the hollow shell of a 'new' Anglican church that was intended to replace St Peter's, which by the mid-1800s had fallen into disrepair. Construction began on this replacement church in 1874 and piecemeal work continued for two decades. Meanwhile bickering between parishioners – some who supported the new church and an increasing number who favored restoring St Peter's – eventually brought the project to a halt.

The Bermuda National Trust, which now maintains the church grounds, has undertaken a restoration to stabilize the walls. Until that work is completed, the Unfinished Church can only be viewed from the outside.

Fort George

Fort George is perched on a hillside about a 15-minute walk west of the town center. Originally erected in 1612 as a watch tower, most of the current structure dates to the early 19th century. It's a small fort with square masonry walls that reach about 150 feet across and a central keep now used as a government communications facility (Bermuda Harbour Radio) to coordinate ocean traffic in Bermuda's waters.

The site remains off tourist maps, as the fort, at least until recently, has been in a state of disrepair and visitors have not been encouraged to explore it. However, the parks department is in the process of bringing Fort George under the national parks umbrella with the hopes of restoring it and eventually opening it to tours.

In the meantime, visitors can take Fort George Hill Rd to the top for a view of St George and St David's, as well as for a peek at the fort and one of its 25-ton, 11-inch guns (a rifled muzzleloader dating to 1871), which is curiously aimed right at the cruise ship dock. It's a fairly steep climb and there's a pesky dog en route, so unless the restoration has moved forward, it's a site that's best appreciated by those with a moped.

Places to Stay

The Town of St George has two accommodations options, both on the north side of town within a 10-minute walk of the center.

The *Hillcrest Guest House* (☎ 297-1630, fax 297-1908), PO Box GE 96, St George's GE BX, is a friendly, family-run place on Nea's Alley in an old established residential neighborhood. There are a dozen rooms, most in the 18th-century main house, although a few are in cottages out back. All have air-conditioning and private bath. Singles/doubles cost an affordable $50/72 year round (no breakfast).

The *St George's Club* (☎ 297-1200, fax 297-8003), PO Box GE 92, St George's GE BX, is a modern timeshare condominium complex with a hilltop location. The 69 units are contemporary and comfortably equipped, each with a living room, complete kitchen, spacious bathroom, TV, phone and air-conditioning. Most are well maintained, but they're renovated piecemeal so conditions vary depending on which unit you get. Many have nice views of the town and surrounding waters. A one-bedroom unit for up to four people costs $165/250 in winter/summer. A two-bedroom unit for up to six people costs $250/450. There are a couple of pools (one heated), tennis courts and a putting green.

Places to Eat

For an early breakfast, there's *Robinson's Coffee Shop*, a cheap cafeteria where you can rub elbows with the locals. It even has a water view. You can get a full breakfast for $5, and lunchtime sandwiches for half that. Robinson's is on Water St, a minute's walk west of King's Square – look carefully, as there's no sign.

Temptations, on York St in the center of town, is a small bakery with a few cafe tables. They sell ice cream and cappuccino, make a nice cup of fish chowder for $3 and have simple sandwiches for around $4. There are also scrumptious, reasonably priced pies, cakes and fruit tarts. It's closed on Sundays, but is otherwise open from 9:30 am to 5 pm, later on cruise ship days.

San Giorgio Ristorante (☎ 297-1307), on Water St, is St George's leading Italian restaurant, with red-checkered tablecloths, Chianti bottles hanging from the ceiling and a full menu of pizzas and pastas. Weekdays from noon to 2:30 pm, diners can opt for pasta dishes or a seafood salad with shrimp, mussels and squid for $9 or pizza by the slice from $2.50. At dinner, from 6:30 to 9:30 pm Monday to Saturday, pasta dishes start at $11, chicken at $16. Full pizzas range from $9 for cheese to $12 for the works.

If you just want something quick and inexpensive, *Pasta Pasta*, to the north on York St, is a simpler eatery with both eat-in and takeout pizza and pasta options.

For atmosphere and setting, it's hard to beat the *White Horse Tavern* (☎ 297-1838), right on King's Square. This casual restaurant and pub has indoor dining as well as an open-air waterfront patio. You can get salads, sandwiches or burgers with fries for around $10; go for an English pub lunch of steak and kidney pie for $13; or get standard meat and fish dishes for around $20. It's open from 11 am to 1 am, with shorter weekday hours in winter.

The *Wharf Tavern* (☎ 297-1515) on Water St is a popular local pub with waterview patio tables in the rear. They have burgers and sandwiches for under $10, a pub menu of simple eats such as shepherd's pie or fish and chips for around $12 and fresh seafood main dishes for around $20. It's open daily from 11:30 am to 1 am.

Margaret Rose (☎ 297-1301) at the St George's Club has an excellent hilltop view and a reasonably priced lunch menu with salads, sandwiches, burgers and light fare such as couscous with grilled vegetables, all for under $10. For a few dollars more, you can get pasta dishes such as chicken breast with sun-dried tomatoes on fettuccine or for $15 there's fresh fish or barbecued ribs. There's also a three-course early-bird dinner from 6:30 to 7 pm that's a good value for $19.

The *Carriage House* (☎ 297-1730), on Water St next to the Carriage Museum, is a large upmarket restaurant in an 18th-century building. Some of the tables have water views, and in warmer weather you can dine al fresco on the harborfront terrace. At lunch, from 11:30 am to 4:30 pm, there are sandwiches and burgers from $7, various salads or quiche for around $10 and English-style fish and chips for $15. At dinner, from 6 to 9:45 pm, chicken or fish dishes begin around $20, or order a four-course early-bird dinner before 6:45 pm (except on Sundays) for the same price. There's also a Sunday brunch buffet for $25; an English-style afternoon tea is served on other days.

You can pick up groceries at *Somers Market*, on the corner of York and Kent Sts. It's open from 7 am to 7 pm Monday to Saturday, from 8 am to 5 pm on Sunday.

Entertainment

The *White Horse Tavern* at King's Square has live entertainment, with a rock band on Friday nights and a jazz band on Saturday nights and Sunday afternoons. Entertainment on other nights can vary; in the past they've had reggae and steel bands, but this may not continue as the locals seem to prefer karaoke.

The *Wharf Tavern* on Water St also has live entertainment on weekends, while the *Carriage House* on Water St often has after-dinner dancing on Saturday nights.

If you want to catch a movie, there's the *New Somers Playhouse* (☎ 297-2821), a cinema at 37 Wellington St at the west side of town.

Things to Buy

All the main Hamilton department stores – Trimingham's, Smith's and AS Cooper & Sons – have branches on the west side of the town center.

The Bridge House Gallery, at the Bridge House, sells quality watercolors of island scenes and various handicrafts and souvenir items.

Frangipani, on Water St, has attractive casual women's clothing, including beachwear, light cottons and batiks.

The Book Cellar, on the corner of Water St and Barbers Alley, is a nice little bookstore with a collection of books on Bermuda, as well as travel books and novels.

Getting Around

Bus Bus Nos 1, 3, 10 and 11 connect St George with the City of Hamilton, while bus No 6 connects St George with St David's.

In addition, the St George's Mini-Bus Service (☎ 297-8199) runs throughout the greater St George area and to St David's. The minibus office is in the St George Town Hall, opposite the tourist office. For more details, see Minibus Service in the Getting Around chapter at the front of the book.

Moped & Bicycle Mopeds and bicycles can be rented from Dowling's Cycles (☎ 297-1614) at 26 York St and from Eve Cycles (☎ 236-6247) at 1 Water St.

St George's Island

Fort St Catherine

At the northeastern tip of St George's Island, Fort St Catherine overlooks the beach where Sir George Somers and his shipwrecked crew scurried ashore in 1609. Bermuda's first governor, a carpenter by the name of Richard Moore, constructed a

---

Invasion Anxiety

The mile-long northeast coast of St George's Island faces The Narrows, a navigable reef channel of strategic importance. Consequently, this stretch of coastline was heavily fortified by British colonists to fend off potential invaders.

The handful of forts that still stand today offer an interesting glimpse of the invasion anxiety that gripped islanders for more than three centuries. Despite the energy exerted on their defenses, Bermuda has never been the object of a foreign attack.

In actuality, only once in its entire history has Bermuda even had the opportunity to fire its guns in anger, and that was way back in 1614, when two small Spanish ships surveying the new British colony decided to launch a skiff near the entrance to Castle Harbour. The skiff drew immediate fire and the Spaniards beat a quick retreat, marking the first and last of Bermuda's military 'skirmishes'. The incident did, however, serve to prompt the construction of some 50 forts in the years that followed. ∎

---

primitive timber fortification here a few years later. The fort has since been rebuilt several times; most of the current concrete structure dates to 1865.

This substantial fort has a drawbridge, a moat, ramparts, a maze of tunnels and five powerful 18-ton muzzleloader guns that have never been fired in anger.

Since the 1950s, Fort St Catherine has been set aside as a museum. Its old powder magazine now contains a collection of period weapons, the artillery storeroom has dioramas depicting colonial history and other rooms have various displays ranging from an audio presentation on Bermuda's forts to a wax figure of Queen Elizabeth II and replicas of Britain's crown jewels. The museum is open every day except Christmas from 10 am to 4:30 pm, with the latest entry allowed at 4 pm. Admission is $2.50 for adults, free for children under 12.

Fort St Catherine is about a mile north of the Town of St George. To get there, turn right on Sapper Lane, north of the Unfinished Church, and continue on Victoria Rd.

Other Fortifications

The remains of two forts can be found on the grounds of the former Club Med hotel, on the hillside southwest of Fort St Catherine. **Fort Victoria**, just south of the hotel, and **Fort Albert**, just east of the tennis courts, both date to the 19th century and are of a similar Wellington construction. The four guns at Fort Albert were of the same class as those displayed at Fort St Catherine, while the guns at Fort Victoria weighed in at 23 tons and shot massive 540-pound shells.

A mile southeast of Fort St Catherine, along the coastal Barry Rd, are two adjacent waterfront fortifications. **Alexandra Battery**, which was begun in the 1870s and extensively remodeled at the turn of the century, has a cannon with a unique cast-iron faceplate that was intended to protect the gun from return fire.

Gates Fort Park, at the point where Barry Rd changes to Cut Rd, holds the remains of a small battery with a couple of

NED FRIARY

Ficus tree at the Bermuda Botanical Gardens, Paget Parish

NED FRIARY

The pineapple-like fruit of the pandanus, or screw pine

NED FRIARY

Frangipani, or plumeria

NED FRIARY

Royal poinciana

NED FRIARY

Lobster claw heliconia

NED FRIARY

Bird of paradise

Aloe, or torch plant

Bougainvillea

Honeycup

Hibiscus

For luck, step through the moongate at Palm Grove Garden.

Palm Grove Garden in Devonshire Parish is a pleasant place for a stroll.

cannons and a lookout tower that offers a view of Town Cut, the strategic channel into St George's Harbour.

Beaches

There are a couple of small sandy beaches on the northeastern tip of the parish that are within walking distance of the Town of St George.

The main public beach, **Tobacco Bay**, can be reached by taking Government Hill Rd north to its end. Tobacco Bay is a good choice for swimming and snorkeling, as it has sheltered waters, interesting rock formations, restroom facilities and a concession stand that sells snacks and rents snorkeling gear from April through October. Tobacco Bay, incidentally, played a part in the American Revolution, when gunpowder stolen from St George's magazine was brought down to this bay and loaded onto small boats that then scurried it across the reef to a waiting American ship, which in turn delivered it to Washington's armies.

At the west side of Fort St Catherine, **Achilles Bay** is a tiny public beach that's also good for swimming and snorkeling, while **St Catherine's Beach**, at the south side of the fort, is a longer and broader beach but with less-protected waters. St Catherine's was formerly the private beach of the now-defunct Club Med.

Railway Trail

The easternmost section of the Railway Trail, a 2.75-mile-long stretch, begins west of the Town of St George, off Wellington Lane, and follows the northern coastline to the western tip of St George's Island at Ferry Point Park. Near the midway point, a section of the trail connects back to the main vehicle road for about half a mile to loop around oil storage facilities that are closed to the public.

Just before Ferry Point, at the south side of picturesque Whalebone Bay, you'll find the foundations of a 19th-century coastal fortification and a circular Martello tower with a powerful cannon that was capable of firing in a complete 360° range. At Ferry Point, waterside concrete footings stand as remnants of a trestle that once provided a rail link across the channel to Coney Island.

At the point, you can either backtrack the same way you came, or simply return via Ferry Rd.

Bermuda Biological Station

Officially named the Bermuda Biological Station for Research (BBSR), this center was founded in 1903 as a joint venture of Harvard University, New York University and the Bermuda Natural History Society. Today the station conducts research on marine science, ranging from coral reef ecology to biological oceanography, and provides facilities for visiting scientists and students.

Free guided tours of the research station, which is west of the Swing Bridge that connects St George's and St David's islands, are given at 10 am on Wednesdays year round. It's possible to stop by at other times, but there may not be anyone available to show you around. The gift shop, which is open at midday on Monday, Wednesday and Friday, sells books on Bermuda's natural history.

The BBSR (☎ 297-1880) is reached by taking Biological Station Lane south from Ferry Rd.

St David's Island

Until 1934, when the first bridge was built between St David's Island and St George's Island, St David's could only be reached by boat. For the most part, it was an isolation that was cherished by its inhabitants, a substantial number of whom are of Mahican ancestry, the descendants of native North Americans taken from the colonies during British Indian raids in the early 17th century.

In 1941, most of St David's Island was turned over to the US military for the development of a naval air station and the residents, reluctant to leave St David's, were concentrated at the eastern end of the island.

In 1995, the US military turned the base lands on St David's back to the Bermudian government. Large tracts of the former base continue to serve as the civilian airport, while the rest is in a state of flux, with the government yet to determine its future use.

The village of St David's, tucked into the eastern flank of the island, maintains a more timeless, unchanged character than other Bermudian communities. Its pastel buildings are not fancy, but they take on a picturesque quality in the late afternoon light. Certainly the town offers a glimpse of one of the least touristed sides of Bermuda.

Gunner Point

A nice way to start an exploration of St David's Island is to drive to the end of the main road, where the small park at Gunner Point offers a notable view of two near-shore islands.

The westernmost one, Smith's Island, is the biggest island in St George's Harbour. The eastern part of Smith's Island, as well as the entire island of Paget, which is immediately north of Smith's Island, are government owned and set aside for preservation. In the 18th century, Smith's Island was used by whalers for boiling down blubber, while Paget Island is best known as the site of Fort Cunningham, one of the most costly forts erected in Bermuda. Unfortunately, the islands aren't readily accessible to visitors who don't have their own boat.

St David's Battery

St David's Battery, an abandoned coastal defense station, sits above Bermuda's highest sea cliffs at the easternmost point of Bermuda. In addition to fine hilltop coastal views, it has the island's most formidable guns – their rusting barrels sitting like silent sentinels above the vast Atlantic. The two largest guns date to the early 1900s, reach 37 feet in length and had a shooting range of more than 20 miles.

The cliff face below contains a number of caves, but because of the steep drop they are not easily accessible. There are good water views, including one of Red Hole Bay that can be reached by walking a few minutes north past the last gun. The south side of Red Hole Bay – like St David's Battery – is encompassed within a 25-acre zone known as Great Head Park.

The quickest way to get to St David's Battery is to take Battery Rd up past the cricket grounds from Great Bay Rd. However, if you're on foot, you can also get to the battery by taking the footpath that begins at the signposted section of Great Head Park on Great Bay Rd. The path, shaded by Bermuda olivewood trees and fiddlewood, begins at the back of the parking area. Continue about 200 yards until you reach a narrow dirt road, onto which you bear right; when the track splits, bear left. En route you'll get glimpses of St David's Lighthouse, pass old military ruins and catch a few coastal views.

St David's Lighthouse

Perched atop a hill at the southeastern side of St David's, this vintage 1879 stone lighthouse offers a panoramic 360° view. Even if the lighthouse is closed – as it often is – it's well worth mopeding up here, as the view can be appreciated from the 485-foot lighthouse hill. Due to tight budgets, the lighthouse is generally open to visitors in summers only, from 10 am to noon Monday to Wednesday; for the latest schedule information call the park ranger's office at ☎ 236-5902.

To get to the lighthouse, take Lighthouse Hill Rd south from Great Bay Rd.

Places to Eat

For a local treat, don't miss *Dennis's Hideaway* (☎ 297-0044), at the end of Cashew City Rd, a little cubbyhole shack overlooking Vaughan's Bay. The thoroughly unpretentious dining room consists of a couple of simple tables with wooden benches, but the food is as fresh as it gets. Dennis Lamb and his son Graham literally catch fish off the rocks and cook them up in the kitchen. You can get a bowl of superb chowder for $2 or tasty fish and chips for $7.50, but if you pack an appetite, the real treat here is to order 'the works', an amazing multicourse feast that includes shark hash, conch fritters, conch stew, mussel stew, fish chowder, shark steak, conch steak, scallops and local fish! The price of $32.50 is quite reasonable when you consider that most of the shellfish has to be imported.

Also in St David's is the *Black Horse Tavern* (☎ 293-9742), a combination bar and restaurant in the center of the village on Great Bay. Open for lunch and dinner every day but Monday, it has sandwiches for around $5 and seafood dishes from $10 to $15.

Getting Around

The only regular public bus to St David's is bus No 6, which runs from the Town of St George about once an hour. For information on the St George's Parish minibus service, see Minibus Service in the Getting Around chapter in the front of the book.

Tucker's Town

Tucker's Town, at the southwest side of Castle Harbour, is one of the most exclusive areas in Bermuda. Much of it is occupied by the members-only Mid Ocean Club, which has Bermuda's top-rated golf course.

There are nice white sandy **beaches**, as well as a seaside natural rock arch, south of the Mid Ocean Club. These beaches, reached via the first right off South Rd after Mid Ocean Drive, are set aside for use by members of the Mid Ocean Club and guests of Marriott's Castle Harbour Resort; in summer, a gatekeeper limits public access to the area.

Tucker's Town Rd, which runs along the narrow peninsula east of the Mid Ocean Club, is bordered by a few dozen homes belonging to wealthy foreigners, including former Italian premier Silvio Berlusconi and American billionaire Ross Perot.

From the end of Tucker's Town Rd, you can look across a narrow strait to **Castle Island**, a nature preserve that contains the stone remains of a British fort, one of the earliest erected in the Western Hemisphere.

Nonsuch Island, to the east, is a bird sanctuary where efforts are being made to reintroduce the Bermuda petrel, or cahow, one of the most endangered birds in the world. To prepare the island for the cahow, exotic predators are being eliminated and efforts are being made to restore the island's precontact ecosystem. Not surprisingly, human access to the island is restricted, though the Bermuda Biological Station and the Bermuda Audubon Society occasionally bring groups over; see Useful Organizations in the Facts for the Visitor chapter.

Getting Around

Bus No 1 connects Tucker's Town with both the City of Hamilton and the Town of St George. The bus goes to the Mid Ocean Club, where it turns around, but goes no farther east.

Hamilton Parish

The parish of Hamilton (not to be confused with the City of Hamilton, which is in Pembroke Parish) wraps around Harrington Sound, Bermuda's largest inland body of water.

Although Harrington Sound may have the appearance of a calm lake, it is in fact a salt-water bay, connected to the sea by a narrow inlet at the village of Flatts. Flatts, with the Bermuda Aquarium, Museum & Zoo, and Bailey's Bay, with its limestone caves, are the parish's two main visitor destinations.

While Hamilton Parish isn't known for its beaches, Shelly Bay Park, on the north shore, is a popular spot for families with children, as the waters are shallow and the park facilities include a playground.

There are some pleasant walks at Blue Hole Park and at the Bermuda Perfumery, both detailed in the Bailey's Bay section, and along the Railway Trail, detailed in the Flatts section.

Grotto Bay Beach Hotel and Marriott's Castle Harbour Resort both have public tennis courts and a wide variety of water sports. The Castle Harbour Golf Club, the Marriott resort's course, is adjacent to the hotel but – because of oddly drawn parish boundaries – lands in St George's Parish. More information on these activities is in the Outdoor Activities chapter in the front of the book.

The population of Hamilton Parish is 4680.

Bailey's Bay

Bailey's Bay, the little village at the north-eastern side of Hamilton Parish, has a couple of enjoyable short trails and an abundance of caves and water-filled grottos. The grandest of them, the Crystal Caves, can be visited on an interesting guided tour with commentary on local geology, or you can see a run of smaller caves by taking a hike in Blue Hole Park. In fact, caves are so abundant that it's not even necessary for some people to leave their resort to see them – there are substantial caves right on the grounds of the Grotto Bay Beach Hotel. One of them, the Cathedral Cave, even has a deep-water pool that's popular with swimmers.

All of the main Bailey's Bay visitor sights – Crystal Caves, the perfume factory and the entrance to Blue Hole Park – are within easy walking distance of each other.

Information
The postage-stamp-size Bailey's Bay post office, at the intersection of Blue Hole Hill and North Shore Rd, is open Monday to Friday from 8 to 11:30 am and 1 to 5 pm.

Bermuda Perfumery
The Bermuda Perfumery (☎ 293-0627) at 212 North Shore Rd, just north of the Bailey's Bay post office, is a small perfume factory that offers free tours of its facilities and invites visitors to stroll around its grounds. The tours, which are available throughout the day and take a scant 10 minutes, include an explanation of the enfleurage processes that fix the flowery scents and end at a little shop where visitors can sample (and purchase) any of the perfumes, colognes and lotions.

A nature trail, which begins at the south side of the factory, loops one-third of a mile around the back side of the property through an area of woods and flower gardens. Some of the flowers grown here, including a patch of fragrant Easter lilies that bloom in spring, are used in making the perfume. Many of the trees and shrubs along the trail are marked with both their common and Latin names, so it makes a particularly enjoyable stroll for those who want to identify some of the flora they've seen around the island. The palmetto palm,

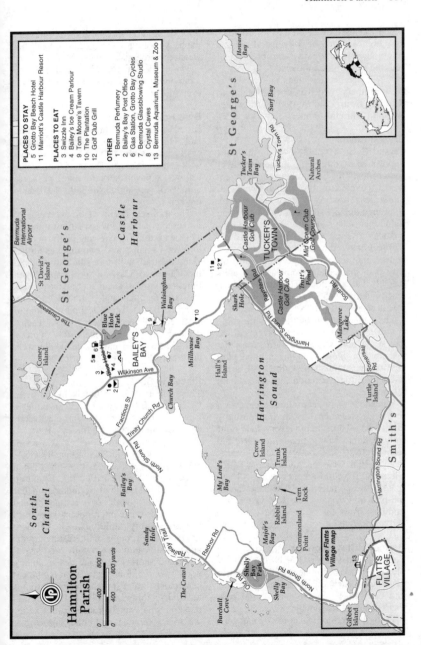

Hamilton Parish

PLACES TO STAY
5 Grotto Bay Beach Hotel
11 Marriott's Castle Harbour Resort

PLACES TO EAT
3 Swizzle Inn
4 Bailey's Ice Cream Parlour
9 Tom Moore's Tavern
10 The Plantation
12 Golf Club Grill

OTHER
1 Bermuda Perfumery
2 Bailey's Bay Post Office
6 Gas Station, Grotto Bay Cycles
7 Bermuda Glassblowing Studio
8 Crystal Caves
13 Bermuda Aquarium, Museum & Zoo

which was used to thatch the earliest colonial homes, and the olivewood tree, a common Bermuda native, are both found near the start of the trailhead.

A free detailed trail map is available at the perfumery, which is open Monday to Saturday from 9 am to 4:30 pm in winter and until 5 pm in summer.

Crystal Caves

Crystal Caves (☎ 293-0640) is the most impressive of the area's numerous caves and grottos. This huge subterranean cavern was discovered in 1907 when two boys, intent on retrieving a stray cricket ball, shimmied down a rope through a hole and found themselves inside.

Today a series of 81 steps leads visitors 120 feet below the surface, past stalactites and stalagmites and onto a pontoon walkway that spans the greenish-blue waters that fill the cave floor. The waters, which reach a depth of 55 feet, are crystal clear, free of marine life and vegetation.

The tour guide provides an enjoyable commentary on the geologic origins of the caves and points out odd formations that resemble profiles, including a good likeness of the Manhattan skyline. All in all, it's a fun little excursion that takes about 20 minutes.

The site is open year round, except for a few weeks in January and during unusually high tides. Tours begin every half hour from 10 am to 3:30 pm daily in winter and from 9 am to 4:30 pm Sunday to Friday from April to October. Admission is $4 for adults, $2 for children ages five to 11 and free for those under four. The caves are at the end of Crystal Cave Rd, just a few minutes from the nearest bus stop on Wilkinson Ave.

Bermuda Glassblowing Studio

The studio, at 16 Blue Hole Hill, is a glassblowing workshop that makes decorative glass items, such as earrings, paperweights and Christmas tree ornaments, and sells them on site at reasonable prices.

From the front of the store you can get a peek of the craftspeople blowing glass in the back room; for $1 you can go back and watch the process up close.

The workshop operates from 9 am to 5 pm on weekdays, while the store is open every day.

Blue Hole Park

Blue Hole Park, off the south side of Blue Hole Hill road near the causeway, is a new, easily accessible 12-acre nature reserve with numerous caves. The main trail, which follows a paved service road, passes a number of very short spur paths that lead to marked sights.

The trailhead begins at the west side of the reserve parking lot and almost immediately leads to a bird-viewing platform overlooking a small pond. Two minutes farther along the trail, a 40-foot side path leads to the Causeway Cave, a fern-draped open limestone cavern. The main trail then passes restroom facilities and continues east to a clearing. Bear left here to find a couple of small coastal caves or bear right to reach a deck overlooking the Blue Grotto, a pretty pond-like sunken cave. The whole walk takes only 20 minutes roundtrip.

Places to Stay

There are two resort hotels in the area: Grotto Bay Beach Hotel, right in Bailey's Bay, and Marriott's Castle Harbour Resort, about two miles south of Bailey's Bay.

Grotto Bay Beach Hotel (☎ 293-8333, fax 293-2306, ☎ 800-582-3190 in the USA, 800-463-0851 in Canada, 0511-5672294 in Germany), 11 Blue Hole Hill, Hamilton Parish CR 04, is one of Bermuda's smaller resort hotels, with 201 rooms spread around a dozen contemporary two-story and three-story buildings. The 21-acre grounds have a couple of interesting grottos and a small sandy beach with good swimming and snorkeling. Facilities include a pool, a hot tub, four tennis courts, a fitness center and a water sports center. The rooms have air-conditioning, cable TV, coffeemakers, small refrigerators, room safes, waterview verandas and either one king or two double beds. Rates for either singles or doubles without meals begin at $110 in winter and $185 in summer.

Marriott's Castle Harbour Resort (☎ 293-2040, fax 293-8288, ☎ 800-223-6388 in the USA and Canada, 0800-221222 in the UK, 69-231-357 in Germany), PO Box HM 841, Hamilton HM CX, has a secluded location overlooking Castle Harbour. Its 250-acre grounds include a well-regarded 18-hole golf course, three heated pools, six tennis courts and a private dock. The hotel, which was recently renovated, has 405 guestrooms with air-conditioning, phone and cable TV, and in many cases waterview balconies. Rates begin at $130/240 for doubles in winter/summer. Add another $15 per person for a breakfast plan. Numerous multiday packages are also available, including golf-and-room plans. The natural shoreline fronting the property is rocky, but the hotel has a choice private beach in the Tucker's Town area that it shuttles guests to and from. The resort has a little shopping arcade, several restaurants, a night club and a water sports facility that arranges boat rentals and diving excursions.

Places to Eat
Bailey's Bay The *Swizzle Inn* (☎ 293-9300), on Blue Hole Hill, serves lunch from noon to 6 pm, with pub grub like shepherd's pie or bangers and mash for around $10, sandwiches with fries for $7 and a selection of reasonably priced soups and salads. At dinner there are a number of entrees for under $15, including fish and chips, vegetarian lasagna and lemon-ginger chicken. Swizzle Inn has both indoor and balcony dining and, as the name implies, the island's most highly touted rum swizzles.

Bailey's Ice Cream Parlour, on Blue Hole Hill opposite the Swizzle Inn, has all-natural ice cream, frozen yogurt, sundaes, milkshakes and simple salads and sandwiches, all for under $5.

Visitors to *Crystal Caves* will find a little snack bar outside the entrance that sells inexpensive burgers and sandwiches.

South of Bailey's Bay *Tom Moore's Tavern* (☎ 293-4222), on secluded Walsingham Bay, is a perennial favorite for fine dining on the east side of the island. The restaurant occupies a historic waterfront house that dates back to 1652 and has several atmospheric dining rooms. The menu is predominantly French-influenced. Appetizers, such as escargots, seafood ceviche, frog legs or scallop mousse, are priced at around $16. Main courses, averaging $30, include island fish with pine nuts, roasted duck in raspberry sauce and standards like scampi and filet mignon. Tom Moore's Tavern is open nightly from 7 to 9:30 pm, and jackets are required. To get there, take Walsingham Rd off Harrington Sound Rd.

The Plantation (☎ 293-1188) on Harrington Sound Rd, about a mile south of Bailey's Bay, serves lunch daily from noon to 2:30 pm and dinner from 6:30 pm. The menu includes salads for around $7, pastas for $17 and local fish for $25. If you have lunch here, with a $10 minimum, you can get a free tour of the adjacent Leamington Caves, which have limestone formations similar to those at Crystal Caves. The restaurant is closed from December to mid-February.

The *Windsor Dining Room* (☎ 293-2040), off the lobby in Marriott's Castle Harbour Resort, is the hotel's main formal dining room. At dinner, served from 6:30 to 9 pm, there's a continental menu with soup, salads and appetizers from $5 to $10 and main dishes such as seafood pasta, catch of the day or veal piccata priced around $25. Jacket and tie are required at dinner. Breakfast, which is more casual, features a grand buffet spread for $15 – or go continental for just $10.50.

Also at the Marriott, the *Golf Club Grill* is a reasonably priced casual lunch restaurant with a hilltop view. It features burgers, salads and pizzas for between $10 to $15, while the hotel's *Mikado* has moderately expensive Japanese dinners, including a sushi bar and such standards as teppanyaki and tempura.

Getting Around
Both the northern (bus Nos 10 and 11) and southern (bus Nos 1 and 3) bus routes around Harrington Sound converge at Bailey's Bay, making the village easy to reach on any bus traveling between the City of Hamilton and the Town of St George. To get to the Castle Harbour Golf Club or the Marriott, take bus No 1, which goes into the resort.

Flatts Village

The village of Flatts, surrounding scenic Flatts Inlet, is home to the island's most visited attraction – the Bermuda Aquarium, Museum & Zoo.

In times past, Flatts had a reputation as a smugglers' haven, while Gibbet Island, the small islet off Flatts, was once used for the execution of islanders accused of witchcraft. Today, Flatts' yacht-filled harbor shows little trace of that more sordid past. The bridge that crosses over the inlet is a good vantage point for views of the harbor and of the rapidly moving tidal waters that rush through the inlet to and from Harrington Sound.

Witchcraft Hysteria
Bermuda was not immune from the witchcraft hysteria that swept Europe and America in the 17th century. The first death sentence given to a 'witch' in Bermuda was in 1651, when a woman accused of evil doings by her neighbors was given a 'trial' in which her feet and hands were tied and she was thrown in the ocean.

In the eyes of her fellow islanders, the fact that the woman managed to float and not drown confirmed that she was indeed a witch, and she was subsequently hanged. Bermudians continued searching for witches in their midst until the hysteria ended in the 1690s. ■

Information
There's a Bank of Butterfield ATM machine outside Four Star Pizza, to the right of the front door. The Flatts post office, which is on Middle Rd, is open Monday to Friday from 8 am to 5 pm.

Bermuda Aquarium, Museum & Zoo
This three-attraction site is under a single roof at the north side of Flatts. The aquarium dates to 1928, while the zoo and natural history museum were added in more recent times. All in all it's quite nicely presented and well worth a visit.

The high point of the complex is the **aquarium**, which contains 26 tanks, each arranged to show a microcosm of Bermuda's underwater ecosystem. The specimens represent more than 100 species of local fish, invertebrates and corals. The tanks, which have drawings and descriptions to identify their occupants, display many of the colorful tropicals you can expect to see while snorkeling or taking a glass-bottom boat cruise. These include bright wrasses, rainbow parrotfish, spotted pufferfish, trumpetfish, angelfish, tangs and damselfish. Be sure to pick up one of the 'Soundstiks' as you enter the room, which plays a recorded commentary as you approach the fish tanks.

There are also tanks with green sea turtles, loggerhead turtles and spiny lobsters. The largest tank displays Nassau groupers – once common in Bermuda's waters but now fished to commercial extinction – and a seven-foot-long green moray eel. An outdoor pool, between the aquarium and natural history museum, contains harbor seals. Incidentally, harbor seals are native to the New England and Canada coast and aren't found in Bermuda waters, but three of the seals were born here at the aquarium.

The **natural history museum** has simple displays on Bermuda's volcanic origins and other aspects of its geology, including dune and cave formations. There's also a presentation on whaling that includes harpoons, blubber spades and the skeleton of a pygmy sperm whale.

The **zoo** is small but interesting, with an aviary of parrots, macaws and other tropical birds, and a collection of primates such as golden lion tamarins and ring-tailed lemurs. There's an invertebrate house with a children's 'touch pool' and a reptile section containing alligators and Galápagos tortoises.

The Bermuda Zoo was the first to breed these giant turtles in captivity, so many of the tortoises you see here have offspring in North American and UK zoos. The zoo has

bred other endangered animals as well, most recently the nene, a Hawaiian goose, which can be seen in the aviary. The Bermuda Aquarium, Museum & Zoo is involved in other conservation efforts, including international sea turtle research, and your visit helps support their work, as do purchases from their well-stocked gift shop.

The Bermuda Aquarium, Museum & Zoo (☎ 293-2727) is open from 9 am to 5 pm daily, with the last entry allowed at 4:30 pm. Admission costs $6 for adults, $3 for children ages five to 12, free for children under five.

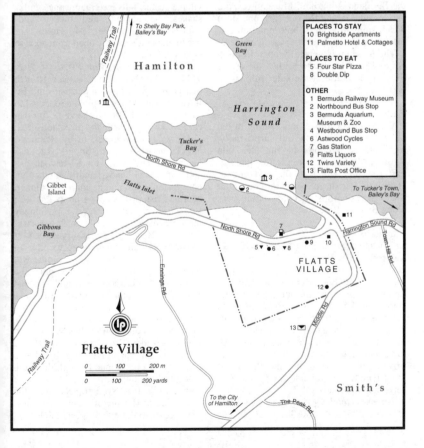

Bermuda Railway Museum

This little 'museum', in a building that once served as a railway station, has a collection of period photos and a few other items relating to Bermuda's railroad, but it's largely a curiosity shop with consignment antiques such as old bottles, china, jewelry and oil lamps. You can also buy a reprinted map ($5) that shows Bermuda's former rail routes and details the history of that rail system, which was built in the early 1930s and defunct by the mid-1940s.

The Bermuda Railway Museum is at 37 North Shore Rd, a 10-minute walk north of the Bermuda Aquarium, Museum & Zoo, but consider taking the bus (just one stop) which stops in front of both museums, as the road is narrow and without sidewalks.

The museum is generally open from 10 am to 4 pm Monday to Friday; the owner lives in the house at the side. Admission is free.

Railway Trail

If you're up for a hike, one section of the old railway trail starts, not surprisingly, right at the grounds of the Bermuda Railway Museum. You can follow it northeast for three miles to the east end of Hamilton Parish, passing the beach at Shelly Bay and other scenic coastal areas along Bailey's Bay.

Places to Stay

Brightside Apartments (☎ 292-8410, fax 295-6968), PO Box FL 319, Smith's FL BX, has a dozen units overlooking picturesque Flatts Inlet. Rates in this friendly, family-run place are the same year round, starting at $75 for a double room, $95 with cooking facilities. Fully equipped two-bedroom, two-bath units with kitchens cost $140 to $200 for up to four people. All have air-conditioning, ceiling fans and private baths. In the winter, monthly apartment rentals are available for $1500/2000 for singles/doubles.

Palmetto Hotel & Cottages (☎ 293-2323, fax 293-8761, ☎ 800-982-0026 in the USA), PO Box FL 54, Flatts FL BX, bordering Harrington Sound, has 42 rooms divided between the main building and a series of cottages. While the units vary, overall the accommodations are straightforward but pleasant. Many units have small balconies with water views and all have air-conditioning and private baths. Single/double rates begin at $91/128 in winter and $120/160 in summer, full breakfast included.

Places to Eat

The *Double Dip*, on North Shore Rd in the village center, sells ice cream cones, milkshakes, cheeseburgers and chicken sandwiches, all for under $4. Hours are irregular, but it's usually open from noon to at least 5:30 pm.

The nearby *Four Star Pizza* (☎ 292-9111), also on North Shore Rd, has 10-inch pizzas from $10, 14-inch pizzas from $16. It's open from 11 am (2 pm on Sundays) to 11 pm (midnight on weekends). You can eat in, take out or have the pizza delivered.

The Inlet Restaurant, in the Palmetto Hotel on Harrington Sound Rd, has lunchtime sandwiches for $7 to $10, fish and chips for $12 and a handful of other hot entrees for a few dollars more. At dinner, beef and fish dishes cost around $22. The best time to eat here, however, is on Sunday mornings between 8 and 11 am, when a traditional codfish breakfast is served for $11.

The most convenient place to pick up groceries is *Twins Variety* on Middle Rd, which is open from 8 am to 11:45 pm daily. You can get juice, beer, wine and spirits at *Flatts Liquors* in the village center.

Getting Around

From the City of Hamilton, bus No 3 goes to Flatts via Middle Rd, while bus Nos 10 and 11 run to Flatts via the North Shore Rd. Bus Nos 10 and 11 continue through the north side of Hamilton Parish along the north shore, while Bus No 3 travels along the south side of Harrington Sound. All three buses go on to Bailey's Bay and St George.

Smith's Parish

Smith's is the smallest of Bermuda's nine parishes, but it does lay claim to the highest point in Bermuda, a 259-foot hill which is somewhat amusingly called The Peak. This hill, on private property near the center of Smith's, is topped with a tower and visible from several points around the parish. The most scenic views in Smith's, however, are not found inland, but are from the shoreline; the parish is bordered on the north and south by the ocean and on the east by Harrington Sound.

While Smith's Parish is primarily residential, it does have a couple of notable sightseeing spots: the Verdmont historic house; a lovely public beach at John Smith's Bay; and Spittal Pond, Bermuda's finest nature reserve.

There are a couple of other green areas in Smith's that are set aside from development: the seven-acre Watch Hill Park near Albuoy's Point, just east of Spittal Pond on the south shore, and the 14-acre Penhurst Park, on the north shore. Watch Hill was once the site of a coastal fortification and has a nice water view, while Penhurst has a small dock and horse trails. Both are used by islanders for picnicking but are of limited interest to most visitors.

The village of Flatts also falls partially in Smith's, but because most of the village is in Hamilton Parish, all information on Flatts is grouped together in the Hamilton Parish chapter.

The population of Smith's Parish is 5261.

Verdmont Museum

Verdmont Museum, off Collectors Hill near its intersection with Sayle Rd, is the crown jewel of historic houses held by the Bermuda National Trust. The house, which enjoys a choice hilltop view, was built in 1710 in a four-squared early Georgian style. It was once the center of a 55-acre estate.

Although Verdmont was lived in until it was sold to the trust in 1951, its owners never significantly altered the property and continued to live without electricity and plumbing. Consequently, Verdmont retains its original character almost free of modifications.

Entering the house is a bit like stepping back in history. It has walls made of Georgia pine captured through privateering, a stairway of native Bermuda cedar and bare-wood floors. Portraits of former residents hang from the walls and finely crafted 17th-century furniture fills the rooms. While some of the items, including Spode pottery and Chinese porcelain, were imported by island traders, most of the furniture was locally made. So much cedar was used within the house that the air is still rich with the scent of the fragrant wood.

You'll notice there's no kitchen; the cottage outside the main house once served as the cookhouse – a fairly common practice in colonial times that provided a measure of insurance from accidental kitchen fires.

The well-versed trust volunteers that staff Verdmont enjoy providing insights on the property. Admission is $4 for adults, with discounts for seniors and students. It's open from 9:30 am to 4:30 pm from April to October and from 10 am to 4 pm the rest of the year. Verdmont is closed on Sundays, Mondays and holidays.

Spittal Pond Nature Reserve

The Spittal Pond Nature Reserve, encompassing some 60 acres, is the largest nature reserve in Bermuda. It centers around Spittal Pond, a nine-acre brackish pond that's the island's finest **birdwatching** venue, attracting scores of migratory shorebirds and waterfowl. Once a favored duck hunting locale, this property is now under the joint protection of the Bermuda National Trust and the government park system, both of which maintain a nature trail for birders and hikers.

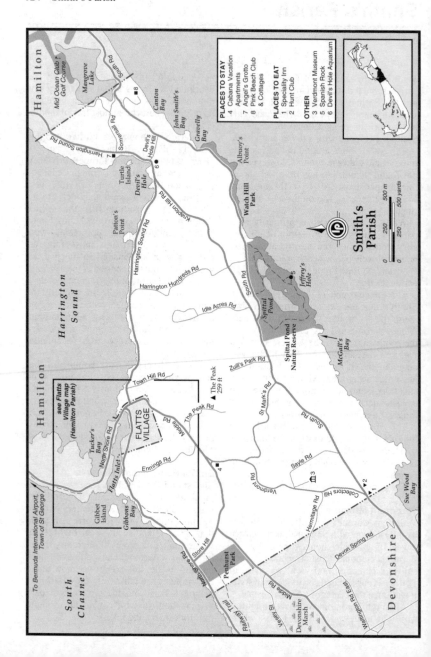

Smith's Parish

PLACES TO STAY
4 Cabana Vacation
  Apartments
7 Angel's Grotto
8 Pink Beach Club
  & Cottages

PLACES TO EAT
1 Speciality Inn
2 Hunt Club

OTHER
3 Verdmont Museum
5 Spanish Rock
6 Devil's Hole Aquarium

In tune with North American bird migration patterns, fall and winter offer the greatest variety of bird life. The earliest arrivals are the shorebirds, which begin making an appearance from August. The most abundant of the two dozen shorebird species that feed at the edge of Spittal Pond is the lesser yellowlegs, which is 10 inches long, has bright yellow legs and flashes a square white rump in flight. From the end of September, egrets and herons – including Louisiana herons, which have long slender necks and a wingspan of more than three feet – can be spotted at the pond. In October, migratory ducks and coots arrive in force.

Although many of the migrants winter over in Bermuda, others merely stop en route to and from the Caribbean, so spring also sees migratory stopovers. In the quieter summer months, Spittal Pond is the domain of resident mallards.

An inviting mile-long **nature trail** runs through the Spittal Pond reserve, passing a dairy farm, mixed woodlands, coastal viewpoints, salt marshes and ponds. There are trailheads at both the east and west sides of the property, with parking areas at each.

It's possible to walk the trail as a loop beginning from either side. As there's no trail along the northwest side of the pond, you'll have to walk a few minutes along South Rd at the end of the 'loop', but otherwise you'll be on a footpath the entire way.

You could of course also take the trail partway from either trailhead and then backtrack the same way. In that case, it's best to begin at the east end of the trail, as that's the most expedient route – just a few minutes walk – to Spittal Pond and the best birdwatching areas.

Along the Trail To walk the entire trail, starting at the west-side trailhead, take the middle route once you reach the cattle fence and continue on that path, which leads through a wooded area of mixed vegetation. You'll also find a few open areas here and elsewhere along the trail where prickly pear cactus thrives – the only cactus native to Bermuda.

Within 10 minutes, you'll reach a sign-posted coastal area that's called the **Checkerboard** because the limestone has weathered into an unusual square-crossed formation. Just after that, a cattle gate leads through the fence as the path continues along the south side of Spittal Pond. The trail passes through a forest of casuarina, an Australian tree that was widely planted throughout Bermuda in the 1950s to replace the groves of native cedars lost to cedar-scale infestation.

The trail then leads into a marshy area with sea lavender, salt grass and a small freshwater pond favored by mallards and teals. A right fork off the main trail makes a short detour to **Jeffrey's Hole**, a sea cave named for an escaped slave who is said to have stowed away there, and then continues to the site of **Spanish Rock**. The original rock, inscribed with the initials TF and the date 1543, is thought to have been carved by a stranded Spanish or Portuguese mariner.

From Spanish Rock, continue back to the main trail, which offers good birding vantages as it passes along the southeast side of Spittal Pond. After reaching the gate, you can either take a short side trail up to the east-side parking area or continue west along the northeast side of the pond until that trail leads into South Rd.

Devil's Hole Aquarium

Devil's Hole Aquarium, on Harrington Sound Rd at the east side of Smith's Parish, is not really an aquarium per se but rather a seawater-filled grotto connected to Harrington Sound by natural tunnels. For $5, visitors can look into the water from a wooden walkway and peer down at stocked sea turtles and tropical fish circling below. It closes in winter but at other times is open daily from 10 am to 4:30 pm, except holidays; a cafe serves sandwiches and ice cream.

John Smith's Bay

This pretty public beach, with its broad swath of white sands, faces east and offers sheltered waters good for swimming and

Sea anemones - like their relatives, the jellyfish - use graceful, waving tentacles to sting and hold their prey.

snorkeling. There are restroom facilities, as well as a lifeguard and a lunch wagon during the season.

The beach is right along the side of South Rd. If you pass by at 6 am, expect to see the members of Bermuda's 'Polar Bear Club' taking their daily morning dip here.

Activities

The best hiking and birdwatching is at Spittal Pond, detailed above. In addition, one section of the Railway Trail, which runs 1.75 miles from Devonshire Parish to the village of Flatts, passes through the north side of Smith's Parish.

For information on the local helmet diving operation, see the Outdoor Activities chapter at the front of the book.

Places to Stay

Cabana Vacation Apartments (☎ 236-6964, fax 236-1829), 61 Verdmont Rd, Smith's FL 02, in the interior off Middle Rd, is a period home that's been converted into seven units. Each has a kitchen, dining room, private bath, air-conditioning, ceiling fan and phone. The cost is $85/99 in winter/ summer for either singles or doubles. There's also a two-bedroom apartment that accommodates four for $152/178. Cabana has a free-form pool, and the bus stop is within walking distance.

Angel's Grotto (☎ 293-1986, fax 293-4164, ☎ 800-637-4116 in the USA, 800-267-7600 in Canada), PO Box HS 81, Smith's HS BX, is a neat little owner-operated complex right on Harrington Sound. It has seven air-conditioned units, each with kitchen, private bath, living room and phone. Winter/ summer prices go from $95/115 for a one-bedroom courtyard unit to $150/190 for a two-bedroom waterview apartment. There's a $30 charge per adult ($15 per child) for over two people. It's not in a village center, but it is on the bus route.

Pink Beach Club & Cottages (☎ 293-1666, fax 293-8935, ☎ 800-355-6161 in the USA and Canada), PO Box HM 1017, Hamilton HM DX, is an attractive complex on the quiet south shore. The 81 units are spread among 25 low-rise pink buildings, most of which face the coast and two sandy beaches. Each has air-conditioning, private bath, phone and patio. The common areas include two tennis courts, a pool, a fireplaced lounge and a seafront dining room. Rates begin at $185/295 in winter/summer for two with breakfast, $225/335 with breakfast and dinner.

For information on Palmetto Hotel and Brightside Apartments, both in Flatts Village, see the Hamilton Parish chapter.

Places to Eat

You'll find a grocery store and a couple of local restaurants on South Rd near its intersection with Collectors Hill.

The most popular of these restaurants is the *Speciality Inn*, which serves breakfast, lunch and dinner. Fish and chips, ribs and other straightforward dishes are under $10. It's open Monday to Saturday from 6 am to 10 pm.

The *Hunt Club*, 100 yards to the east along South Rd, has breakfast omelettes, sandwiches and lunch offerings for around $10 and dinners from $20 to $25.

Getting Around

Three main roads run west to east across Smith's Parish: North Shore Rd along the north coast, South Rd along the south coast and Middle Rd through the interior.

Buses that run between the City of Hamilton and the Town of St George cross Smith's on all three of these west-east roads. Bus No 1 takes South Rd, stopping at the Verdmont Museum, Spittal Pond Nature Reserve and John Smith's Bay. Bus No 3 takes Middle Rd to Flatts and then edges along the south shore of Harrington Sound. Bus Nos 10 and 11 operate along the North Shore Rd.

Devonshire Parish

In the center of the island, sandwiched between Pembroke, Paget and Smith's parishes, Devonshire is one of Bermuda's less-touristed areas, but it does have a few gardens and historic sights.

Up on North Shore Rd, the Bermuda National Trust maintains the early 18th-century **Palmetto House**, which was built in the shape of a cross. The house has a few rooms displaying period furnishings, but has very limited opening hours; call the Trust (☎ 236-6483) for information.

On North Shore Rd, west of Palmetto House, are two adjacent parks. The 17-acre **Palmetto Park** is a relatively large green space with water views that's popular with islanders as a picnicking spot. The tiny **Robinson Bay Park**, right at Robinson Bay, has a rocky and not terribly well-maintained beach.

South of Palmetto House is the **Devonshire Marsh** area, part of which is under the auspices of the Bermuda Audubon Society. Although the wet marsh is difficult to enter, there are birding possibilities along the narrow roads that border the marsh, particularly along Vesey St.

The **Old Devonshire Church**, at the intersection of Middle and Brighton Hill Rds, dates to 1716 but has been rebuilt a few times, most recently following an explosion in 1970. Still, it's a Devonshire landmark of sorts and has some 16th-century silver on display.

The population of Devonshire Parish is 7371.

Palm Grove Garden

This pleasant private garden, just off South Rd opposite Brighton Hill Rd, has lawns with statues, lots of flowering shrubs and trees, tropical plants, a moongate and a wishing well.

Up the hill, beyond cages of exotic parrots and toucans, is a unique reflecting pool that contains a map of Bermuda out-lined in concrete and given an element of relief with a cover of green turf.

The property is owned by one of Bermuda's more prominent families, the Gibbons, who open the garden to the public Monday to Thursday from 8 am to 5 pm. Admission is free.

Devonshire Bay Park

Just 300 yards east of the Palm Grove Garden is Devonshire Bay Rd, which leads south to Devonshire Bay Park. A three-minute walk from road's end takes you to the top of a casuarina-shaded hill. This was once the site of the Devonshire Bay Battery, built in the 1860s during the US Civil War, when tensions were high between the British and the Americans. Remnants of the battery, mainly some partial walls, can still be seen, but the main attraction these days is the fine hilltop coastal view and the crashing surf of the Atlantic below.

The park also has a little cove that's used primarily by fishermen to harbor their boats and clean fish.

Arboretum

This 20-acre property, occupying a valley at the corner of Middle and Montpelier Rds, was developed into an arboretum in the late 1950s, after being turned over to the island government by the British War Department.

The concept for the new arboretum was to gather a collection of trees and shrubs that were capable of flourishing in Bermuda. Specimens were brought in from countries as far flung as Japan, New Guinea and Canada, in addition to others presented by Queen Elizabeth II from the Royal Botanic Gardens in Kew. The trees include conifers, palms, fruit and nut trees, and such exotics as rubber trees and black ebony.

Managed by the Department of Agriculture, the Arboretum is not as developed or

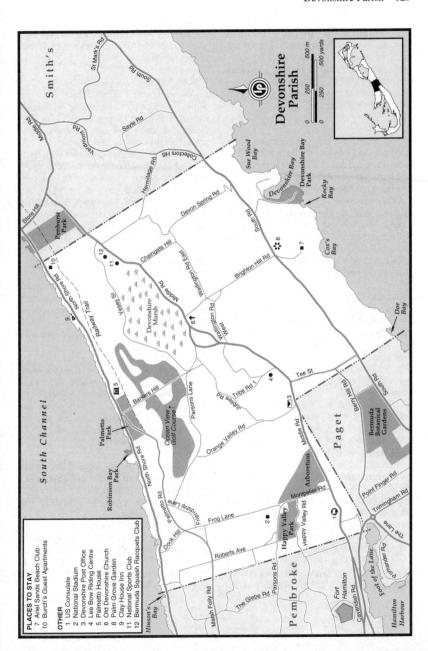

PLACES TO STAY
7 Ariel Sands Beach Club
10 Burch's Guest Apartments

OTHER
1 US Consulate
2 National Stadium
3 Devonshire Post Office
4 Lee Bow Riding Centre
5 Palmetto House
6 Old Devonshire Church
8 Palm Grove Garden
9 Clay House Inn
11 National Sports Club
12 Bermuda Squash Racquets Club

Devonshire Parish

500 m
500 yards

well utilized as the Bermuda Botanical Gardens in Paget. Nonetheless, it's a pleasant spot crossed by shaded walking paths and visitors are free to stroll the grounds any day between sunrise and sunset. There's a bus stop on Middle Rd directly in front of the Arboretum.

Activities

If you're up for a hike, one section of the Railway Trail starts at the back side of Palmetto Park and runs 1.75 miles to the village of Flatts, passing Palmetto House en route and taking in coastal and inland views.

Other recreation options in Devonshire include golf at the Ocean View Golf Course, horseback riding at Lee Bow Riding Centre and squash at the Bermuda Squash Racquets Club. More information is in the Outdoor Activities chapter at the front of the book.

Places to Stay

Burch's Guest Apartments (☎ 292-5746), 110 North Shore Rd, Devonshire FL 03, has 10 units with kitchenettes. While it's not central to restaurants and tourist facilities, there is a nearby bus stop. Singles/doubles cost $55/80, and there's an apartment for three people for $90. Rates are the same year round.

Ariel Sands Beach Club (☎ 236-1010, fax 236-0087, ☎ 800-468-6610 in the USA, 800-267-7000 in Canada), PO Box HM 334, Hamilton HM BX, on Devonshire's south shore, is a quiet hotel on a private white-sand beach. The 51 rooms, which are spread around the grounds in a dozen buildings, have private baths, air-conditioning and in most cases seaview verandas. Facilities include freshwater and saltwater pools, three tennis courts, a fireplaced guest lounge and a bar and restaurant. Some of the guestrooms, as well as the commons building with the restaurant and lounge, are wheelchair accessible. Rates are from $154/238 in winter/summer

for a double without meals; for another $50 you can add a MAP plan with breakfast and dinner for two.

Places to Eat

Caliban's at Ariel Sands Beach Club on South Rd has a pleasant setting, with both indoor and patio dining overlooking the beach. At lunch you can get reasonably priced soups, salads and sandwiches. A chicken breast and brie sandwich with fries or salad costs $10, and there are a couple of hot lunches such as pan-fried fish topped with bananas and almonds for $15. At dinner, appetizers like duck strudel or blackened beef carpaccio cost $9, while main dishes such as grilled salmon or chicken with risotto begin at $20.

Entertainment

The Clay House Inn (☎ 292-3193), 77 North Shore Rd, is the area's main music spot. It usually offers a nightly show that includes steel band and calypso music, as well as limbo dancing. It's open from April to November and has a $15 cover charge.

Spectator Sports

Devonshire is the site of the National Stadium, on Frog Lane, where Bermuda-wide and international sporting events are held, and the National Sports Club, on Middle Rd, where rugby clubs compete on weekends from September to April.

Getting Around

Devonshire Parish is crossed by three main roads that run west to east: South Rd along the south coast, North Shore Rd along the north coast and Middle Rd through the interior.

Buses that run between the City of Hamilton and the Town of St George cross Devonshire on all three of these west-east roads. Bus No 1 operates along South Rd, bus No 3 along Middle Rd and bus Nos 10 and 11 along the North Shore Rd.

Paget Parish

Paget is one of the more popular parishes for visitors, not only due to its proximity to the City of Hamilton but also because of Elbow Beach, the first of a string of sandy beaches that extends along Bermuda's southwest shore. The parish also has an appealing botanical gardens that shouldn't be missed.

Paget has a good variety of accommodations, ranging from moderately priced guesthouses to expensive resort hotels.

There are two main visitor areas. Most accommodations are centered between Elbow Beach and Paget village, the tiny commercial center at the intersection of Middle and South Rds.

While the parish's south shore attracts the beachgoers, the north side, along Hamilton Harbour, is suited for those looking to get away from the tourist crowd. The north shore's Salt Kettle area, a quiet established neighborhood of older homes and well-to-do families, has a handful of small hotels with picturesque views across the harbor to the City of Hamilton.

The parish population is 4877.

Information

Money Rural Hill Plaza on South Rd, about 200 yards east of Middle Rd, has a 24-hour ATM that accepts MasterCard, Visa and Cirrus and Plus bank cards.

Post The Paget post office, on Middle Rd near its intersection with South Rd, is open Monday to Friday from 8 am to 5 pm.

Medical Services King Edward VII Memorial Hospital (☎ 911 for emergencies, 236-2345 for nonemergencies), Bermuda's general hospital, is on Point Finger Rd just south of Berry Hill Rd.

Paget Pharmacy, in the Rural Hill Plaza on South Rd, is open Monday through Saturday from 8 am to 8 pm, Sundays from 2 to 6 pm.

Bermuda Botanical Gardens

The 36-acre Bermuda Botanical Gardens, which is bordered by South Rd and Berry Hill Rd, is the finest place on Bermuda for enjoying and identifying the island's varied flora. Originally opened in 1898, these delightful gardens encompass everything from formal plantings of roses and perennials to lofty trees and an aviary.

If you enter from the main gate on Berry Hill Rd, you'll immediately pass a cacti collection that features native prickly pear cactus, as well as aloes and other succulents that tolerate Bermuda's humid climate. Opposite the cacti collection is a section of conifer trees – both subtropical and temperate varieties thrive here.

Just 100 yards south of the gate is the visitor center, open daily from 10 am to 4 pm, which shows a 30-minute video of Bermuda and distributes a free brochure with a garden map and site descriptions. It also has a gift shop that sells souvenirs, books, drinks and snacks.

Some of the highlights include a palm garden with native palmetto trees, a subtropical fruit garden, a garden for the blind that features scented plants, a plumeria collection, a section of endemic and native plants, a ficus collection with rubber and banyan trees and a flowering hibiscus garden. There's also an orchard area with large fruit trees, including mangos, soursops and Bermuda's oldest avocado tree. In addition, there are greenhouses with orchids, bromeliads and a variety of flowering houseplants.

All in all, it's a delightful place to stroll. Because the plants are labeled, you can see and identify much of what the gardens have to offer on your own. However, if you want more insights into the gardens, the visitor center offers guided tours on Tuesdays, Wednesdays and Fridays at 10:30 am. Call the center (☎ 236-5291) for more information.

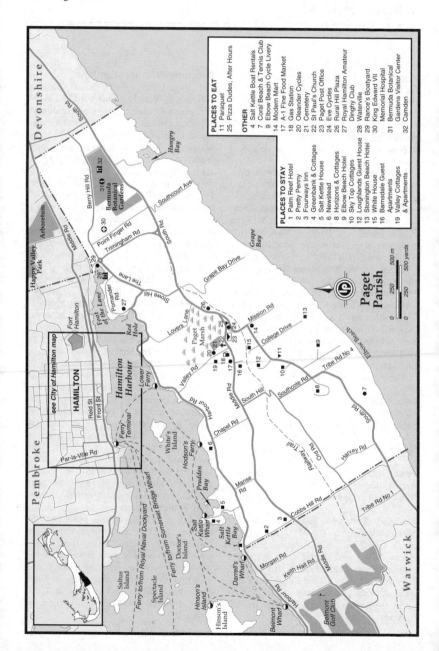

Paget Parish

PLACES TO STAY
1 Palm Reef Hotel
2 Pretty Penny
3 Fourways Inn
4 Greenbank & Cottages
5 Salt Kettle House
6 Newstead
8 Horizons & Cottages
9 Elbow Beach Hotel
10 Sky Top Cottages
12 Loughlands Guest House
13 Stonington Beach Hotel
15 White House
16 Barnsdale Guest Apartments
19 Valley Cottages & Apartments

PLACES TO EAT
11 Paraquet
25 Pizza Dudes, After Hours

OTHER
4 Salt Kettle Boat Rentals
7 Coral Beach & Tennis Club
9 Elbow Beach Cycle Livery
14 Modem Mart
17 A-1 Fine Food Market
18 Gas Station
20 Oleander Cycles
21 Cemetery
22 St Paul's Church
23 Paget Post Office
24 Eve Cycles
26 Rural Hill Plaza
27 Royal Hamilton Amateur Dinghy Club
28 Waterville
29 Rance's Boatyard
30 King Edward VII Memorial Hospital
31 Bermuda Botanical Gardens Visitor Center
32 Camden

Double Fantasy

In 1980, while John Lennon was in Bermuda working on compositions for an upcoming album, he took a break to stroll through the Bermuda Botanical Gardens. Here he spotted a beautiful freesia in bloom and bent down to take a closer look. The flower was labeled 'Double Fantasy'. When Lennon stood up, he reportedly smiled and jotted down the flower's name – he had found the perfect title for his new album.

'Double Fantasy', Lennon's last album, was released in 1980. After the story broke, Lennon fans made efforts to seek out the little flower, and for years the botanical gardens' staff stayed busy replacing the flower's identifying label, which kept disappearing.

The park eventually decided to deal with the souvenir issue by printing T-shirts with an attractive 'Double Fantasy' flower design and stocking them in the visitor center gift shop. ∎

If you're taking a bus, the easiest way to get into the heart of the gardens is to get off at the hospital on Point Finger Rd. The path south of the hospital leads right into the gardens. The gardens are open daily year round from sunrise to sunset.

Camden

Camden, the official residence of Bermuda's premier, is located at the northeast corner of the Bermuda Botanical Gardens. This graceful plantation house was built in the early 1700s, though its front verandas and bow windows were added in the 19th century. In 1823, the house was bought by the Tuckers, one of Bermuda's most prestigious families. One of the occupants was Henry James Tucker, who served as the mayor of Hamilton from 1851 to 1870 and started an arrowroot factory on the property.

In more recent times, Camden was turned over to the Bermuda government to be incorporated into the botanical gardens. The house was restored in the 1970s and set aside for the premier, although in actuality it is not used as a living quarters but rather for official receptions.

The house has an informal yet gracious interior that reflects its history, with period cedar furniture, a Waterford crystal chandelier, gilt mirrors, the portraits of former premiers, porcelain plates decorated with Bermuda flora and the like.

You don't have to wait for a formal invitation to peek inside – just stop by on Tuesday or Friday between noon and 2 pm, when Camden opens its doors to the general public. Admission is free.

Waterville

Dating to the early 1700s, Waterville is one of the oldest buildings in Bermuda; quite suitably, it's the headquarters for the Bermuda National Trust. In addition to housing the trust's administrative offices, Waterville contains two rooms of period furnishings, including a Jamaican mahogany sideboard, antique Staffordshire figurines and portraits of the Trimingham family, who owned the two-story house for more than two centuries. There's a noteworthy rose garden at the side of the building and a 300-year-old tamarind tree out front. Waterville is open Monday to Friday from 9 am to 5 pm. There's no admission charge.

Also on the property is Trustworthy, the trust's gift shop, which sells books and pamphlets on trust properties, as well as

Arrowroot

The rhizomes of the arrowroot plant *(Maranta arundinacea)* yield a nutritious, easily digestible starch that can be used as a thickener in gravies, puddings and other dishes. In modern times, less-expensive cornstarch has largely replaced the use of arrowroot in the kitchen, but in days past, arrowroot was one of Bermuda's major exports.

There were two main arrowroot factories on Bermuda, one of them started by Henry James Tucker, the mayor of Hamilton in the mid-19th century. Tucker lived in Camden, a plantation house at the current Bermuda Botanical Gardens, and the arrowroot factory – where the starch was soaked from the plants and dried in the sun – was built in back of the house. The arrowroot starch exported by the Tuckers was well-regarded in both England and America for its high quality.

Although arrowroot starch is no longer produced in Bermuda, Tucker's arrowroot factory still remains – these days it harbors a collection of endemic and native ferns and is one of the sights that visitors can take in at the botanical gardens. ■

gift items. Waterville is at the head of Hamilton Harbour, on The Lane just west of the roundabout.

Paget Marsh

Paget Marsh, a 25-acre wetland nature reserve, is bordered on the south by South Rd and on the west by Valley Rd. Despite having the appearance of an inhospitable overgrown swamp, it is one of the least-disturbed natural areas in Bermuda and contains the last virgin forest of two endemic trees, the Bermuda palmetto and the Bermuda cedar. In addition, Paget Marsh holds the full range of Bermudian marsh habitat, including a mangrove swamp. The area has survived intact not only because the spongy ground has deterred human use, but also because most exotic flora has been unable to take root in this wet, acidic ecosystem.

It is possible to enter the marsh. The main entrance is from the cemetery behind St Paul's Church, where steps lead to a trail. However, damp and overgrown trail conditions as well as widespread poison ivy deter most visitors. Those who do go in should be careful not to stray from the trails, as rare ferns and other flora could be trampled.

The property is owned jointly by the Bermuda National Trust and the Bermuda Audubon Society. You can get views into Paget Marsh from Valley Rd, as well as from South Rd and the Railway Trail.

Elbow Beach

Elbow Beach, which extends for more than half a mile, is a lovely beach of soft beige sands. The Elbow Beach Hotel sits at the east end of the beach and claims that section for its guests, but the rest of the beach is public and can be accessed from Tribe Rd No 4, which begins at a sharp curve on South Rd, west of the Elbow Beach Hotel.

Being the closest noteworthy beach to Hamilton, Elbow Beach attracts a crowd of locals and visitors alike. Not only is it a popular swimming and sunbathing locale, but it's a good beach for strolling as well. The west side of the beach is backed by limestone cliffs that provide habitat for sea-grape trees and birds.

The public beach has a daytime lunch wagon (see Places to Eat) and free showers and toilets. Should you prefer to hang out in front of the Elbow Beach Hotel, non-guests are allowed to use the beach and facilities there for a $3 fee.

Activities

Sailboats and motorboats can be rented at Rance's Boatyard at the head of Hamilton Harbour and at Salt Kettle Boat Rentals at the west end of the parish. Salt Kettle Boat Rentals also arranges snorkeling excursions.

There are tennis courts open to the public at Elbow Beach Hotel, Horizons, Newstead, Palm Reef Hotel and Stonington

Beach Hotel. The tennis and squash courts at the private Coral Beach & Tennis Club are open only to members or by introduction from a member.

For long walks, there's a two-mile section of the Railway Trail that crosses Paget. Going from west to east, the Railway Trail runs between Middle Rd and South Rd until Paget village and from there continues south of South Rd. Along the trail you'll get glimpses of old Bermudian estates, Paget Marsh and vegetable gardens where carrots and cabbages grow.

More detailed information on these activities is in the Outdoor Activities chapter near the front of the book.

Places to Stay

South Shore If you want to be near the beach, there are two resort hotels right on Elbow Beach, while most of the other south shore accommodations listed below are a 10- to 15-minute walk away.

Loughlands Guest House (☎ 236-1253), 79 South Rd, Paget PG 03, is a classic old guesthouse between Elbow Beach and Paget village. Most of the 25 rooms are in the main building, a Bermudian estate house with columned porches that look out upon acres of green lawn. The common areas are furnished with antiques. Guestrooms, which are sufficient if perhaps a bit tired, have private baths, coffeemakers, radios and air-conditioning. A continental breakfast, with cereal and pastries, is included in the rate of $58/75 for singles/doubles in winter, $75/118 in summer. There's a pool and tennis courts.

Sky Top Cottages (☎ 236-7984), PO Box PG 227, Paget PG BX, has a lot of appeal with its quiet hilltop location, well-maintained accommodations, friendly management and reasonable rates. The 11 units have English-style cottage decor, private baths and cooking facilities. The cheapest is a small bedroom with a mini-refrigerator, toaster oven and coffee pot that costs $75/95 in winter/summer. Comfortable studio cottages with full kitchens cost $85/115 and spacious apartments,

which have separate living rooms and kitchens, cost $95/125. In winter there are also weekly and monthly rates available. It's a five-minute walk from the bus stop, grocery store and Elbow Beach.

Barnsdale Guest Apartments (☎ 236-0164, fax 236-4709), PO Box DV 628, Devonshire DV BX, is in the village of Paget on the corner of Middle Rd and Barnes Valley Rd. This is an attractive, well-maintained complex with seven studio apartments. Two units have twin beds, the rest have queen beds; all have TVs, phones, full kitchens and private baths. It's close to bus routes, a grocery store and two cycle-rental shops, and there's a pool on site. Popular with repeat guests, winter rates are $60/80 for singles/doubles, while summer rates are $100/120. It can be a good value if you're staying awhile, as the seventh night is free in summer, while in winter every fifth night is free.

Valley Cottages & Apartments (☎ 236-0628, fax 236-3895), PO Box PG 214, Paget PG BX, is a little apartment complex off Valley Rd, just north of Middle Rd in the village of Paget. There are nine air-conditioned units, each with a phone and cooking facilities. TVs can be rented for $2 a day. Studio rooms start at a reasonable $65/70 in winter/summer for singles, $73/80 for doubles. One- and two-bedroom cottages with separate living rooms cost $90/110 in winter/summer for two people; add $37 for each additional person.

The *White House* (☎ /fax 236-4957), 6 Southlyn Lane, Paget PG 03, is a bed and breakfast run by Odette and André Rémond, who were born in France but have lived in Bermuda for 40 years. Located just north of South Rd, this two-story house has three simple but pleasant guestrooms, each with a private bath and either two twins or one double bed. There's a nice little pool. Singles cost $60/80 in winter/summer, doubles cost $80/100, including taxes, a service charge and a continental breakfast.

Stonington Beach Hotel (☎ 236-5416, 800-447-7462 in the USA and Canada), PO Box HM 523, Hamilton HM CX, is a

64-room resort hotel at the east end of Elbow Beach. The rooms are contemporary with 1st-class amenities, including ceiling fan, cable TV, small refrigerator, phone, two twin beds or one king and a sofabed. All rooms have ocean views. The hotel has a heated pool and tennis courts. Because it's run by students from the local college as part of the hospitality and culinary program, the service is quite attentive – but then rates are steep, starting at $148/168 for singles/doubles in winter, $285/305 in summer. Full breakfast and afternoon tea are included, and a dinner plan can be added at additional cost.

Horizons & Cottages (☎ 236-0048, fax 236-1981, ☎ 800-468-0022 in the USA), 33 South Rd, PO Box PG 198, Paget PG BX, is an upmarket cottage colony on a peaceful 25-acre estate. Nine guestrooms are in the atmospheric main house, while the other 41 are in 13 attractive cottages spread around the grounds. Each cottage has a maximum of five bedrooms, and most have a fireplaced sitting room for common use by the guests. All rooms have private baths and pleasant decor; many have nice hilltop views. Rates for doubles, which include breakfast and dinner, are from $230 in winter, $300 in summer. It's $50 less with dinner omitted, but that's not recommended as Horizons has a superb restaurant as well as two good sister restaurants – Newstead and Waterloo – where guests can dine on the meal plan. There's a heated pool, a nine-hole golf course and tennis courts. Elbow Beach is about a five-minute walk away. The hotel is a member of the Relais et Chateaux chain.

Elbow Beach Hotel (☎ 236-3535, fax 236-8043, ☎ 800-344-3526 in the USA), PO Box HM 455, Hamilton HM BX, is an old-fashioned resort with a prime location on Elbow Beach. Although the hotel dates to 1908, many of the buildings scattered around the grounds are more recent additions. There are 295 rooms and cottages in all. Facilities include a small health club, a large free-form heated pool, tennis courts, a pub and a couple of waterview restaurants.

Rooms are comfortable, if understated, with one king or two twin beds, a desk, a phone and an armoire with cable TV. Early risers are treated to complimentary juice, coffee, tea and pastry, complete with a fax of the day's *New York Times*, and there's complimentary afternoon tea. Rates without breakfast begin at $135 in winter for singles or doubles. In summer, rates include breakfast and begin at $250/280 for singles/doubles. It's a member of the Rafael chain.

North Shore *Salt Kettle House* (☎ 236-0407, fax 236-8639), 10 Salt Kettle Rd, Paget PG 01, is a comfortable, friendly and refreshingly informal 11-room guesthouse right on the water between Prudden and Salt Kettle bays. Rooms vary, but all have private baths, access to kitchen facilities and interesting nooks and crannies. Rooms in the cottages, which are apartment-like in layout, cost $50 per person, with a minimum of two guests; the largest can accommodate four people. Rooms in the historic main house, including a 'tower room' with water views in both directions, cost $85/92 for singles/doubles. A full breakfast is included; in winter, owner Hazel Lowe offers guests slight discounts. The Salt Kettle ferry stop is just a few minutes' walk away.

Pretty Penny (☎ 236-1194, fax 236-1662, ☎ 800-637-4116 in the USA, 800-267-7600 in Canada), PO Box PG 137, Paget PG BX, is a pleasant little apartment complex on Cobbs Hill Rd, 300 yards south of Darrell's Wharf. There are seven air-conditioned studio units, all with combined bedroom and living room areas, private baths, patios and kitchenettes that include stove tops (no ovens) and small refrigerators. Rates for up to two people are $90/125 in winter/summer. The complex has a pool. Although it's in the midst of a residential area, it's within walking distance of a Middle Rd bus stop as well as the ferry.

Greenbank & Cottages (☎ 236-3615, fax 236-2427, ☎ 800-637-4116 in the USA, 800-267-7600 in Canada), PO Box PG 201,

Paget PG BX, is comprised of an old Bermuda home and a handful of waterside cottages. All of the 11 units have air-conditioning and phones; nine have kitchens and most have water views. Each is different, but all are quite pleasant for the money. Rates in summer are $95 for a double room with continental breakfast and from $110 to $125 for the cottages with kitchens (no breakfast). There are also a couple of units that can accommodate four people for $200. Rates are about 20% lower in winter. A private dock and boat rentals are available; the Salt Kettle ferry dock is a minute's walk away.

Palm Reef Hotel (☎ 236-1000, fax 236-6392, ☎ 800-221-1294 in the USA and Canada), PO Box HM 1189, Hamilton HM EX, is a moderately priced 60-unit hotel on the water adjacent to Darrell's Wharf, at the Paget/Warwick parish line. All rooms have air-conditioning, phones and private baths; TVs can be rented for $6. Standard rooms have land views and cost $96/124 for doubles in winter/summer; moderate rooms, which are a bit bigger and have partial ocean views, cost $106/150; and deluxe rooms, which have the addition of a harborview balcony, cost $116/190. Singles cost $20 to $30 less. These rates are without meals; breakfast can be added for $12 per person and dinner plans are also available. The hotel has a saltwater pool and a waterfront restaurant. Palm Reef closes each year for the month of December.

Fourways Inn (☎ 236-6517, fax 236-5528, ☎ 800-962-7654 in the USA), PO Box PG 294, Paget PG BX, has 10 contemporary rooms and suites in a handful of poolside buildings behind the exclusive Fourways restaurant at the intersection of Middle and Cobbs Hill Rds. All units have a king-size bed, cable TV, minibar, phone, small kitchenette and little extras like bathrobes and fresh cut flowers. The suites have a spacious living room with a queen sofabed as well. In winter, doubles cost $140 for rooms and $180 for suites, while in summer the rooms/suites cost $230/325. Singles are $30 cheaper in both seasons. A continental breakfast of bread and pastries from the inn's bakery is included in the rates.

Newstead (☎ 236-6060, fax 236-7454, ☎ 800-468-4111 in the USA, 800-236-2451 in Canada), PO Box PG 196, Paget PG BX, is a small waterfront hotel centered around an old manor house. It has manicured grounds, a little putting green on the front lawn, inviting sitting rooms with Victorian furnishings, a library and lovely harbor views. Some of the 52 rooms are in the main house but most are in a handful of separate buildings. While the decor varies, all rooms have air-conditioning and phones, and some have cable TV. Newstead has a sizable following of return guests, particularly among retirees. There's a pool and tennis court. The public ferry docks beside the hotel, making it easy to get to Hamilton. Year-round rates begin at $160/216 for singles/doubles, breakfast included. Add another $25 per person for dinner, which allows you to eat here or at the well-regarded sister restaurants, Waterloo and Horizons.

Places to Eat

The *Modern Mart*, a midsize grocery store at 104 South Rd, has wine and produce sections and a deli that sells baked chicken and other takeout foods. It's open Monday to Saturday from 8 am to 8:30 pm. There's another grocery store, the *A-1 Fine Food Market*, on Middle Rd near its intersection with Valley Rd.

Pizza Dudes (☎ 232-3833), at the intersection of South and Middle Rds, has reasonable takeout food. There are four pizza sizes, from $10 for a 10-inch cheese to $20 for an 18-inch, plus optional toppings. A tasty chicken or lamb gyro in pita bread costs $5 and there are a dozen varieties of sub sandwiches for a few dollars more. It's open from 5 to 10 pm Monday to Thursday, from 11 am to 1 am on Fridays and Saturdays and from noon to 10 pm on Sundays. Best of all, they deliver.

If you don't want take out, *After Hours*, an unpretentious place next to Pizza Dudes at 117 South Rd, has pizza as well as West

Indian items, including chicken or lamb roti sandwiches for $8 and curry dishes with meat, vegetables, rice and mango chutney for $10. It also has breakfast fare at similar prices, though it's open at night only, from 6:30 pm to 12:30 am (to 4 am in summer) daily, except on Sundays.

Ice Queen, next to Paget Pharmacy in the Rural Hill Plaza on South Rd, has ice cream, hot dogs, burgers and sandwiches for around $3. It's open daily from 10 am to 5 am and is a popular place to stop in the wee hours after the bars close.

Dinty's Lunch Wagon parks along Elbow Beach, at the end of Tribe Rd No 4, from 10 am to 7 pm daily in summer only. Beach-goers can buy soft drinks as well as inexpensive hot dogs, fish cakes and burgers.

Paraquet (☎ 236-9742) on South Rd, a few minutes' walk northeast of the Elbow Beach Hotel, is a local diner with straight-forward food, open daily from 9:30 am to 1 am. Until 11 am, you can get pancakes, French toast or eggs with bacon for $7, juice and coffee included. At other times, there are sandwiches, soups and chowder for under $5 and various fish dishes for $10 to $18. There's a dining room, but you'll strike up the best conversations by sitting at the counter and rubbing elbows with the locals.

Cafe Lido (☎ 236-9884) at the Elbow Beach Hotel is a pleasant beachside restaurant with tempting Mediterranean food, generous portions and attentive service – certainly a good choice for a night of fine dining. The shrimp and mango cocktail ($14) is a tasty appetizer, as is the grilled vegetables with roasted garlic and goat cheese ($12). Pastas, such as penne with smoked salmon or angel hair with blackened shrimp, cost $13 as an appetizer and around $20 as a main course. Other main dishes include local fish, rack of lamb and braised duck, each about $27. Dinner is from 6:30 to 10 pm. When making reservations, request one of the waterview tables. Cafe Lido is also open for lunch from noon to 2:45 pm, with salads, sandwiches and pastas for under $15.

Ondine's (☎ 236-3535), the main dining room at the Elbow Beach Hotel, has a decent breakfast buffet (from 7:30 to 10:30 am) of fresh fruits, pastries, omelettes to order etc, although it's a bit pricey at $15. The Sunday brunch, however, is an exceptional affair, with jumbo shrimp, smoked salmon, steamship round of beef, hot dishes, a dozen salads and a luscious dessert table with fruits, cakes, pies and tarts. It costs $25, including a glass of wine, and is served from noon to 2 pm. At dinner, nightly from 6:30 to 9:30 pm, there are pastas from $20 and chicken, fish and red-meat dishes for around $25.

Horizons (☎ 236-0048), at 33 South Rd, is an appealing fine-dining option with a traditional Bermudian setting, a hilltop ocean view and good service and food. The fixed-price ($48), five-course menu changes daily but maintains a distinctively French accent. You can generally choose from two soups, three starters and five main dishes, with offerings such as ginger-poached salmon or duck breast on polenta. Coffee and dessert are included. There's an extensive wine list.

Newstead (☎ 236-6060), 27 Harbour Rd, has good food and fine harbor views from both its regular dining room and its seasonal patio. From 8 to 10 am, you can get a continental breakfast for $7.50 and various full breakfast plates for double that. From 12:30 to 4 pm, there are sandwiches priced around $10. Dinner, from 7:30 to 9 pm, features a five-course, fixed-price menu ($45) that includes a selection of appetizers and main dishes such as grilled local fish or duck with cherry rum sauce. In summer there's a barbecue on Tuesday and Thursday evenings when dress is casual; at other times a jacket and tie are requested for dinner.

Fourways Inn (☎ 236-6517), 1 Middle Rd, at the Warwick Parish line, is one of Bermuda's most highly regarded fine-dining spots. This highbrow restaurant, which occupies a 1727 manor house, boasts haute cuisine and a formal setting. There are various dining rooms, as well as an outdoor courtyard with tables set around a water fountain. Lunch, from noon to 3 pm Monday to Saturday, is affordable, with sandwiches under $10, a spinach and goat cheese salad for $12 and hot dishes for a few dollars more. On Sundays from 11:30 am to 2:30 pm, there's a popular $30 barbecue with soups, salads, chicken, roast beef, fish, desserts and a 'complimentary' rum swizzle. At dinner, from 6:30 to 9:30 pm, the menu is more elaborate – starters such as lobster terrine or salmon tartare cost around $20 and main dishes are around $30 for vegetarian offerings and $40 for steak, venison and lamb. There's a pianist nightly.

Fourways Inn also has a shop out back where you can get fine pastries for takeout.

Getting Around
Paget Parish is crossed from west to east by three main roads: Harbour Rd along the north shore, Middle Rd in the central area and South Rd along the south shore.

Bus & Ferry There's no bus service along Harbour Rd, but that area is connected to the City of Hamilton by public ferry and sections of it are within walking distance of Middle Rd bus stops.

The two main bus routes are No 8, which runs from Hamilton to the Royal Naval Dockyard via Middle Rd, and bus No 7, which runs a similar route via South Rd. Bus No 7 is the one to take to get to Elbow Beach.

If you're coming from the City of Hamilton, you can take bus No 1, 2 or 7 to get to the hospital or botanical gardens. Bus Nos 2, 7 and 8 stop at Paget village.

There are ferry terminals at Hodson's Ferry, near the Newstead hotel; at Salt Kettle Wharf, in the midst of the Salt Kettle area; and nearby at Darrell's Wharf, at the Paget/Warwick parish line.

Moped & Bicycle Mopeds and bicycles can be rented at the Elbow Beach Cycle Livery (☎ 236-3535) at the Elbow Beach Hotel. Mopeds can also be rented in the village of Paget at Eve Cycles on Middle Rd and Oleander Cycles on Village Rd.

Warwick Parish

Warwick is the second most populated parish in Bermuda, with 7900 inhabitants.

The parish's central village, on Middle Rd, has a quaint period church and a wetland nature preserve, but for most people the highlight of a visit to Warwick is found along the south shore, which boasts some of Bermuda's loveliest pink-sand beaches. Collectively, they offer beachgoers a splendid range of options, from the quiet little coves found at Astwood Park, Jobson Cove and Chaplin Bay to the long, straight stretch of open shoreline at Warwick Long Bay.

While you don't need to stay in Warwick to use the beaches, which are conveniently on the South Rd bus route, Warwick would make a good base for those who want to be on the water. Warwick has no large seaside resorts but rather a nice collection of smaller guesthouse and apartment-style places – some a mere stone's throw from the beach. Restaurant choices in the parish are limited, but most Warwick accommodations are equipped with kitchens.

Information

The Warwick post office on Middle Rd is open Monday to Friday from 8 am to 5 pm.

There's a laundrette on Middle Rd, west of Hayward's Grocery in the village center.

Astwood Park

This 23-acre park has panoramic ocean views, an inviting little sandy cove and a grassy picnic area on a coastal knoll. Because of its scenic nature, the park is one of the most popular spots on Bermuda for outdoor weddings.

Astwood had once been earmarked as the site of a large new resort. To make room for the new development, South Rd, which dipped down to the coast here, had to first be rerouted north. After the road work was completed, islanders began to have second thoughts about the desirability of another

resort and in 1984 the government negotiated the purchase of the property, for $2.2 million, from the would-be developers. Today, instead of leading visitors down to a mega-hotel, the faded asphalt of the old South Rd is the entryway into a national park.

The park is well-utilized by both visitors and islanders. The beach is small, but the swimming is good and the nearshore rocks and reef provide snorkeling options. The cliffs at the east side of the park are a favorite area for local shore fishers. In spring and fall, migratory birds can be seen among the stand of casuarina trees inland of the cliffs, as well as at the west extent of the park, where native palmetto trees and Bermuda cedars have been planted.

Astwood Park has toilets and moped parking; the entrance to the park is just west of Tribe Rd No 3.

Warwick Long Bay

Warwick Long Bay, which forms the eastern extent of South Shore Park, is a splendid beach of pink and white coral sands that extends unbroken for half a mile, making it a fine choice for those who enjoy long beach strolls. Also, because it's open to the ocean, it often has more surf action than the rest of South Shore Park and can be a good place for bodysurfing.

There are a couple of entrances. If you enter at the east side of Warwick Long Bay, you'll find several short footpaths that lead from the parking area down to the beach.

Best, however, is the entrance at the west end of Warwick Long Bay, as the walkway from the parking lot leads to a rocky outcropping that separates the expansive beach from a run of secluded coves and bays to the west. This gives you a nice variety of tempting beach options.

Jobson Cove, which is just minutes from the westside parking lot, is the smallest of the coves and has a tiny white-sand beach that's nearly encircled by shoreline

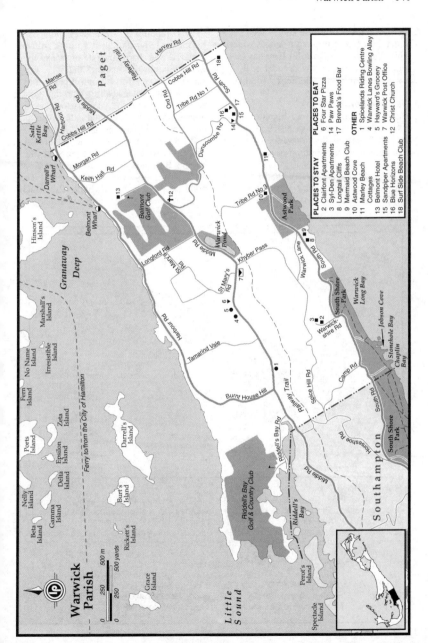

Warwick Parish

PLACES TO STAY
2 Clairfont Apartments
3 Syl-Den Apartments
8 Longtail Cliffs
9 Mermaid Beach Club
10 Astwood Cove
11 Marley Beach
    Cottages
13 Belmont Hotel
15 Sandpiper Apartments
16 Blue Horizons
18 Surf Side Beach Club

PLACES TO EAT
6 Four Star Pizza
14 Paw Paws
17 Brenda's Food Bar

OTHER
1 Spicelands Riding Centre
4 Warwick Lanes Bowling Alley
5 Hayward's Grocery
7 Warwick Post Office
12 Christ Church

rocks. Next is **Stonehole Bay**, which has a wider beach and bright turquoise waters, while the adjacent **Chaplin Bay** has inviting double coves and is broader still. All are connected to one another by footpaths.

Warwick Pond

Warwick Pond, in the parish center about 100 yards east of the post office, is one of the best places on this side of the island for spotting migratory shorebirds and wintering teal.

Once part of a network of shallow ponds and marshes that extended east to Spittal Pond, Warwick Pond is now one of the largest remaining freshwater ponds in Bermuda. Even though it's in the village center, it was spared the fate of many other wetland ponds and marshes that were long ago filled in an effort to control pesky mosquitoes. The water level in Warwick Pond varies throughout the year, as the pond is reliant upon rainwater, and extensive mud flats form during dry spells.

Because of its environmental significance, Warwick Pond was acquired in 1988 by the Bermuda National Trust and set aside as a nine-acre nature preserve. The pond can be seen from Middle Rd, which forms the preserve's northern boundary.

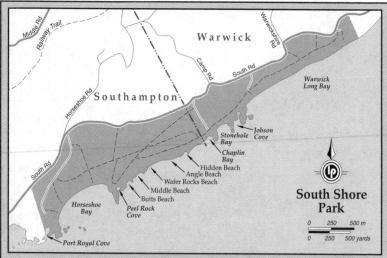

South Shore Park

South Shore Park is a 1½-mile-long coastal park that encompasses some of Bermuda's finest beaches. The park stretches into two parishes. Its eastern boundary begins with the expansive Warwick Long Bay in Warwick Parish, while the western boundary runs just beyond picturesque Horseshoe Bay in Southampton Parish. In between, outcroppings of craggy rocks give rise to a series of coves and small bays that offer protected swimming and more seclusion than the longer bookend beaches. A coastal trail links the beaches, making it a tidy package that's easy to explore.

In all, South Shore Park contains 12 sandy beaches, albeit a few are just postage-stamp size. From east to west they are: Warwick Long Bay, Jobson Cove, Stonehole Bay, Chaplin Bay, Hidden Beach, Angle Beach, Wafer Rocks Beach, Middle Beach, Butts Beach, Peel Rock Cove, Horseshoe Bay and Port Royal Cove. ■

Christ Church

This historic church, on Middle Rd opposite the Belmont Golf Club, dates to 1719, making it one of the oldest Presbyterian churches in the Western Hemisphere. The interior has stained-glass windows and a period pulpit. Equally intriguing is the churchyard, where you'll find old gravestones, many with poignant epitaphs that provide insights into the early inhabitants of Bermuda.

Activities

Since beaches are Warwick's prime attraction, the most popular activities are water sports, such as swimming, snorkeling and bodysurfing.

If you're up for a scenic hike, it's hard to beat the coastal paths that connect the lovely beaches of South Shore Park. While not as dynamic, the other option is the Railway Trail, which crosses the length of Warwick Parish two miles from west to east, running between Middle Rd and South Rd. En route, it passes the south side of Warwick Pond and the Belmont Golf Club.

Bowling is available at Warwick Lanes on Middle Rd in the village center. One of Bermuda's four diving operations, Fantasea Diving, is based at Darrell's Wharf on Warwick's north shore. Snorkel sets can be rented at Fantasea Diving and several snorkel cruises depart from Darrell's Wharf and Belmont Wharf.

Warwick has two golf courses: the public Belmont Golf Club, at the Belmont Hotel, and the private Riddell's Bay Golf & Country Club, which occupies the parish's northwestern peninsula. There are public tennis courts at the Belmont Hotel. Spicelands Riding Centre on Middle Rd offers horseback rides.

For more details on these activities see the Outdoor Activities chapter near the front of the book.

Places to Stay

Astwood Cove (☎ 236-0984, fax 236-1164, ☎ 800-441-7087 in the USA and Canada), 49 South Rd, Warwick WK 07, is a thoroughly recommendable apartment-style place opposite Astwood Park. Run by a congenial, well-traveled Bermudian couple, Nicky and Gaby Lewin, the 20 modern studio and suite units are thoughtfully designed and laid out. Each unit has a phone, air-conditioning, ceiling fan, private bath, veranda, extra sofabed and a full kitchen that's equipped right down to the wine glasses. The grounds have a swimming pool, barbecue grills, a sauna (extra charge) and a coin laundry. Rates for up to two people are from $76/108 in winter/summer for a studio and $86/128 for a suite with a living room. For just $4 more in winter and $10 more in summer, you can get a 2nd-story unit with a cathedral ceiling and a view. A $60 singles rate is available on the studios in winter only. From December through February there's a 30% discount on stays of one month, if booked direct.

Syl-Den Apartments (☎ 238-1834, fax 238-3205), 8 Warwickshire Rd, Warwick WK 02, has five attractive units that are a good value for those who don't mind being a couple of blocks inland from the beach. The apartments are modern and comfortably furnished, with air-conditioning, ceiling fans, phones, kitchens and private baths. Rates for two are $75/90 in winter/summer. There's a pool and sundeck, and the beach at Warwick Long Bay is within walking distance.

A similar deal can be found next door at the *Clairfont Apartments* (☎ /fax 238-0149), PO Box WK 84, Warwick WK BX. Its eight modern apartments each have a kitchen, private bath, air-conditioned bedroom, TV and phone. Corner units are notably big, but all are comfortable and reasonably priced at $80 to $100 year round. There's a pool.

The family-run *Blue Horizons* (☎ 236-6350), 93 South Rd, Warwick WK 10, at the east side of Warwick Parish, has a half-dozen units, each a bit different but all comfortable with private baths. Rates are the same year round. A room alone costs $60, while one with a kitchen costs $80. There's also a three-room apartment big enough for a family with a couple of children for $90. Rates are $5 less for singles and $5 more for each additional person beyond two (no charge for children under age four). There's a pool and snack bar. The house is set back from South Rd just far enough to be beyond the sound of traffic.

The nearby *Sandpiper Apartments* (☎ 236-7093, fax 236-3898), PO Box HM 685, Hamilton HM CX, is a small apartment complex right on South Rd. All 14 units have air-conditioning, two double beds, a single sofabed, a private bath and a room with full kitchen. Some of the units also have separate living rooms for no additional cost. The rate of $120 for up to two people, $160 for three, is the same year round, making it a much better deal in summer. While it's not near the beach, there's a pool out back.

Surf Side Beach Club (☎ 236-7100, fax 236-9765, ☎ 800-553-9990 in the USA), PO Box WK 101, Warwick WK BX, is a pleasant family-run place on a private beach at the southeastern edge of Warwick Parish. The 37 units, which range from studios to two-bedroom apartments, are in contemporary one-story and two-story buildings spread across the five-acre grounds. All are comfortable and have air-conditioning, cable TV, a balcony and a fully equipped kitchen with both a conventional oven and a microwave. It has a quiet setting but is only a few minutes' walk from the nearest bus stop. The beach offers good swimming and there's even a nearshore shipwreck that can be snorkeled. Facilities include a pool, sauna and hot tub; during the summer, there's a poolside coffee bar that serves breakfast and lunch. Rates for studios are $105/185 in winter/summer for up to two people. Two-bedroom units cost $200/300 for up to four people. From December to March, there are discounts for longer stays, ranging from 10% for eight days to around 40% for a month's stay.

The *Mermaid Beach Club* (☎ 236-5031, fax 236-8784, ☎ 800-441-7087 in the USA and Canada), PO Box WK 250, Warwick

WK BX, is a condominium-like property on a sandy cove just east of Warwick Long Bay. The 77 units are adequate, if a bit generic in appearance, and range from hotel rooms with refrigerators to two-bedroom suites with full kitchens. All are air-conditioned and have phones and oceanfront balconies or patios. There's a heated pool, a nice little private beach and a bar and restaurant. Standard rates for either singles or doubles begin at a rather pricey $102/224 in winter/summer, but there are various packages that work out cheaper.

Just west of the Mermaid Beach Club is *Longtail Cliffs* (☎ 236-2864, fax 236-5178, ☎ 800-637-4116 in the USA, 800-267-7600 in Canada), PO Box HM 836, Hamilton HM CX, a small seaside apartment complex that's especially suitable for two couples traveling together. All 13 units have two bedrooms, two baths, air-conditioning, wall safe, phone with free local calls, TV, kitchen, living room and covered veranda. There's a pool and a small private beach out back, and Warwick Long Bay is a short walk away. Winter rates are $130 for doubles plus $20 for each additional person. Summer rates are $215 for doubles plus $40 for each additional person. Request a 2nd-floor unit for the best sea views.

Marley Beach Cottages (☎ 236-1143, fax 236-1984, ☎ 800-637-4116 from the USA), PO Box PG 278, Paget PG BX, consists of a dozen bluffside cottages scenically set above a sandy beach. Each unit has air-conditioning, TV, kitchen, private bath and patio. There's a heated pool and a whirlpool. Rates for doubles begin at $138/172 in winter/summer. The private beach below the cottages is available to guests.

The 150-room *Belmont Hotel* (☎ 236-1301, fax 236-6867, ☎ 800-225-5843 in the USA and Canada, 0345-404-040 in the UK, 69-239-190 in Germany), PO Box WK 251, Warwick WK BX, is perched on a hillside above the Belmont Golf Club. Even though it's the cheapest of the island's 'resort' hotels, it has a pleasant, old-fashioned character and less bustle than other large hotels. The rooms are quite suit-

NED FRIARY
Galápagos tortoises can live over 200 years.

NED FRIARY
The colorful kiskadee is a Trinidadian import.

NED FRIARY
Jamaican anoles have built-in warning flags.

CATHI BELOW
A young green sea turtle at the Bermuda Aquarium, Museum & Zoo, Flatts Village

St Peter's segregated churchyard, St George

St Peter's churchyard, Town of St George

Scaur Hill Fort Park, Sandys Parish

Shipwrecks, Southampton Parish

Somerset Bridge, Sandys Parish

NED FRIARY
Replica of *Deliverance,* Town of St George

NED FRIARY
View from Astwood Park, Warwick Parish

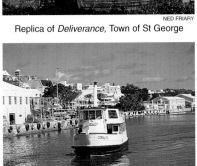
NED FRIARY
Public ferry leaving the Hamilton terminal

BERMUDA DEPARTMENT OF TOURISM
Bobby in the birdcage, City of Hamilton

NED FRIARY
Blue Hole Park, Hamilton Parish

Cycling in the Town of St George

Cycle shop, Town of St George

Tobacco Bay, St George's Parish

Water gate at the Bermuda Maritime Museum

able, each with air-conditioning, cable TV, phones and either two doubles or a king-size bed. Many also have views of the Great Sound. The 114-acre property includes three night-lit tennis courts, a billiards room and a pool, as well as the 18-hole golf course. The Belmont Wharf ferry dock and a public bus stop are both an easy walk from the hotel. In summer, there's a free shuttle to Horseshoe Bay. In part because the property is on a golf course rather than a beach, it tends to attract an older crowd. Singles/doubles begin at $110/149 in winter and $127/174 in summer, without meals. By booking at least a month in advance, you can get a discounted MAP meal plan that adds breakfast and dinner for nearly the same rate as the room only. In winter, you can sometimes get steeply discounted promotional rates by calling the hotel direct instead of using the toll-free number. All guests are entitled to free unlimited golf.

Places to Eat

Side by side on Middle Rd in Warwick center, there's *Hayward's Grocery*, open daily from 8 am to 5 pm, and *Four Star Pizza* (☎ 232-0123), which offers free delivery and the standard variety of pizzas for dine-in or takeout. A 10-inch pizza with the works, either meat or vegetarian, will set you back $13, a 14-inch version $21; opening hours are from 11 am (2 pm on Sundays) to 11 pm (midnight on weekends).

Paw Paws (☎ 236-7459) is an informal local restaurant at 87 South Rd, at the corner of Dunscombe Rd. At lunch, from 11 am to 5 pm, there are sandwiches with fries for around $8 and hot dishes, such as fettuccine Alfredo or fish, for $10 to $15. At dinner, from 6 to 10 pm, main dishes average $20 and include the likes of crab-meat fritters, shark steak with Creole sauce and Paw Montespan – a baked green papaya (paw paw) dish with ground beef, cheese and tomato. It's also open for breakfast from 8:30 am.

A hundred yards to the east of Paw Paws on South Rd is *Brenda's Food Bar*, a little

---

Eugene O'Neill

Famed American playwright Eugene O'Neill had a house on Harbour Rd in Warwick for a time, and it was here that he wrote *Mourning Becomes Electra, Lazarus Laughed, Strange Interlude* and *The Great God Brown*. O'Neill's daughter Oona, who married silent-film actor Charlie Chaplin, was born in Bermuda in 1925.

The book *Eugene O'Neill & Family, The Bermuda Interlude* by Joy Bluck Waters (Granaway Books) details the author's life on the island. ■

---

snack bar with inexpensive sandwiches, fries and other simple eats.

The Jolly Lobster (☎ 236-5031) is a casual waterfront restaurant at the Mermaid Beach Club on South Rd. Appetizers like clams casino or seafood ravioli cost around $10, while seafood and steak main dishes are $20 to $25. Lobster, a house specialty, is sold at market price. It's open nightly from 6:45 to 9 pm, but closed in January and February.

Tree Frogs Restaurant (☎ 236-1301), the main dining room at the Belmont Hotel on Middle Rd, offers a $16 breakfast buffet and a full-course dinner of soup or salad, a main dish, dessert and coffee for $30 – or order à la carte, with pasta at $12 and roast beef at $18. At lunch the bar serves sandwiches and other simple fare.

Getting Around

Warwick is crossed from east to west by three main roads: Harbour Rd on the north shore, Middle Rd through the interior and South Rd along the south shore.

Bus No 8 travels along Middle Rd and bus No 7 travels along South Rd; both of the routes connect Warwick with Sandys Parish to the west and the City of Hamilton. On average, the buses along both routes run about every 15 minutes. There's no bus service on Harbour Rd, but there's public ferry service to Hamilton from Belmont Wharf and Darrell's Wharf at the northeast side of the parish.

Southampton Parish

Southampton Parish comprises the western elbow of Bermuda, bordered on the north by Little Sound and on the south by the Atlantic. The north side is mainly residential, while the south side is a prime visitor destination dotted by a series of bays and coves with attractive pink-sand beaches.

Bordered by Sandys Parish to the north and Warwick Parish to the east, Southampton is relatively long and thin, with a width that tapers to a mere one-third of a mile at its narrowest point. In addition to beautiful beaches, the parish has a couple of historic sites – Gibbs Hill Lighthouse and Whale Bay Battery – and a brewery that welcomes visitors.

Southampton has the largest share of hotel rooms of any of the island's nine parishes. Two of Bermuda's largest resort hotels are on Southampton's south shore and there are a number of smaller hotels and guesthouses, many of them on or near the waterfront.

The parish population is 5804.

Gibbs Hill Lighthouse

The Gibbs Hill Lighthouse, erected in 1846 after a rash of shipwrecks along Bermuda's treacherous western shoals, is the area's most significant landmark, towering nearly 120 feet above its hilltop site.

Pink Sand

Bermuda's sand is made up of particles of coral, marine invertebrates and various shells, but it takes its distinctive light pink hue from the bodies of one particular sea creature, a member of the order Foraminifera. A marine protozoan abundant on Bermudian reefs, foraminifers have hard, tiny shells that wash up on shore after the animal within dies. These pink shell fragments provide the dominant color in what would otherwise be a confetti of bleached white coral and ivory-colored calcium carbonate shells. ∎

Not only is it an attractive building, but it is unique in being the tallest cast-iron lighthouse in the world. It was one of just a handful of cast-iron lighthouses erected by the British in the mid-18th century, though most, including two surviving ones in Scotland, were only about a third as high.

The lens, which consists of concentric prisms, weighs 2¾ tons and is capable of generating a half-million candlepower. Using a 1000-watt electric bulb, it emits a beam that can be seen 40 miles out to sea.

You can climb the eight flights of stairs to the top – some 185 steps in all – where you'll be rewarded with a panoramic view. En route, you'll also find some interesting shipwreck-related displays. The lighthouse is open daily from 9 am to 4:30 pm. Admission is $2, free for children under five.

On the same grounds, about 100 feet north of the lighthouse, is a lookout that's been known as the Queen's View ever since Queen Elizabeth II paused there in 1953 to admire the scenery; a plaque duly notes the event.

The Gibbs Hill Lighthouse is on Lighthouse Rd, which begins just west of the Henry VIII restaurant on South Rd. If you don't have a moped, it's about a 10-minute uphill walk.

For information on the atmospheric lighthouse tea room, see the Places to Eat section later in this chapter.

Horseshoe Bay

This horseshoe-shaped bay, with its wide crescent of soft pink sand, is arguably the most beautiful beach in Bermuda. It's certainly the most popular, and it's the only beach in the South Shore Park (see the sidebar in the Warwick Parish chapter) that is staffed with lifeguards. There's a large parking lot, restrooms, showers, snorkel rentals and a little cafe that sells $3 sandwiches, ice cream and a few other simple eats. All of the facilities are available in the

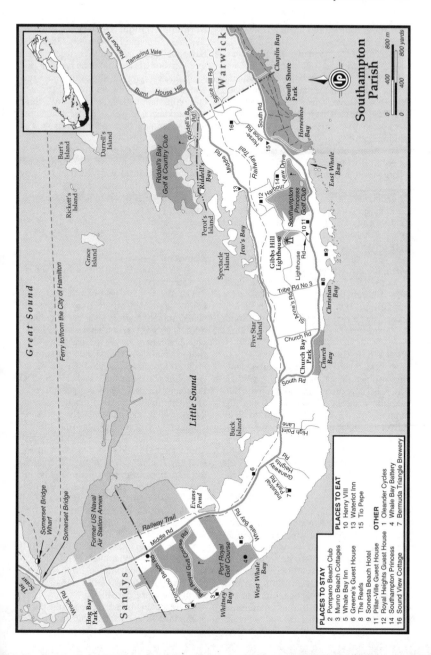

Southampton Parish

PLACES TO STAY
2 Pompano Beach Club
3 Munro Beach Cottages
5 Whale Bay Inn
6 Greene's Guest House
8 The Reefs
9 Sonesta Beach Hotel
11 Pillar-Ville Guest House
12 Royal Heights Guest House
14 Southampton Princess
16 Sound View Cottage

PLACES TO EAT
10 Henry VIII
13 Waterlot Inn
15 Tio Pepe

OTHER
1 Oleander Cycles
4 Whale Bay Battery
7 Bermuda Triangle Brewery

eats. All of the facilities are available in the tourist season only.

You can get a nice angle on Horseshoe Bay by walking out onto the peninsula at the west end of the beach. On the west side of this peninsula is the small rock-protected **Port Royal Cove**. This cove, as well as the tiny **Peel Rock Cove** at the east end of Horseshoe Bay, offer relatively secluded bathing options.

The main entrance to Horseshoe Bay is on South Rd, opposite Tio Pepe restaurant, where you'll also find a bus stop.

Church Bay Park

Church Bay is a pretty little beach at the western end of South Rd. In early colonial times, a coastal fort was built here; if you walk up onto the knoll at the east side of the bay, you'll find a plaque marking the spot where the fort was erected in 1612.

As the reef comes in close to the shore here, Church Bay is a favorite place for snorkeling. It's also an easy beach to access, just a two-minute walk from South Rd. There are restrooms and a telephone.

West Whale Bay

West Whale Bay is a pleasant little sandy cove in a natural setting at the end of Whale Bay Rd. There are picnic tables on the hillside above the beach, and you'll find the remains of a small fort, **Whale Bay Battery**, a mere three-minute walk up the hill to the northwest. This small fortification now overlooks the Port Royal Golf Course and offers a nice view of the endless turquoise and cobalt waters of the Atlantic.

The gun battery was built in the 1870s to defend Hog Fish Cut, a channel through the reefs leading to the Royal Naval Dockyard. The battery's original nine-inch cannons weighed 12 tons and provided a hefty defense against potential raids on the Dockyard. Whale Bay Battery was also used as a lookout station during WWII. Although the guns are gone, you can still rummage through the former ammunition magazines and barracks.

Bermuda Triangle Brewery

Bermuda Triangle Brewing (☎ 238-2430), Bermuda's first and only brewery, offers free tours of its operations on weekdays at 4 pm and on Saturdays at noon and 3 pm. Tours, which explain the brewing process, end with samples of the company's three standard beers, as well as any seasonal ones that they might be experimenting with at the time.

To get to the brewery, take bus No 7 or 8, which stop on Middle Rd near its intersection with Industrial Park Rd. The brewery is in the SAL industrial center, which is about 200 yards down Industrial Park Rd; when you see two large warehouses on the south side of the road, follow the gravel road around the warehouse on the left.

Activities

Southampton offers visitors a wide variety of water activities.

The West Side's best easy-access snorkeling spot is Church Bay, where the nearshore reef harbors a variety of colorful tropical fish. If you don't have snorkel gear, you can rent it at the parish's two dive shops: Nautilus Diving at the Southampton Princess hotel and South Side Scuba Watersports at the Sonesta Beach Hotel. The Pompano Beach Club Watersports Centre, at the Pompano Beach Club hotel, rents kayaks, sailboats and windsurfing gear.

Hikers will find a coastal trail running from Horseshoe Bay east through South Shore Park. In addition, a section of the Railway Trail runs clear through Southampton Parish, connecting it with neighboring Sandys Parish to the northwest and Warwick Parish to the east. The Railway Trail parallels Middle Rd most of the way, offering views of Southampton's less-touristed north shore and the Little Sound.

Southampton has two 18-hole golf courses: the Southampton Princess Golf Club, at the Southampton Princess hotel, and the Port Royal Golf Course, at the north side of the parish.

There are tennis courts open to the public at the Port Royal Tennis Club (at the Port

The Bermuda Triangle

Few terms conjure up images of the paranormal the way that 'Bermuda Triangle' does.

The name is given to a triangular section of the Atlantic Ocean that's bound by Bermuda to the north, Florida to the west and Puerto Rico to the south. It's thought that as many as 100 ships and planes have vanished in the triangle. The mysterious disappearances in this zone, which is also known as the Devil's Triangle, date back to the mid-19th century, but it wasn't until the 1970s, when a popular interest in UFOs and other unexplained phenomena arose, that the disappearances drew international attention and the term Bermuda Triangle came into common use.

What makes the triangle unusual is that not only are the disappearances quite substantial for an area of this size, but many of the vessels have gone down without so much as emitting a distress signal – and with no subsequent trace of the craft ever appearing. In other cases, ships have reappeared intact months after disappearing, but with no trace of the crew ever found.

The largest single disappearance in the Bermuda Triangle was that of the infamous Flight 19, a group of five US Navy torpedo bombers that flew out of Florida on a routine flight in December 1945 and vanished; a search plane sent in their wake also disappeared.

Various theories have been advanced to explain the disappearances, ranging from atmospheric disturbances and erratic magnetic forces to time warps and extra-terrestrial kidnappings. Others just write most of it off as coincidence and the usual combination of mechanical failure, bad weather and human error.

However you look at it, the Bermuda Triangle gives those with a rich imagination plenty to work with. ■

Royal Golf Course), the Sonesta Beach Hotel and the Southampton Princess.

More information on these activities is in the Outdoor Activities chapter near the front of the book.

Places to Stay

Sound View Cottage (☎ 238-0064), 9 Bowe Lane, Southampton SN 04, is a small hilltop place in a residential neighborhood midway between Middle Rd and South Shore Park. It has three compact studio units, each with private bath, kitchenette and air-conditioning. You'll also find a swimming pool in the backyard and a patio with a barbecue. All in all, it's a particularly good value at $50 for up to two people, $75 for three. It's open from April through October only.

The informal *Pillar-Ville Guest House* (☎ 238-0445), PO Box SN2, Southampton SN BX, is on South Rd between the Sonesta Beach Hotel and the Southampton Princess. There are seven straightforward studios and two-bedroom units with kitchens, private bath, TV and radios. Summer rates range from $50/80 for singles/doubles in studio units to $130 for four people in a two-bedroom cottage with a living room and two baths; there's a slight discount in winter. Guests have access to a private beach.

Royal Heights Guest House (☎ 238-0043, fax 238-8445), PO Box SN 144, Southampton SN BX, on a hill between the Southampton Princess golf course and Middle Rd, is a contemporary home with friendly hosts and a half-dozen guestrooms. All rooms have cable TV, air-conditioning, coffeemakers, refrigerators and balconies. Some of the rooms have connecting doors that can be opened for use by families. There are picturesque views of Great Sound from the poolside patio and from most of the rooms. Because of its hilltop location, it's best suited for guests who plan to rent mopeds. Singles/doubles cost $100/125 year round, continental breakfast included.

Greene's Guest House (☎ 238-0834, fax 238-8980), PO Box SM 395, Southampton SN BX, is on Middle Rd at the north side of the parish. Managed by an East Indian family from Trinidad, it has six air-conditioned guestrooms with private bath, phone, mini-refrigerator, coffeemaker, TV and VCR. While it's not terribly close to the south shore's sandy beaches, there's a pool and it's on a bus route. Rates, which include a full breakfast, are $90/100 for singles/doubles year round, although you can generally negotiate a small discount in the winter if you book direct.

Whale Bay Inn (☎ 238-0469, fax 238-1224), PO Box SN 544, Southampton SN BX, is a pleasant little place with a peaceful location at the southern edge of the Port Royal Golf Course. Despite its seclusion, both the beach at West Whale Bay and the bus stop on Middle Rd are within a 10-minute walk. The five comfortably furnished units each have air-conditioning, ceiling fans, TV, phone, private bath, a separate bedroom, kitchen and patio. The rates are a reasonable $65/80 in winter/summer for singles and $80/110 for doubles.

Munro Beach Cottages (☎ 234-1175, fax 234-3528), PO Box SN 99, Southampton SN BX, is comprised of nine duplex units spread in an arc along low cliffs overlooking the ocean. This quiet, secluded complex is bordered by the Port Royal Golf Course, making it an ideal spot for golfers. The units are modern, with full kitchens, private baths, air-conditioning, oceanfront patios, TV and phones. A path leads down to a small, private beach at Whitney Bay, and tennis is available nearby. Rates for one or two people are $102 in winter, $168 in summer.

The *Pompano Beach Club* (☎ 234-0222, fax 234-1694, ☎ 800-343-4155 in the USA and Canada), 36 Pompano Beach Rd, Southampton SB 03, is a friendly family-run hotel with 52 pleasant rooms in a handful of two-story buildings. It has a private location on a coastal cliff at the north side of the Port Royal Golf Course. Facilities include five tennis courts, two hot tubs, a heated pool and a small fitness room. There's a small beach fronting shallow waters that are good for snorkeling. The rooms have ceiling fans, rattan furnishings, king-size beds, private baths, phones and oceanview balconies. Double rates, with breakfast and dinner included, begin at $220 in winter and $345 in summer. Room-and-golf packages are also available.

The Reefs (☎ 238-0222, fax 238-8372, ☎ 800-742-2008 in the USA and Canada), 56 South Rd, Southampton SN 02, is an attractive small hotel on a nice private beach at Christian Bay, just west of the Sonesta resort. There are 65 upscale rooms in a series of terraced hillside buildings. Most rooms have waterview balconies and all have cheery tropical decor, air-conditioning, refrigerators, room safes and phones with free local calls. The grounds have two tennis courts, a shuffleboard court, a pool and a small fitness center. Rates vary with the category of accommodations, beginning at $264/336 for doubles in winter/summer, including breakfast and dinner.

The *Sonesta Beach Hotel* (☎ 238-8122, fax 238-8463, ☎ 800-766-3728 in the

USA), PO Box HM 1070, Hamilton HM EX, is perched on a rocky outcrop that separates two protected bays, each with nice sandy beaches. The 403 rooms have the usual amenities and decor of a large resort hotel, including TVs, phones, room safes, air-conditioning and balconies, most with water views. There are six tennis courts, heated indoor and outdoor pools, a croquet lawn, a health spa (extra charge), diving facilities and shops. A shuttle bus runs around the 25-acre property and up to the public bus stop. Rates for a standard room without meals begin at $130/250 in winter/summer for either singles or doubles. Add another $15 per person for the breakfast plan or $55 for the breakfast-and-dinner plan – however, if you're not a big eater, there are cheaper options in the hotel restaurants.

The *Southampton Princess* (☎ 238-8000, fax 238-8968, ☎ 800-223-1818 in the USA, 800-268-7176 in Canada, 0171-407-1010 in the U.K), PO Box HM 1379, Hamilton HM FX, is Bermuda's largest resort hotel. Opened in 1972, the hotel has a quiet hilltop location amidst an 18-hole golf course. Other facilities include a fitness center, two swimming pools, 11 tennis courts, a pro shop and several restaurants. The 600 rooms and suites are pleasantly upscale with air-conditioning, cable TV, phones, room safes, waterview balconies and little extras like hair dryers and bathrobes. The entire 3rd floor is set aside as a smoke-free area. The lobby and common areas have a relaxing traditional decor with dark woods and Victorian furnishings. Although the hotel is about a half-mile inland, its private white-sand beach – and anywhere else on the 100-acre grounds – can be reached by a complimentary shuttle. Free transport is provided to the City of Hamilton as well, where the Princess' sister hotel is located. Room rates begin at $150 for singles or doubles in winter (no meals) and at $269/319 for singles/doubles in summer, when the rates include breakfast and dinner.

Places to Eat

The quaint *Lighthouse Tea Room* (☎ 238-8679) at the Gibbs Hill Lighthouse has a lovely setting and view, making it a perfect spot for afternoon tea or a traditional English breakfast. There are tempting cakes and pastries, including warm scones, toasted crumpets and currant teacakes, all served with butter and jam and priced under $3. At midday you can also order Cornish pasties, pork pies or finger sandwiches for $7. The tearoom is open daily from 9 am to 5 pm.

Tio Pepe (☎ 238-1897), on South Rd opposite Horseshoe Bay, is an Italian restaurant with a variety of nine-inch pizzas, including vegetarian, for $10. You can also order lasagna, fettuccine or other pastas for $14 and meat dishes for around $20. It's open daily from 10 am to 10 pm. Ask about the nightly special, which includes salad and a main course for $16. Takeout is available. At dinner there's a minimum charge of $15 per person.

The popular *Henry VIII* (☎ 238-1977), on South Rd opposite the Sonesta Beach Hotel, plays up a convivial Olde English ambiance, all burgundy and dark wood, with waitresses in Tudor-style dress. At lunch, from noon to 2:30 pm, you can get a sandwich or burger with fries for $7 or a few hot items, such as steak and kidney pie, for double that. Dinner, served from 7 to 10:30 pm, offers an extensive menu. If you're a big meat eater, you'll find the prime rib with Yorkshire pudding ($23.50) to be filling, or for the same price you can order a choice cut of filet mignon or broiled local rockfish. Add another $5 for soup or a simple salad. There is a good variety of moderately priced wines, and the adjoining pub features English lagers and Bermuda Triangle ale on tap.

The cheapest place to eat at the Sonesta Beach Hotel, *The Cafe* is in the hotel's shopping arcade. It has fresh-baked pastries and muffins for $1.25, coffee for $2 and fruit cups for $3, as well as sandwiches, Häagen-Dazs ice cream, frozen yogurt and other light snacks. The Cafe is open from 6:30 am to 10 pm.

The Sonesta's main dinner restaurant, *Lillian's* (☎ 238-8122), has a Northern Italian-influenced à la carte menu with chicken and pasta dishes for around $20, steaks and fish from around $25. Add another $6 for soup or salad and another $10 for starters such as carpaccio or grilled portabello mushrooms. It's open from 6:30 to 9 pm; jackets and ties are optional.

The *Cedar Room* in the Pompano Beach Club (☎ 234-0222), at the end of Pompano Beach Rd, has fine dining, a nice ocean view and good food. At lunch there are sandwiches, a variety of salads and a few hot dishes such as fish and chips, all for under $10. At dinner there's a five-course meal for $39, which includes a choice of appetizers, a hot or chilled soup, a salad, a selection of tempting desserts and a half-dozen main dishes, such as lobster cannelloni, beef Wellington and Cajun catfish. The dress code is jacket and tie on Tuesday, Thursday and Saturday nights and 'smart casual' at other times.

Coconuts (☎ 238-0222) at The Reefs hotel has a romantic seaview setting that makes it a favorite south shore dinner spot. There's a changing menu, with starters that include the likes of escargots Bourguignonne, gravlax or gazpacho soup and main courses such as filet mignon, seared local wahoo and breast of duck with cilantro pancakes. At lunch there's a simpler menu of sandwiches and salads. Expect lunch for two to run around $25, dinner for two around $100.

Windows on the Sound, the main dining room at the Southampton Princess hotel (☎ 238-2555), takes its name from the dining room's wall of windows that look across the croquet lawn towards the Little Sound. From 7 to 11 am daily, you can get a continental breakfast for $6 or a full breakfast for $12. At lunch there are sandwiches for around $7 and hot dishes for about double that. Dinner includes appetizers such as an antipasto plate for under $10

and main dishes like prime rib or grilled swordfish with sun-dried tomatoes for around $20. Dress is smart casual.

For a jacket-and-tie dinner in the Southampton Princess, the *Newport Room* serves French and continental cuisine with a nouvelle accent. Starters such as foie gras or smoked salmon are around $20, while main dishes, including steaks and fresh fish, are around $30. It's closed during winter.

Still, the most popular restaurant affiliated with the Southampton Princess is the *Waterlot Inn* (☎ 238-0510), which is not on the hotel grounds, but just north of the property on Middle Rd. Located in a historic dockside inn, the restaurant has a pleasant water view and is a favorite for its indulgent Bermuda-style Sunday brunch, which is accompanied by a Dixieland jazz band. The brunch costs $28 and is served from 11:30 am to 1 pm from March to November; reservations are often essential. The restaurant is also open from 6:30 to 9:30 pm for dinner, with a blend of French, Mediterranean and Bermudian fare. Dishes include the likes of pan-fried fish with juniper berry sauce, bouillabaisse and rack of lamb. Appetizers average $15, main courses $30 and tantalizing flambéed desserts $9. Jackets and ties are required at dinner.

Entertainment

The two resort hotels, *Southampton Princess* and *Sonesta Beach Hotel*, often have some sort of entertainment, particularly during the summer season. *Henry VIII* restaurant, opposite the Sonesta Beach Hotel, has entertainment most nights, varying from rock groups to mellow instrumentals.

Getting Around

Bus Middle Rd runs along the Little Sound and is served by bus No 8, while South Rd runs along Southampton's south shore and is served by bus No 7.

South Rd merges with Middle Rd about midway in the parish, at a spot called

Barnes Corner. Note that a number of buses terminate at Barnes Corner, so if you're going any farther west make sure you take a bus that's marked 'Dockyard' or 'Somerset'. Things are simple if you're heading east, as all No 7 and 8 buses terminate in the City of Hamilton.

Moped Mopeds can be rented from Oleander Cycles, on Middle Rd just north of the Port Royal Golf Course and at The Reefs hotel; from Astwood Cycles at the Sonesta Beach Hotel; and from Wheels Cycles at the Southampton Princess.

Sandys Parish

Sandys (pronounced 'sands'), the western-most parish in Bermuda, is comprised of the northern part of Bermuda Island as well as Somerset Island, Watford Island, Boaz Island, Ireland Island South and Ireland Island North, all of which are connected by bridges.

The main village is Somerset, at the northern side of Somerset Island. It has its roots in colonial agriculture and retains an unabashedly local character.

Watford Island, Boaz Island and the Ireland Islands were once occupied by the British Royal Navy. Today, testimony to that past is found in the naval cemeteries that flank the road leading to the Royal Naval Dockyard.

At the southern tip of Ireland Island North is the former HMS Malabar, a British naval base that closed in March 1995, ending a 200-year presence on Bermuda by British forces.

The rest of Ireland Island North is occupied by the 75-acre Royal Naval Dockyard. With its collection of 19th-century buildings, this former military dockyard and fort has been turned into one of Bermuda's foremost visitor destinations, with its own cruise ship dock, a small boat marina, craft galleries, a shopping center and a handful of restaurants.

Sandys Parish is also referred to by Bermudians as the West End. The parish population is 6437.

Somerset & Around

Somerset, the largest island in Sandys Parish, derives its name from Bermuda's founding father, Sir George Somers.

Somerset Bridge, which was built in the 17th century to connect Bermuda's main island with Somerset Island, has as its claim to fame the distinction of being the world's smallest drawbridge. Its 30-inch span opens just wide enough to allow the mast of a sailboat to pass through as the boat sails between the Great Sound and Ely's Harbour. Obviously, the sailor needs to have a good command and steady hand!

The heart of Somerset Island is sleepy **Somerset Village**, abutting Mangrove Bay, where there's a small sandy beach that's favored by fishers. Unlike St George at the other end of Bermuda, Somerset's facilities are geared more for locals than tourists. If you have extra time, Somerset can be a pleasant enough spot to poke around, and it can make a good place to break for lunch on the way to the Royal Naval Dockyard. The most prominent sight on the island is Scaur Hill Fort Park, but there are a couple of other parks and nature reserves.

'Where fate would take us', reads Bermuda's coat-of-arms.

Bermuda Lights

On an island that was 'accidentally' discovered by shipwrecked castaways, it comes as no surprise that marine safety has long been a major concern. Indeed, shortly after the English established the first settlement on Bermuda in the early 17th century, a handful of simple light beacons were set on prominent hills in order to help guide approaching ships through Bermuda's tricky reefs.

By the 18th century, increased sea traffic brought a sharp rise in the frequency of shipwrecks off Bermuda. Alarmed at the situation, the British Navy erected the first lighthouse at Wreck Hill, on the westernmost tip of Sandys Parish. An elementary structure that burned tar, the Wreck Hill Lighthouse overlooked Western Ledge Flats, a site so notorious for claiming ships that mariners nicknamed it 'the graveyard'.

The light's strength proved insufficient, however, and in December 1838 the French frigate *L'Herminie*, a 300-foot vessel with 60 cannons and a crew of nearly 500 men, went down on the reef just four miles west of Wreck Hill. In all, some 39 shipwrecks occurred during that decade off the west side of Bermuda. In 1840, the British administration responded by appropriating funds to erect Bermuda's first modern lighthouse.

Situated in Southampton Parish atop the 245-foot Gibbs Hill, the new lighthouse began operation in May 1846. The tower, constructed of cast iron, extended a lofty 117 feet from the base to the light. Fired by sperm whale oil that burned from four concentric wicks, the revolving light had the capacity to reach not only the treacherous western shoals, but substantial sections of the northern and southern shoals as well.

In the years that followed, attention shifted to the northeastern side of the island, where Sir George Somers had wrecked the *Sea Venture* some 250 years earlier and which remained beyond the reach of the Gibbs Hill light. In the 1870s, following a rash of shipwrecks on the reefs north of St George's, Bermuda's second lighthouse, St David's Lighthouse, was built atop a hill at the eastern side of that parish.

This second light filled in the former blind spot. Furthermore, when viewed together, the two lights being cast from opposite ends of Bermuda now allowed captains to gauge their ship's exact position. In the decades that followed, the frequency of shipwrecks off Bermuda dropped significantly – with some of the more notorious ones occurring in times of mechanical failures at the lighthouses.

Both of Bermuda's 19th-century lighthouses stand largely unchanged, except for the modernization of their light mechanisms. Instead of burning whale oil, they now operate on 1000-watt electric bulbs, which cast beams 40 miles out to sea. Bermuda's lighthouses also serve as landmarks for airplane pilots, who can spot the lights from more than 100 miles away. ∎

Information

Money In Somerset Village, there are branches of both the Bank of Bermuda and the Bank of Butterfield on Mangrove Bay Rd, opposite the Somerset Country Squire restaurant. Both banks are open Monday to Thursday from 9:30 am to 3 pm, Fridays from 9:30 am to 4:30 pm.

Post The Mangrove Bay Post Office, in Somerset Village, is open Monday to Friday from 8 to 11:30 am and 1 to 5 pm. There's another post office at the south side of the Somerset Bridge with the same hours.

Newspapers Somerset News Agency, on Somerset Rd next to Thel's Cafe in Somerset Village, sells Bermuda newspapers and a few British tabloids.

Scaur Hill Fort Park

Scaur Hill Fort is a monument to the tensions that existed between the British and the Americans in the mid-19th century. During the US Civil War, the British had backed the defeated Confederacy, and, despite the fact that the victorious North had emerged from the war in such a battle-weary condition that it posed little threat to anyone,

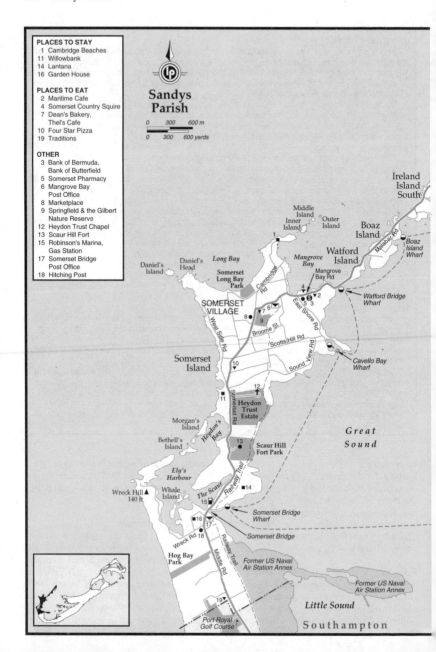

PLACES TO STAY
1 Cambridge Beaches
11 Willowbank
14 Lantana
16 Garden House

PLACES TO EAT
2 Maritime Cafe
4 Somerset Country Squire
7 Dean's Bakery,
    Thel's Cafe
10 Four Star Pizza
19 Traditions

OTHER
3 Bank of Bermuda,
    Bank of Butterfield
5 Somerset Pharmacy
6 Mangrove Bay
    Post Office
8 Marketplace
9 Springfield & the Gilbert
    Nature Reserve
12 Heydon Trust Chapel
13 Scaur Hill Fort
15 Robinson's Marina,
    Gas Station
17 Somerset Bridge
    Post Office
18 Hitching Post

Sandys Parish

0   300   600 m

0   300   600 yards

Ireland
Island
South

Middle
Island
Inner
Island   Outer
                Island   Boaz
                                Island   Boaz
                                                Island
                                                Wharf

Daniel's
Island

Daniel's
Head   Long Bay   Mangrove
                                 Bay   Watford
                                                  Island

Somerset
Long Bay
Park   Mangrove
              Bay Rd

SOMERSET
VILLAGE   Watford Bridge
              Wharf

Cambridge Rd

East Shore Rd

West Side Rd

Broome St

Scotts Hill Rd

Cavello Bay
Wharf

Somerset
Island

Sound View Rd

Heydon
Trust
Estate

Morgan's
Island

Bethell's
Island

Ely's
Harbour

Great
Sound

Scaur Hill
Fort Park

Somerset Rd

Heydon's Bay

Railway Trail

Wreck Hill ▲
140 ft   Whale
              Island

The Scaur

Somerset Bridge
Wharf

Somerset Bridge

Wreck Rd

Railway Trail

Middle Rd

Hog Bay
Park

Former US Naval
Air Station Annex

Former US Naval
Air Station Annex

Little Sound

Port Royal
Golf Course

Southampton

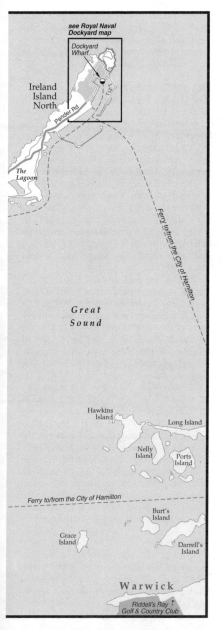

the British were fearful of the possibility of a retaliatory US invasion of Bermuda.

Britain, which still had colonial ties with Canada as well as possessions in the West Indies, looked upon Bermuda as a forward citadel of its naval power in the New World. Consequently, in 1865 the British allocated a hefty sum for fortifying Bermuda and in 1868 work began on Scaur Hill Fort, the most ambitious of several such projects.

Scaur Hill Fort was built at the south side of Somerset Island, on the crest of its highest hill, with the express purpose of protecting the Royal Naval Dockyard from a land invasion. In keeping with that intent, a deep ditch was dug from Ely's Harbour in the west to Great Harbour in the east – effectively slicing Somerset Island in two. Ramparts were built along the elevated northern side of the ditch, where platforms were installed for use by infantry men who – theoretically, at least – could mow down invading soldiers as they leaped into the ditch from the south.

So ambitious was the design of the fort that it took the better part of two decades to complete the work. By the time it was finished it was obsolete, but, considering Bermuda's history of nonexistent military confrontations, that seemed to be beside the point.

The fort was equipped with two 64-pound rifled muzzleloader (RML) cannons mounted on Moncrieff 'disappearing' carriages that recoiled down into recesses for reloading after firing; five-ton counterweights then raised the carriages to position.

In an interesting twist of fate, American troops finally did come to occupy Scaur Hill Fort, albeit by British invitation, when the 52nd Coast Artillery Battalion of the US Army took up station at the fort during WWII.

Visitors can explore the old parade grounds, march along the ditch, view the stone galleries with their cannon and rifle windows and peer into the concrete emplacements that held the disappearing

RML cannons. However, true to their names, the big guns themselves have disappeared from the site.

Scaur Hill Fort is open daily from 9 am to 4 pm (to 4:30 pm from May through October). Admission is free, and there's an on-site caretaker who can answer questions.

Springfield & the Gilbert Nature Reserve

This combined historic site and nature reserve, on Somerset Rd at the south side of Somerset Village, once comprised a small plantation. The manor house, known as Springfield, dates to the 17th century and was purchased by the Bermuda National Trust in 1967. Today Springfield holds a library, nursery school and private apartments.

The adjacent five-acre property, the Gilbert Nature Reserve, was purchased by the Trust in 1973 to protect its rural nature from potential development. The reserve is crossed with short footpaths that begin at the southwest side of the parking lot. The paths start in thick brush and wind past wooded areas that include mature native cedar trees as well as more recently planted cedar and palmetto trees.

Somerset Long Bay Park

Sandys is not endowed with the same type of glorious beaches found in neighboring parishes to its south. The main public bathing spot is Somerset Long Bay Park, off Cambridge Rd at the northwest side of Somerset Island. It has a sandy beach with shallow waters that are generally suitable for children; there's parking, toilets and picnic facilities.

Perhaps more interesting than the beach is the adjacent **Somerset Long Bay Nature Reserve**. A former dump site that's now owned by the Bermuda Audubon Society, this wetland habitat serves as an important nesting site for resident waterfowl and also attracts migratory birds. A trail through tall grasses at the southwest side of Somerset Long Bay Park leads into the sanctuary. Just two minutes

along that trail will bring you to a good duck-viewing area. At various times of the year, you might also spot migratory herons, egrets, warblers and kingfishers, as well as resident catbirds and cardinals.

Heydon Trust Estate

The Heydon Trust, along Middle Rd north of Scaur Hill Fort, is a privately held 43-acre tract of undeveloped open space. The property has banana groves, citrus orchards, gardens and wooded areas, the latter including one of the island's finest remaining stands of Bermuda cedar trees.

The centerpiece of the Heydon Trust is a hilltop **chapel**, which occupies a little limestone cottage that is one of Bermuda's oldest structures, dating back to 1616. Inspired by its peaceful setting, an interdenominational Christian organization has been using the cottage as a chapel since 1974.

Visitors are free to take a look at the chapel, which is used for informal sunrise and afternoon prayer services. At the east side of the chapel is a lookout point with a vista of the Great Sound. If you look to the southeast you'll get a bird's-eye view of Tucker's Peninsula, which until recently served as home to the US Naval Air Station Annex.

In addition to the views and tranquility near the chapel, you'll also find a handful of short trails running off the main road that can make for pleasant strolls. During the spring and autumn migratory seasons, the property is a good spot for birdwatching.

The road into the property, Heydon Drive, begins opposite the Willowbank hotel on Middle Rd and leads east about 500 yards, where it makes a loop around the chapel. The Heydon Trust Estate is open free to the public during daylight hours.

Hog Bay Park

Hog Bay Park, at the south side of Sandys, is one of Bermuda's newest public parks. The 38-acre property was purchased during the past decade from three adjoining estates.

Bermuda Cedar

The Bermuda cedar tree *(Juniperus bermudiana)*, endemic to Bermuda, was abundant on the islands when the first settlers shipwrecked in 1609. In fact, it was cedar that the settlers used to craft the ships that took them on to the New World. Not only did this native cedar prove suitable for shipbuilding but it was also harvested for the construction of homes, forts and furniture. So important was the cedar to the well-being of the colonists that they issued legislation to protect the trees and also outlawed the export of cedar timber.

Until 50 years ago, the Bermuda cedar was still the most predominant tree on the islands. Then in 1942 a scale insect was accidentally introduced and an epidemic spread like wildfire. Within a decade over 95% of the island's cedar trees had succumbed to the cedar-scale epidemic.

Biological controls, such as the release of insects that naturally prey upon the scale insect, were introduced in an attempt to stop the devastation. In time, those Bermuda cedars that did survive began to develop a resistance to the scale insect. Seeds from these healthy surviving trees have been intensely propagated in recent years as part of a successful community-wide campaign to bring the Bermuda cedar back from near-extinction.

Much of the hands-on work of raising and planting the seedlings has been done by volunteers, ranging from the local Rotary Club to school and garden organizations. Thanks to their efforts, young Bermuda cedars are becoming an increasingly common sight in island parks and gardens. ∎

The three estates had kept the land in a natural state, free of 20th-century development; consequently, the park is a repository for Bermuda's rural past and holds many relics dating to the early colonial period. During that period, Sandys and nearby Southampton Parish encompassed a substantial number of Bermuda's farms; Hog Bay Park incorporates a block of that original agricultural land. In the early 1990s, before the property was opened as a public park, researchers from the College of William and Mary in Williamsburg, Virginia, uncovered a number of artifacts and identified some of the uses of former sites.

The new park, which extends from Middle Rd to the Atlantic Ocean, makes a fun place to explore for those who enjoy walking about old house sites and the like. Spread around the property are fallow fields that once grew tobacco and cassava, abandoned cottages, a lime kiln and some mature stands of native trees. The path begins at the roadside parking area and can be followed all the way down to the bay, where hikers will be rewarded with a fine coastal view. Look for a map at the trailhead.

Activities

Mangrove Marina Ltd, at Robinson's Marina at Somerset Bridge, rents kayaks, canoes, motorboats, snorkel sets and fishing gear. Blue Water Divers, which also operates out of Robinson's Marina, arranges diving. Greg Hartley's Under Sea Adventure conducts helmet-diving trips from May through October from the Watford Bridge dock.

For more information on the activities listed above, see the Outdoor Activities chapter near the front of the book.

A 2¼-mile stretch of the Railway Trail runs from Southampton Parish to Somerset Village. The section on Somerset Island is open to both hikers and motorbikes and is quite a pretty route, with views of the Great Sound along the way. En route the Railway Trail passes the eastern sides of Scaur Hill Fort Park, the Heydon Trust Estate and the Gilbert Nature Reserve, offering hikers some nice diversions.

Places to Stay

Garden House (☎ 234-1435, fax 234-3006), 4 Middle Rd, Somerset Bridge, Sandys SB 01, is an old Bermuda home with a handful of rental units in a quiet setting just south of Somerset Bridge. Accommodations include a studio unit with private bath and kitchen, as well as a one-bedroom one-bath cottage and a two-bedroom two-bath cottage, both with living rooms, kitchens and private baths. All units have radios, phones, TVs and VCRs. The owner's Doberman handles security on this quiet two-acre estate, which contains a pool and fruit trees. Smoking is not allowed indoors. Rates for the one-bedroom cottage and studio range from $92 to $117, while the two-bedroom cottage costs from $199 to $229 for up to four people. The higher prices are in effect during midsummer.

Willowbank (☎ 234-1616, 800-752-8493 in the USA, 800-463-8444 in Canada), PO Box MA 296, Sandys MA BX, is a 65-unit complex on a small beach southwest of Somerset Village. This is a nondenominational Christian hotel with an alcohol-free environment that caters to families. There are some religious services, mainly a morning Bible study, but they are optional. Accommodations, which are in cottages and low-rise buildings spread around the six-acre grounds, are comfortable enough but basic. Rooms have private baths but no TVs, radios or phones. Rates for doubles begin at $144/208 in winter/summer, breakfast and dinner included. There's a coffee shop that serves soup and sandwiches at lunchtime, and there are two tennis courts.

Lantana (☎ 234-0141, fax 234-2562, ☎ 800-468-3733 in the USA, 800-463-0036 in Canada), PO Box SB 90, Sandys SB BX, is a popular upmarket complex overlooking the Great Sound at the south end of Sandys. It has 61 air-conditioned suites and cottages on 20 acres of carefully tended grounds. The units have private baths and living rooms and are equipped with phones and radios; TVs are available for an extra charge. There's a small enclosed beach, a pool and tennis courts, and water-sports activities can be arranged. Rates that include breakfast and dinner begin at $180/210 for singles/doubles in

winter, $245/310 in summer. In summer, you can also get a plan without meals for $215/250 for singles/doubles.

Cambridge Beaches (☎ 234-0331, fax 234-3352, ☎ 800-468-7300 in the USA, 800-463-5990 in Canada), Somerset MA 02, is an exclusive cottage community spread out along a 25-acre peninsula at the northernmost point of Somerset Island. It's bordered by sandy beaches and has its own marina with a private shuttle to Hamilton. All 82 of the units have air-conditioning, private baths, radios and phones; TVs are available for an extra charge. Rates for singles begin at $209/305 in winter/summer, doubles at $230/335, breakfast and dinner included. Children under age five are accepted if they're accompanied by a nanny; credit cards aren't accepted at all. An array of activities are available for guests, ranging from lawn croquet and tennis to deep-sea fishing. In addition to the ground's five private beaches, there's a heated pool and a health spa.

Places to Eat

The village of Somerset is not a dining destination per se, but if you're wandering around the area at mealtime there are several places where you can grab a quick bite.

On Somerset Rd, west of the post office, you'll find *Dean's Bakery*, which has inexpensive sandwiches and meat pies, and *Thel's Cafe*, with $5 omelettes and dishes such as fried chicken for double that.

Down near the waterfront in the village center there's a cluster of eateries, including an inexpensive snack bar in the *Somerset Pharmacy*, at the corner of Mangrove Bay and East Shore Rds, which sells scones, Danish pastries, sandwiches and other simple eats. The *Maritime Cafe*, a small cubbyhole on Mangrove Bay Rd, has burgers and sandwiches for under $5 and a couple of sidewalk tables where you can sit and eat.

The *Somerset Country Squire*, a basement pub on Mangrove Bay Rd opposite the pharmacy, has sandwiches for $6 and steak and kidney pie or fish and chips for around $12; at dinner, seafood and steak dishes are priced around $20. In summer, you can also opt to sit at the outdoor patio that overlooks Mangrove Bay.

Four Star Pizza (☎ 234-2626), on Somerset Rd south of Somerset Village, charges $10 for a 10-inch cheese pizza or $15 for one loaded with toppings; it stays open until at least 10 pm daily.

At the very southern part of the parish, on Middle Rd opposite the gate to the former US Naval Air Station Annex, is *Traditions*, a neighborhood restaurant with affordable prices. You can get a range of breakfast options, including omelettes, pancakes or bacon and eggs for around $6, burgers and fries for $8 and steak and seafood dishes for $15.

There is a couple of grocery stores in the parish, including the *Marketplace* on Somerset Rd, opposite the Gilbert Nature Reserve, and the smaller *Hitching Post*, on Middle Rd at the south end of the parish.

Getting Around

The main road through Sandys is Middle Rd, which changes its name to Somerset Rd as it crosses Somerset Bridge, to Mangrove Bay Rd as it passes the village of Somerset, and to Malabar Rd as it continues toward the Royal Naval Dockyard.

Bus Bus Nos 7 and 8 operate along the main road. When you're boarding in Hamilton, take note of the destination marked on the front of the bus, as some of these buses only go as far as Barnes Corner in Southampton Parish, while others stop in Somerset Village and still others go on to the Royal Naval Dockyard.

If you're traveling between Somerset Village and the Dockyard, there's also a parish minibus service; for information see Minibus Service in the Getting Around chapter near the front of the book.

Ferry The Somerset/Dockyard route provides service between the City of Hamilton and Sandys Parish, with stops at the Royal Naval Dockyard, Boaz Island, Watford Bridge, Cavello Bay and Somerset Bridge. The order of stops varies with the sailing, so check the schedule beforehand. The schedule is most frequent on weekdays, least frequent on Sundays. For more detailed information, see Ferry in the Getting Around chapter near the front of the book.

Royal Naval Dockyard

After the American Revolution in 1776, the British were no longer able to use ports in the former American colony and needed a new dockyard facility and resupply depot that had the capacity to repair naval vessels and also serve as a midway station between Nova Scotia and the British West Indies.

To serve this purpose, hilly Ireland Island, at the western tip of Bermuda, was earmarked to become a new 'Gibraltar of the West'. The location was selected because it had a deepwater cove, a huge sheltered anchorage and commanding land and sea views of all approaches. Surveys and drawings by military architects and engineers were undertaken and in 1810 construction began.

Much of the back-breaking work was carried out by convicts who were brought from Britain and quartered in 'prison ships' – old, permanently docked hulks with unspeakably crowded conditions and wretched sanitation. Outbreak of diseases, including yellow fever, claimed hundreds of prisoners. In all, nearly 10,000 convicts were sent to Bermuda between 1814 and 1863 to work on the Dockyard and related projects.

The main elements of the fort – built in Georgian style of limestone block – were completed in the 1820s, while construction on other buildings, including many of the magazines, continued until the 1860s.

One of the Royal Naval Dockyard's first military operations took place while the fort was still under construction: During the War of 1812, a British fleet set sail from

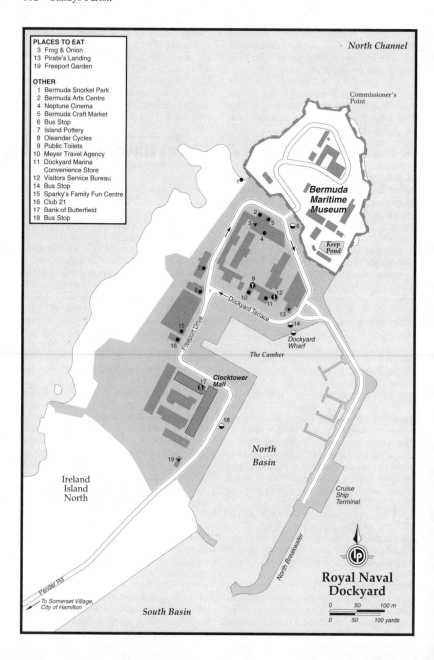

PLACES TO EAT
3 Frog & Onion
13 Pirate's Landing
19 Freeport Garden

OTHER
1 Bermuda Snorkel Park
2 Bermuda Arts Centre
4 Neptune Cinema
5 Bermuda Craft Market
6 Bus Stop
7 Island Pottery
8 Oleander Cycles
9 Public Toilets
10 Meyer Travel Agency
11 Dockyard Marina
Convenience Store
12 Visitors Service Bureau
14 Bus Stop
15 Sparky's Family Fun Centre
16 Club 21
17 Bank of Butterfield
18 Bus Stop

North Channel

Commissioner's Point

Bermuda Maritime Museum

Keep Pond

Dockyard Terrace

Dockyard Wharf

The Camber

Freeport Drive

Clocktower Mall

North Basin

Ireland Island North

Cruise Ship Terminal

North Breakwater

Pender Rd

To Somerset Village, City of Hamilton

South Basin

Royal Naval Dockyard

0   50   100 m
0   50   100 yards

the Dockyard in August 1814 on the infamous raid that sacked and burned Washington DC. In the years that followed, the Dockyard not only kept tabs on American activities in the Atlantic, but also on French privateers in the West Indies.

In the 20th century, the Royal Naval Dockyard served as a North Atlantic base during WWI and WWII and was used briefly by NATO during the postwar period. Still, with the collapse of the British Empire, activities at the Dockyard base tapered off. Strapped for cash, the British Admiralty decided it no longer needed the remote outpost and in 1951 the Royal Naval Dockyard was closed and the property abandoned.

Since then, its buildings have been renovated and given a second life. The Bermuda Maritime Museum occupies the buildings in the former Keep. The Cooperage, where barrels were made, is now the site of an atmospheric pub, a movie theater and the Bermuda Craft Market. The attractive twin-towered naval administration building on the waterfront has been turned into a shopping center, called the Clocktower Mall. You may notice that the clocks on the two towers read differently – that's because one was designed to show actual time and the other to indicate the time of high tide.

Most people visit the Royal Naval Dockyard to have lunch at one of the restaurants, browse for souvenirs at the crafts shops or shop at the Clocktower Mall. In addition to the Bermuda Maritime Museum, you can pleasantly pass an hour or two simply strolling about the rest of the Dockyard grounds. For those who care to explore the water as well, there's a small beach where masks and snorkels can be rented.

There's no admission charge to the Royal Naval Dockyard, except for entry into the Bermuda Maritime Museum.

Information
Tourist Offices There's a small Visitors Service Bureau in the old Cooperage where you can get brochures and general tourist information. It's open weekdays from 9 am to 4 pm and Sundays from 11 am to 3 pm, with slightly reduced hours from November to March.

Money The Bank of Butterfield in the Clocktower Mall is open weekdays from 9:30 am to 3 pm and has an ATM that's accessible at other times.

Post & Communications The Ship Inn Book Gallery in the Clocktower Mall sells postage stamps and phone cards. There are pay phones at a number of points around the Dockyard, including the cruise ship terminal and Clocktower Mall.

Other There's a coin laundry next to the tourist office and a travel agency, Meyer Travel, nearby in the same cluster of buildings.

The Admiral's Locker shop in the Clocktower Mall sells bus tokens and bus passes.

The Dockyard Marina Convenience Store, adjacent to the tourist office and open daily from 8 am to 6 pm, sells soda, beer and snacks and also carries snorkeling gear.

Bermuda Maritime Museum
Bermuda's most significant historic museum, the Bermuda Maritime Museum, was inaugurated by Queen Elizabeth II in 1975. The museum occupies the Dockyard's six-acre Keep, which retains its original fortress character, separated from the rest of the Dockyard by a moat. Indeed, to enter the gate of the Keep today, you must still walk across the moat footbridge.

Many of the exhibits are in ordnance buildings, the high-vaulted brick ceilings of which were once stacked with munitions; these days, each building contains displays on different themes.

Building No 1, known as the Queen's Exhibition Hall, has exhibits on the naval ties between Canada and Bermuda, displays on whaling and navigation, and model ships, including one of the *Deliverance* and others of Bermudian-built two-masted schooners. Take note of the bitumen (tar) floor in this hall. The bitumen, which came from Pitch Lake in Trinidad, was spread on the floor to prevent sparking when barrels were rolled across it. Nearly 5000 barrels of gunpowder were stored in Building No 1. In the event that bitumen alone didn't handle the situation, the limestone walls were constructed a full four feet thick in the hopes of minimizing damage from a potential explosion.

Out back, Building No 2 is the former Shifting House, erected in 1837 to temporarily store munitions unloaded from ships that were being repaired in the Dockyard. Today it houses a fascinating collection of artifacts from shipwrecks, including pieces of pewter and pottery from the *Sea Venture* and gold coins, bars and jewelry recovered from 16th-century Spanish shipwrecks.

Building No 3, to the immediate south, contains a collection of Bermuda bills and coins, including the island's unique hog money. Building No 4, at the southeast corner, has exhibits on the early explorers who came to Bermuda and the New World.

Building No 5, the Forster Cooper Building, is a former cooperage that made the all-essential barrels that were once used to store virtually everything from ale to gunpowder. Today the building houses exhibits on shipbuilding and the history of the Dockyard; a separate entrance leads to an interesting collection of 2000 antique bottles.

The largest collection of items can be found in Building No 6, the Boatloft, at the east side of the Keep Yard. Here you'll find an extensive display on Bermuda dinghies, 14-foot boats made of Bermuda cedar and driven by oversized sails. In addition to a completely fitted dinghy and other related displays, you'll find a thought-provoking exhibit on turtle fishing, which continued in Bermuda until the 1970s and resulted in the loss of all sea turtle nesting on the island.

Beyond the indoor exhibits, visitors can also wander around the Keep Pond, view the statue of Neptune, which stands in the Keep Yard and walk through the gate to the upper grounds, where sheep graze. The upper grounds contain old cannons that still point out to sea, rusting anchors and the once-elaborate Commissioner's House, which is now closed to the public, although it's earmarked for eventual renovation.

The museum is open daily from 10 am (9:30 am in summer) to 5 pm, with the last entry allowed at 4:30 pm. Admission is $7.50 for adults, $6 for senior citizens and university students, $3 for children ages five to 18, and free for children under five.

Activities

The Bermuda Snorkel Park, at the north side of the Royal Naval Dockyard, has a shallow lagoon with a little beach that's suitable for children and a nearshore reef that can be snorkeled. For $2 you can go in and use the beach or for $17.50 rent a snorkel, mask, fins and buoyancy vest. There are showers and changing rooms. It's open only during the peak tourist season, from mid-April through October. Hours are from 10 am to 5 pm.

Sparky's Family Fun Centre on Freeport Rd has video games, pinball machines and simple kiddie

Brain coral, one of Bermuda's 24 species of hard coral

rides. It's open Monday to Thursday from 10 am to 2 pm and on weekends from at least 11 am to 8 pm.

Places to Eat

The cheapest, though not necessarily the best, place to grab a quick eat is the fast-food counter at *Sparky's Family Fun Centre*, on Freeport Rd, which has inexpensive fries, hot dogs and burgers.

Frog & Onion – which takes its name from its two owners, one French and one Bermudian – has a period pub atmosphere and good food. This is the Dockyard's most popular dining spot. At lunch there are salads for $5, including a nice tabouleh plate, and sandwiches and burgers for around $8. You'll also find all the usual pub standards, including fish and chips, meat pies and bangers and mash at moderate prices. In addition, there's a full dinner menu with the likes of grilled chicken or lamb chops for $15 to $21. Lunch is served from 11 am to 3 pm and dinner from 6 to around 9:30 pm; the bar stays open until midnight. It's closed on Mondays in winter.

Pirate's Landing, a cafe opposite the ferry landing, has simple lunch fare, including burgers and salads for around $7. Between 6 and 7 pm there's an early-bird three-course meal for $17; otherwise, dinner entrees range from $13 for pasta to $22 for steak. It's open from 11:30 am to 10 pm.

In the Clocktower Mall you'll find a *Häagen-Dazs* ice cream shop, where a small scoop will set you back just $2. Also in the Clocktower Mall, *La Brioche* is a small cafe with typical cafe fare, including carrot cake, croissants and coffee. Prices are moderate – you can get a slice of lasagna or quiche, a sandwich or a calzone for around $6.

Freeport Garden, opposite the south side of the Clocktower Mall, is an unpretentious restaurant that serves three-egg omelettes with bacon, toast and coffee, or a hamburger plate with fries and cole slaw, for a reasonable $7. It also has salads, submarine sandwiches and pastas for under $10 and fish and chips and a few other hot entrees for a few dollars more.

Entertainment

The *Frog & Onion* (☎ 234-2900) has pool tables and live music on Saturdays year round. *Club 21* (☎ 234-2721) is the Dockyard's other nightspot.

The *Neptune Cinema* (☎ 234-2923), opposite the Frog & Onion, shows first-run Hollywood movies.

Things to Buy

Cooperage Area The Bermuda Craft Market has an extensive selection of handicrafts made by local artists. There are various stalls selling jewelry at moderate prices, glasswork, candles, pottery, watercolors, stained glass and other items that could make nice souvenirs. In summer it's open daily from 10 am to 5 pm; November through March it's open Tuesday to Sunday from 10:30 am to 4:30 pm.

The Bermuda Arts Centre at the north side of the craft market has changing exhibits by local artists in a variety of media. All of the items on display are for sale, including paintings, sculpture, pottery, woodwork, batiks, prints and note cards. Three artists have permanent studios in the center. One specializes in creative jewelry and quilted wall hangings; a second paints in watercolors, acrylics and oils; and the third sculpts fragrant native Bermuda cedar. It's open daily from 10 am to 5 pm.

At Island Pottery on Freeport Rd, artisans in the rear of the shop hand-make the pottery that is sold in the front. Most pieces have floral designs, ranging from splashy island motifs to more delicate detail. Mugs cost $15, while vases are priced from around $40. It's open daily from 9 am to 5 pm.

Clocktower Mall The Clocktower Mall (also called the Clocktower Centre) contains an array of shops and galleries. It's open Monday to Saturday from 10 am to 5 pm and on Sundays from 11 am to 5 pm.

The Admiral's Locker has an eclectic collection of nautical-related items, as well as imported objects such as Buddha statues and Russian nesting dolls. Gombey Trader has souvenir items, some locally made, including Gombey rag dolls. The Michael Swan Gallery specializes in prints of pastel Bermuda scenes, with some nice choices for around $50, and the Carole Holding Studio also has watercolors. Ships Inn Book Gallery specializes in used books on Bermuda, including rare and antique books. Calypso has stylish clothing, swimwear, leather bags and jewelry. Davidson's of Bermuda has T-shirts and other casual wear. Dockyard Linens sells tea towels and place mats with Bermuda designs.

The Clocktower Mall also has branches of a couple of Hamilton's largest stores, including AS Cooper & Sons, which has everything from fashionable clothing and perfume to Waterford crystal and Royal Copenhagen porcelain. Archie Brown & Sons, which features Shetland wools and cashmere sweaters, is together with a branch of Britain's Marks & Spencer department store, where you can get items ranging from European fashions to British jams and cookies.

Also in the mall is Ratteray's Wines & Spirits, which has a small collection of wines, beers and spirits and can deliver duty-free liquor to your ship.

Getting Around

Bus Bus No 7, which travels via the south shore, leaves the Royal Naval Dockyard for the City of Hamilton at 20 and 50 minutes past the hour, while bus No 8, which travels to Hamilton via Middle Rd, leaves the Dockyard at 5 and 35 minutes past the hour. On weekdays, buses operate on this schedule from 6:35 am to 6:20 pm although there are also a couple of later staggered night buses, the last leaving the Dockyard at 11:50 pm. Sunday schedules are lighter.

If you pick up a No 7 or 8 bus in Hamilton, make sure it reads 'Dockyard', as not all buses continue that far.

Ferry The ferry between Hamilton and the Royal Naval Dockyard makes an interesting alternative to the bus – you might want to take the ferry one way and the bus the other.

The ferry runs 11 times a day on weekdays. It takes between 30 and 75 minutes, depending on whether you catch a nonstop boat or one that stops at various places in Sandys Parish en route. Boats are slightly less frequent on Saturdays and half as frequent on Sundays. For more details, see Ferry in the Getting Around chapter near the front of the book.

Moped During the tourist season, Oleander Cycles (☎ 234-2764) rents mopeds at the west side of the Royal Naval Dockyard.

Index

MAPS

TEXT

LONELY PLANET TRAVEL ATLASES

Lonely Planet has long been famous for the number and quality of its guidebook maps. Now we've gone one step further and in conjunction with Steinhart Katzir Publishers produced a handy companion series: Lonely Planet travel atlases – maps of a country produced in book form.

Unlike other maps, which look good but lead travellers astray, our travel atlases have been researched on the road by Lonely Planet's experienced team of writers. All details are carefully checked to ensure the atlas corresponds with the equivalent Lonely Planet guidebook.

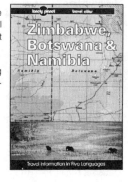

The handy atlas format means no holes, wrinkles, torn sections or constant folding and unfolding. These atlases can survive long periods on the road, unlike cumbersome fold-out maps. The comprehensive index ensures easy reference.

- full-colour throughout
- maps researched and checked by Lonely Planet authors
- place names correspond with Lonely Planet guidebooks
  – no confusing spelling differences
- legend and travelling information in English, French, German, Japanese and Spanish
- size: 230 x 160 mm

Available now:
Chile & Easter Island • Egypt • India & Bangladesh • Israel & the Palestinian Territories • Jordan, Syria & Lebanon • Kenya • Laos • Thailand • Vietnam • Zimbabwe, Botswana & Namibia

---

LONELY PLANET TV SERIES & VIDEOS

Lonely Planet travel guides have been brought to life on television screens around the world. Like our guides, the programmes are based on the joy of independent travel, and look honestly at some of the most exciting, picturesque and frustrating places in the world. Each show is presented by one of three travellers from Australia, England or the USA and combines an innovative mixture of video, Super-8 film, atmospheric soundscapes and original music.

Videos of each episode – containing additional footage not shown on television – are available from good book and video shops, but the availability of individual videos varies with regional screening schedules.

Video destinations include: Alaska • American Rockies • Australia – The South-East • Baja California & the Copper Canyon • Brazil • Central Asia • Chile & Easter Island • Corsica, Sicily & Sardinia – The Mediterranean Islands • East Africa (Tanzania & Zanzibar) • Ecuador & the Galapagos Islands • Greenland & Iceland • Indonesia • Israel & the Sinai Desert • Jamaica • Japan • La Ruta Maya • Morocco • New York • North India • Pacific Islands (Fiji, Solomon Islands & Vanuatu) • South India • South West China • Turkey • Vietnam • West Africa • Zimbabwe, Botswana & Namibia

The Lonely Planet TV series is produced by:
Pilot Productions
Duke of Sussex Studios
44 Uxbridge St
London W8 7TG UK

Lonely Planet videos are distributed by:
IVN Communications Inc
2246 Camino Ramon
California 94583, USA

107 Power Road, Chiswick
London W4 5PL UK

Music from the TV series is available on CD & cassette.
For video availability and ordering information contact your nearest Lonely Planet office.

PLANET TALK

Lonely Planet's FREE quarterly newsletter

We love hearing from you and think you'd like to hear from us.
When... is the right time to see reindeer in Finland?
Where... can you hear the best palm-wine music in Ghana?
How... do you get from Asunción to Areguá by steam train?
What... is the best way to see India?

For the answer to these and many other questions read PLANET TALK.

Every issue is packed with up-to-date travel news and advice including:

* a letter from Lonely Planet founders Tony and Maureen Wheeler
* travel diary from a Lonely Planet author–find out what it's really like out on the road
* feature article on an important and topical travel issue
* a selection of recent letters from our readers
* the latest travel news from all over the world
* details on Lonely Planet's new and forthcoming releases

To join our mailing list contact any Lonely Planet office .

Also available: Lonely Planet T-shirts. 100% heavyweight cotton (S, M, L, XL)

LONELY PLANET ONLINE

Get the latest travel information before you leave or while you're on the road

Whether you've just begun planning your next trip, or you're chasing down specific info on currency regulations or visa requirements, check out the Lonely Planet World Wide Web site for up-to-the-minute travel information.

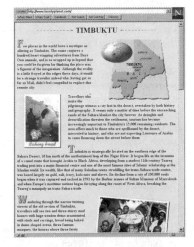

As well as travel profiles of your favorite destinations (including interactive maps and full-color photos), you'll find current reports from our army of researchers and other travelers, updates on health and visas, travel advisories, and the ecological and political issues you need to be aware of as you travel.

There's an online travelers' forum (the Thorn Tree) where you can share your experiences of life on the road, meet travel companions and ask other travelers for their recommendations and advice. We also have plenty of links to other Web sites useful to independent travelers.

With tens of thousands of visitors a month, the Lonely Planet Web site is one of the most popular on the Internet and has won a number of awards including GNN's Best of the Net travel award.

www.lonelyplanet.com

LONELY PLANET PRODUCTS

Lonely Planet is known worldwide for publishing practical, reliable and no-nonsense travel information in our guides and on our web site. The Lonely Planet list covers just about every accessible part of the world. Currently there are eight series: *travel guides, shoestring guides, walking guides, city guides, phrasebooks, audio packs, travel atlases* and *Journeys* – a unique collection of travel writing.

EUROPE

Austria • Baltic States & Kaliningrad • Baltic States phrasebook • Britain • Central Europe on a shoestring • Central Europe phrasebook • Czech & Slovak Republics • Denmark • Dublin city guide • Eastern Europe on a shoestring • Eastern Europe phrasebook • Finland • France • Greece • Greek phrasebook • Hungary • Iceland, Greenland & the Faroe Islands • Ireland • Italy • Mediterranean Europe on a shoestring • Mediterranean Europe phrasebook • Paris city guide • Poland • Portugal • Prague city guide • Russia, Ukraine & Belarus • Russian phrasebook • Scandinavian & Baltic Europe on a shoestring • Scandinavian Europe phrasebook • Slovenia • Spain • St Petersburg city guide • Switzerland • Trekking in Greece • Trekking in Spain • Ukrainian phrasebook • Vienna city guide • Walking in Britain • Walking in Switzerland • Western Europe on shoestring • Western Europe phrasebook

NORTH AMERICA

Alaska • Backpacking in Alaska • Baja California• California & Nevada • Canada • Florida • Hawaii • Honolulu city guide • Los Angeles city guide • Mexico • Miami city guide • New England • New Orleans city guide • Pacific Northwest USA • Rocky Mountain States • San Francisco city guide • Southwest USA • USA phrasebook • Washington, DC & the Capital Region

CENTRAL AMERICA & THE CARIBBEAN

Bermuda • Central America on a shoestring • Costa Rica • Cuba • Eastern Caribbean • Guatemala, Belize & Yucatán: La Ruta Maya • Jamaica

SOUTH AMERICA

Argentina, Uruguay & Paraguay • Bolivia • Brazil • Brazilian phrasebook • Buenos Aires city guide • Chile & Easter Island • Chile & Easter Island travel atlas • Colombia • Ecuador & the Galápagos Islands • Latin American Spanish phrasebook • Peru • Quechua phrasebook • Rio de Janeiro city guide • South America on a shoestring • Trekking in the Patagonian Andes • Venezuela

Travel Literature: Full Circle: A South American Journey

ANTARCTICA

Antarctica

ISLANDS OF THE INDIAN OCEAN

Madagascar & Comoros • Maldives & Islands of the East Indian Ocean • Mauritius, Réunion & Seychelles

AFRICA

Arabic (Moroccan) phrasebook • Africa on a shoestring • Cape Town city guide • Central Africa • East Africa • Egypt • Egypt travel atlas• Ethiopian (Amharic) phrasebook • Kenya • Kenya travel atlas • Morocco • North Africa • South Africa, Lesotho & Swaziland • Swahili phrasebook • Trekking in East Africa • West Africa • Zimbabwe, Botswana & Namibia • Zimbabwe, Botswana & Namibia travel atlas

Travel Literature: The Rainbird: A Central African Journey • Songs to an African Sunset: A Zimbabwean Story